JOHN WOO'S

7 BROTHERS

Created by
JOHN WOO

Script
GARTH ENNIS
with additional scenes from the cutting
room floor of Tiger Hill Productions

Art
JEEVAN KANG

Cover Art
YOSHITAKA AMANO

Variant Cover Art
JONATHAN HICKMAN

Original Series Cover Art
YOSHITAKA AMANO

Additional Covers
GREG HORN
JEEVAN KANG

Colors
S.SUNDARAKANNAN
and **JEEVAN KANG**

Letters
B.S. RAVI KIRAN
and **NILESH S. MAHADIK**

Project Manager
REUBEN THOMAS

Assistant Editors
MAHESH KAMATH,
DAN HERNANDEZ,
CHARLIE BECKERMAN
and **SANA AMANAT**

Editors
GOTHAM CHOPRA and
MACKENZIE CADENHEAD

Consulting Editor
LORI TILKIN

7 BROTHERS™

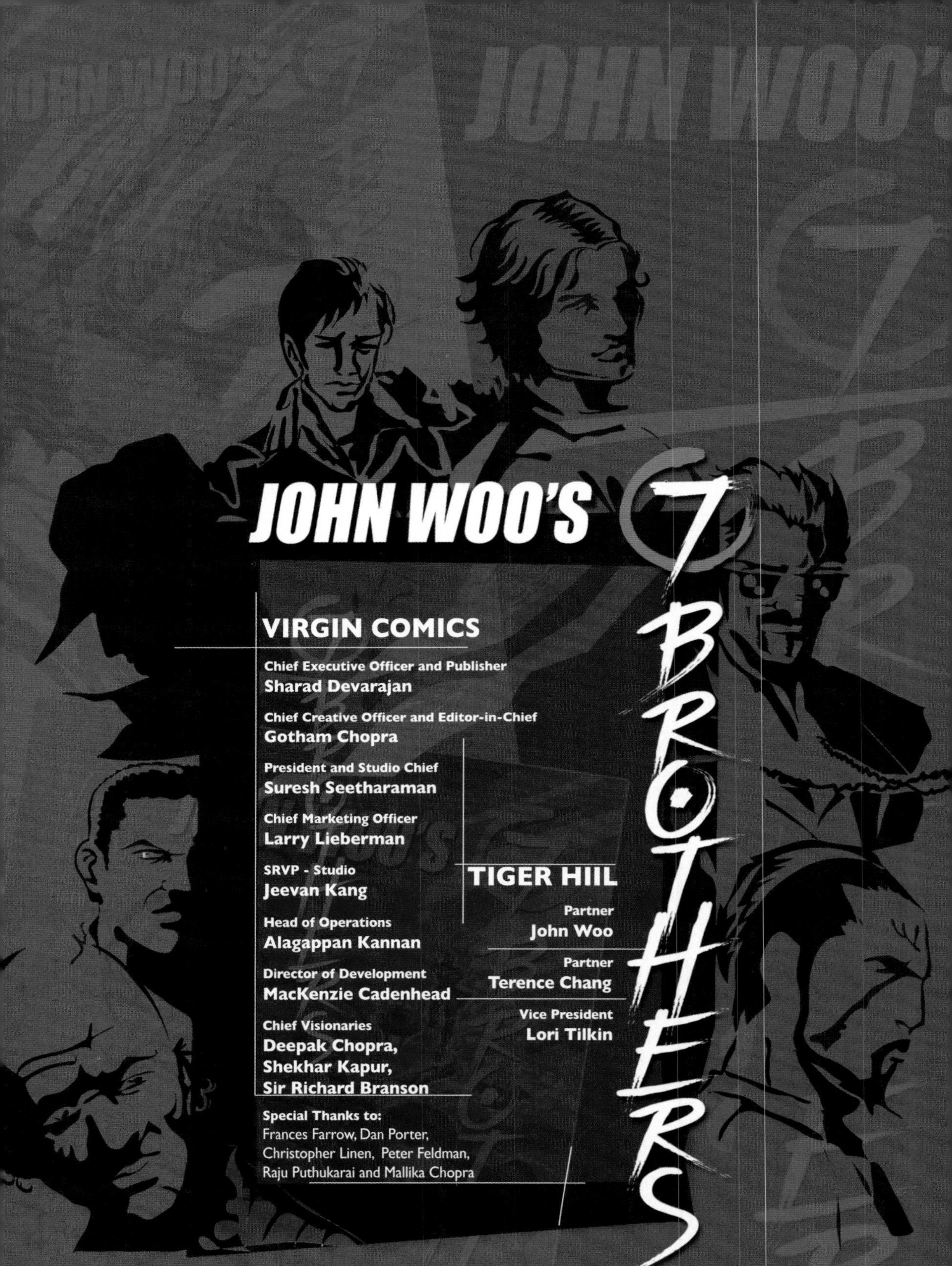
JOHN WOO'S
7 BROTHERS™

VIRGIN COMICS

Chief Executive Officer and Publisher
Sharad Devarajan

Chief Creative Officer and Editor-in-Chief
Gotham Chopra

President and Studio Chief
Suresh Seetharaman

Chief Marketing Officer
Larry Lieberman

SRVP - Studio
Jeevan Kang

Head of Operations
Alagappan Kannan

Director of Development
MacKenzie Cadenhead

Chief Visionaries
Deepak Chopra,
Shekhar Kapur,
Sir Richard Branson

Special Thanks to:
Frances Farrow, Dan Porter,
Christopher Linen, Peter Feldman,
Raju Puthukarai and Mallika Chopra

TIGER HIIL

Partner
John Woo

Partner
Terence Chang

Vice President
Lori Tilkin

SEVEN BROTHERS TPB, Vol: 1 , June 2007 published by VIRGIN COMICS L.L.C. OFFICE OF PUBLICATION: 594 Broadway, New York, NY 10012 (text) The characters included in this issue, SEVEN BROTHERS, and the distinctive likenesses thereof are properties of Virgin Comics L.L.C. No similarity between any of the names, characters, persons, and/or institutions in this magazine with those of any living or dead person or institution is intended, and any such similarity which may exist is purely coincidental. Printed in Canada.
For advertising, licensing and sales info please contact: info@virgincomics.com or (212)584-4040. www.virgincomics.com

IT USED TO BE SO DIFFERENT...

Comic book artists cowered and begged for scraps while the movie guys strutted like peacocks. But along came a generation of directors and producers who truly loved comic books for what they are, at their best, and these creative folk changed everything, turning an illicit, even an abusive affair into a full-blown marriage. No longer were we simply strip-mined or treated as a joke. Richard Donner and Marlon Brando rewarded Joe Schuster and Jerry Siegel's Superman myth with gravitas and verisimilitude: as the slogan went, you really did believe a man can fly. And Tim Burton's *Batman* looked downright scary, a far cry from the loveable, wisecracking, but utterly insipid Adam West TV show.

But that was just a bare beginning. Along came Sam Raimi to bring Steve Ditko and Stan Lee's *Spider-Man* to vivid life; Bryan Singer to recreate John Byrne and Chris Claremont's epic *X-Men*; reincarnations of *The Crow* and *Men In Black* that thrilled audiences who never would've guessed they were based on comic books. Even Harvey Pekar's sarcastic, drowned-in-reality *American Splendor* passed muster. And Robert Rodriguez hunted me down like a stray dog to convince me to co-direct my precious baby *Sin City*.

The inmates were taking over the asylum. And the asylum was taking over the inmates.

Sam Raimi has now written comic books. So has Darren Aranofsky, director of *Pi* and *Requiem for a Dream* and *The Fountain*. The list goes on, and grows.

Enter John Woo, celebrated director, who brings outrageous vitality to the movies, as well as dazzling technical verve.

Welcome to the neighborhood, John. I'm sure we'll learn a lot from you.

FRANK MILLER
NEW YORK CITY, 2007

"To put the world in order, we must first put the nation in order. To put the nation in order, we must first put the family in order. To put the family in order...we must first set our hearts right."

—Confucius

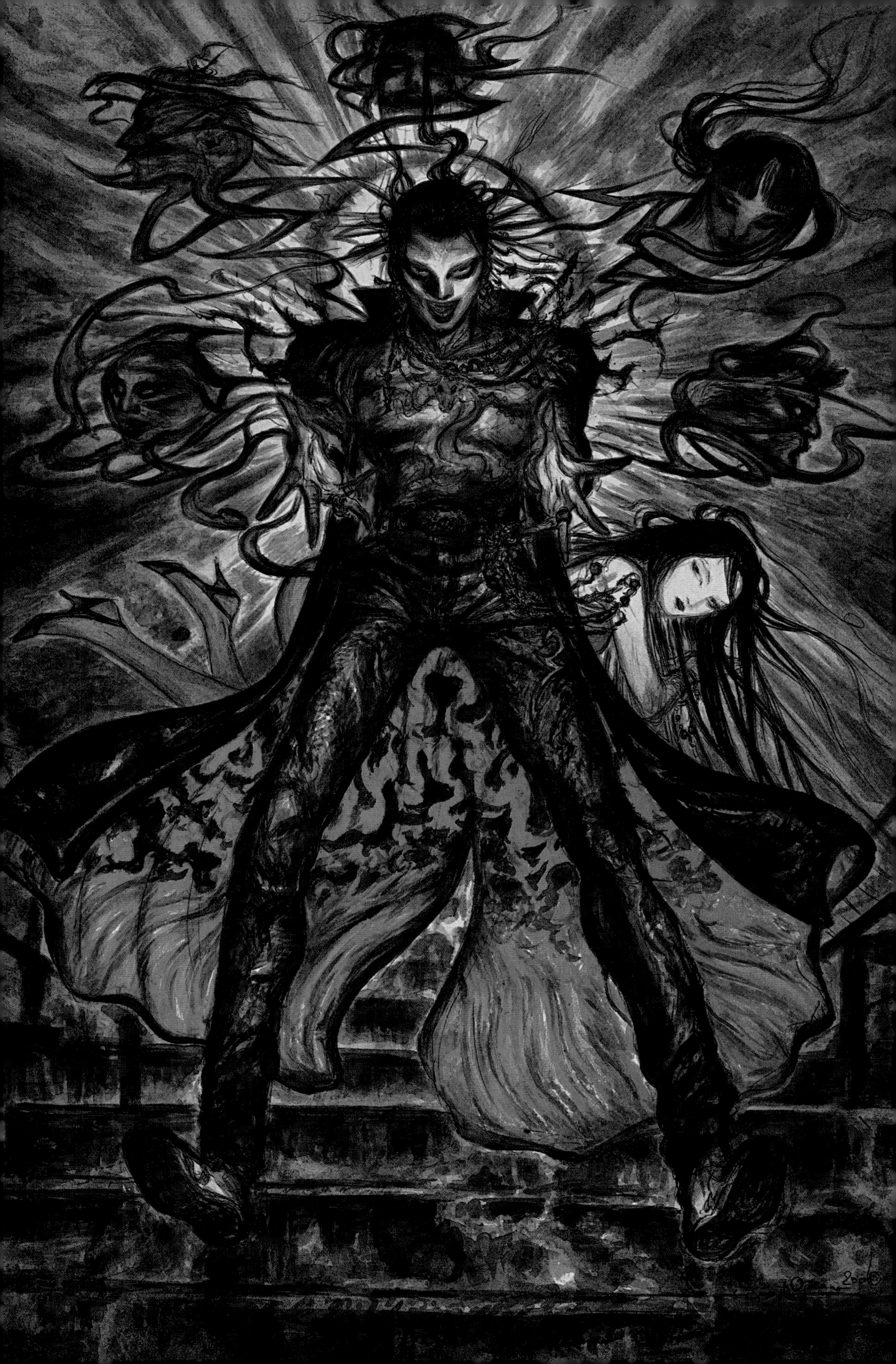

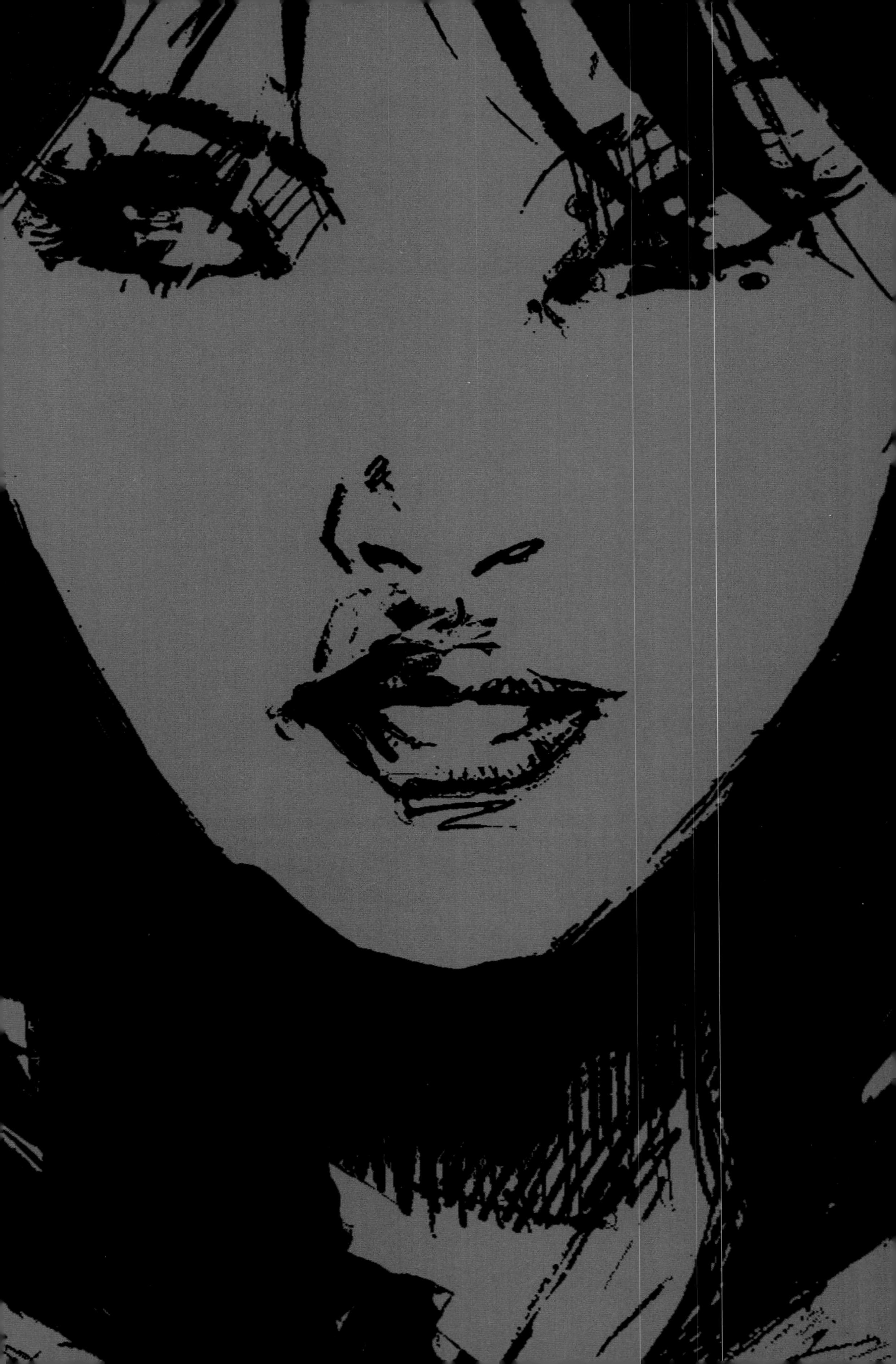

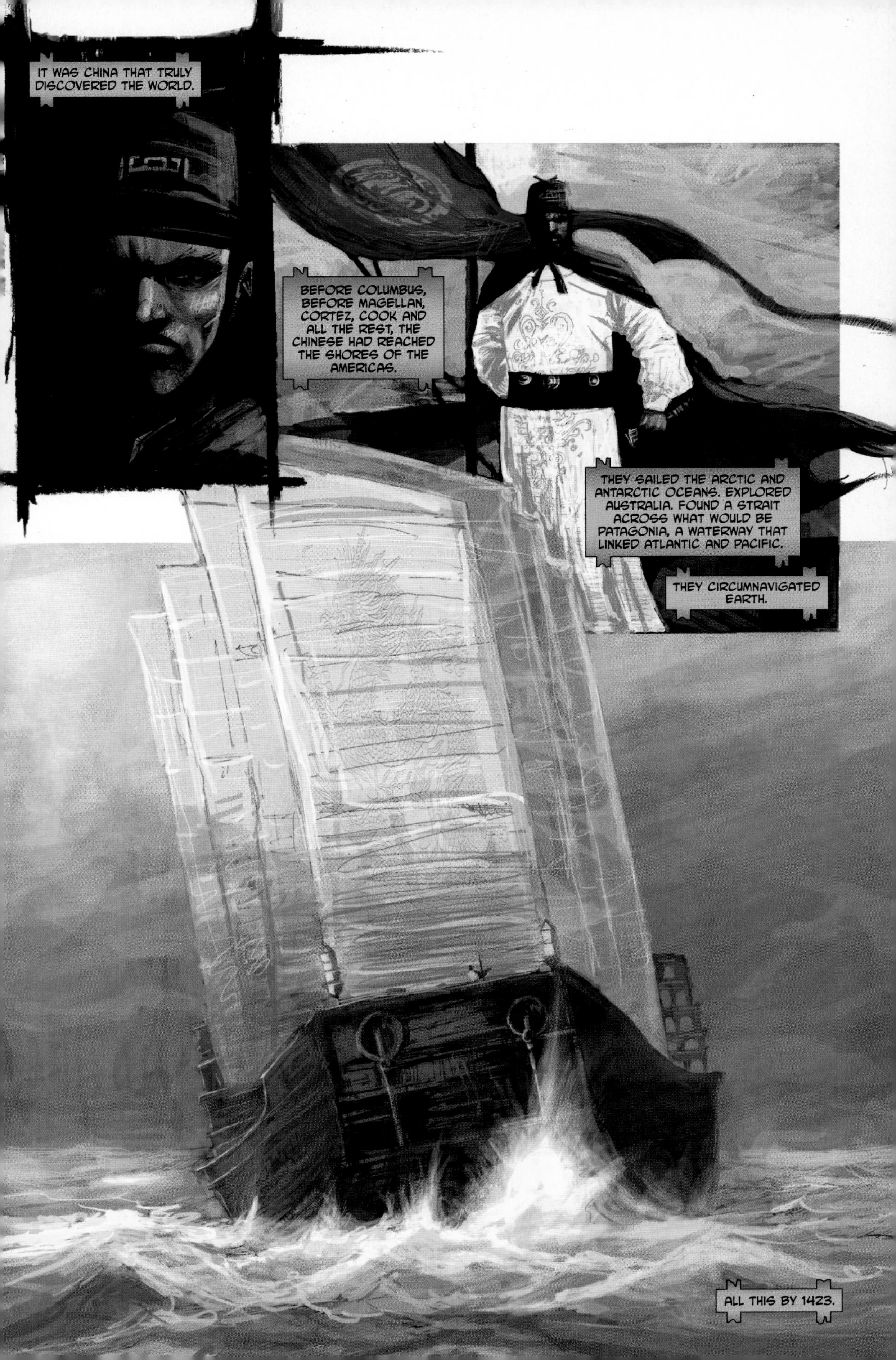
IT WAS CHINA THAT TRULY DISCOVERED THE WORLD.
BEFORE COLUMBUS, BEFORE MAGELLAN, CORTEZ, COOK AND ALL THE REST, THE CHINESE HAD REACHED THE SHORES OF THE AMERICAS.
THEY SAILED THE ARCTIC AND ANTARCTIC OCEANS. EXPLORED AUSTRALIA. FOUND A STRAIT ACROSS WHAT WOULD BE PATAGONIA, A WATERWAY THAT LINKED ATLANTIC AND PACIFIC.
THEY CIRCUMNAVIGATED EARTH.
ALL THIS BY 1423.

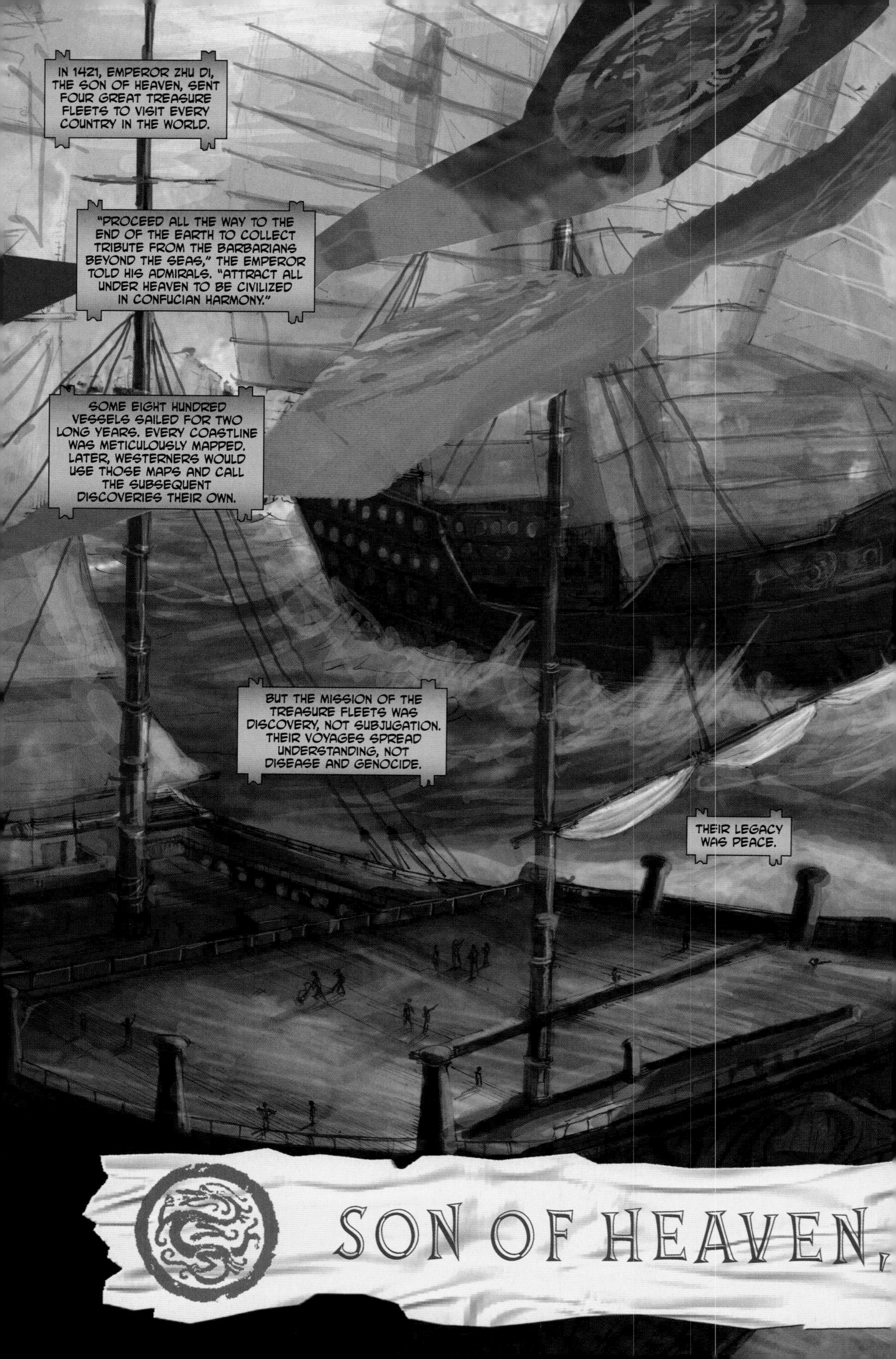
IN 1421, EMPEROR ZHU DI, THE SON OF HEAVEN, SENT FOUR GREAT TREASURE FLEETS TO VISIT EVERY COUNTRY IN THE WORLD.
"PROCEED ALL THE WAY TO THE END OF THE EARTH TO COLLECT TRIBUTE FROM THE BARBARIANS BEYOND THE SEAS," THE EMPEROR TOLD HIS ADMIRALS. "ATTRACT ALL UNDER HEAVEN TO BE CIVILIZED IN CONFUCIAN HARMONY."
SOME EIGHT HUNDRED VESSELS SAILED FOR TWO LONG YEARS. EVERY COASTLINE WAS METICULOUSLY MAPPED. LATER, WESTERNERS WOULD USE THOSE MAPS AND CALL THE SUBSEQUENT DISCOVERIES THEIR OWN.
BUT THE MISSION OF THE TREASURE FLEETS WAS DISCOVERY, NOT SUBJUGATION. THEIR VOYAGES SPREAD UNDERSTANDING, NOT DISEASE AND GENOCIDE.
THEIR LEGACY WAS PEACE.
SON OF HEAVEN,

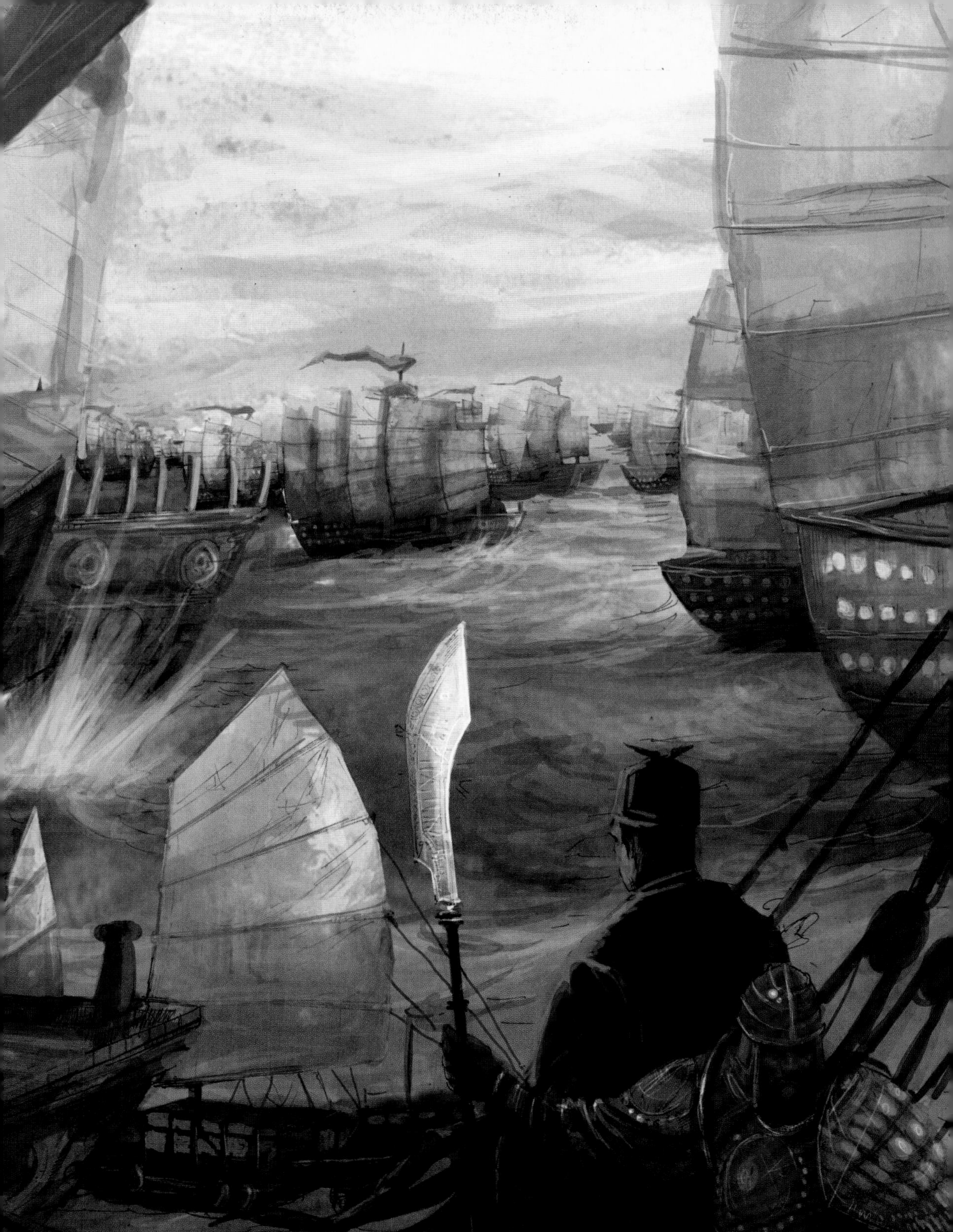

SON OF HELL

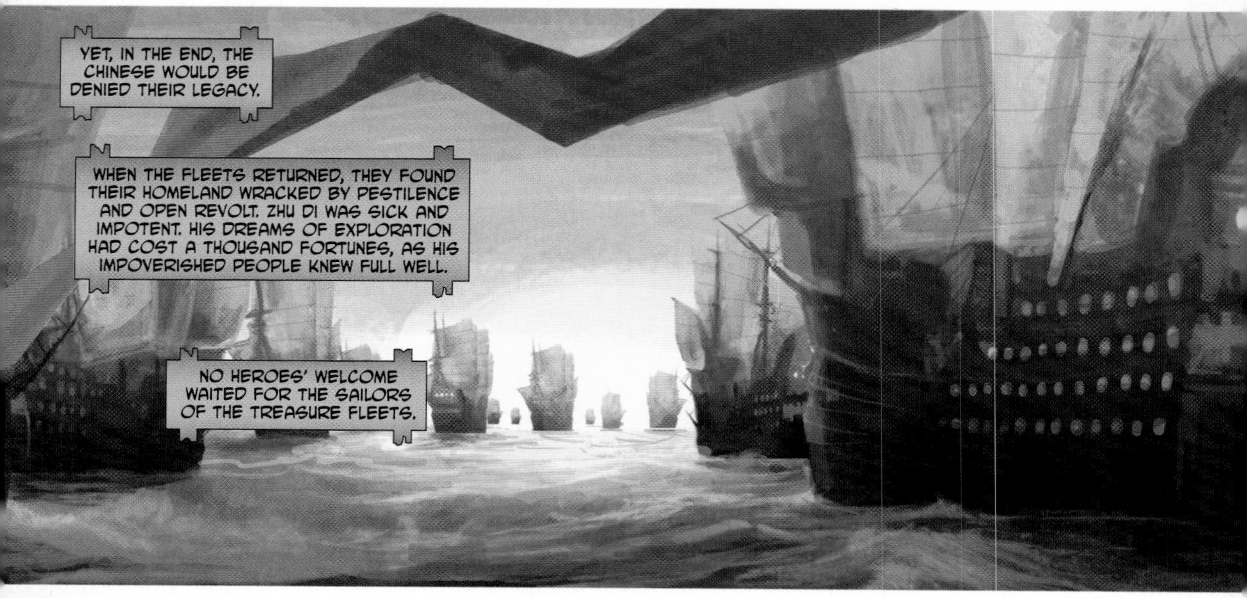
YET, IN THE END, THE CHINESE WOULD BE DENIED THEIR LEGACY.
WHEN THE FLEETS RETURNED, THEY FOUND THEIR HOMELAND WRACKED BY PESTILENCE AND OPEN REVOLT. ZHU DI WAS SICK AND IMPOTENT. HIS DREAMS OF EXPLORATION HAD COST A THOUSAND FORTUNES, AS HIS IMPOVERISHED PEOPLE KNEW FULL WELL.
NO HEROES' WELCOME WAITED FOR THE SAILORS OF THE TREASURE FLEETS.

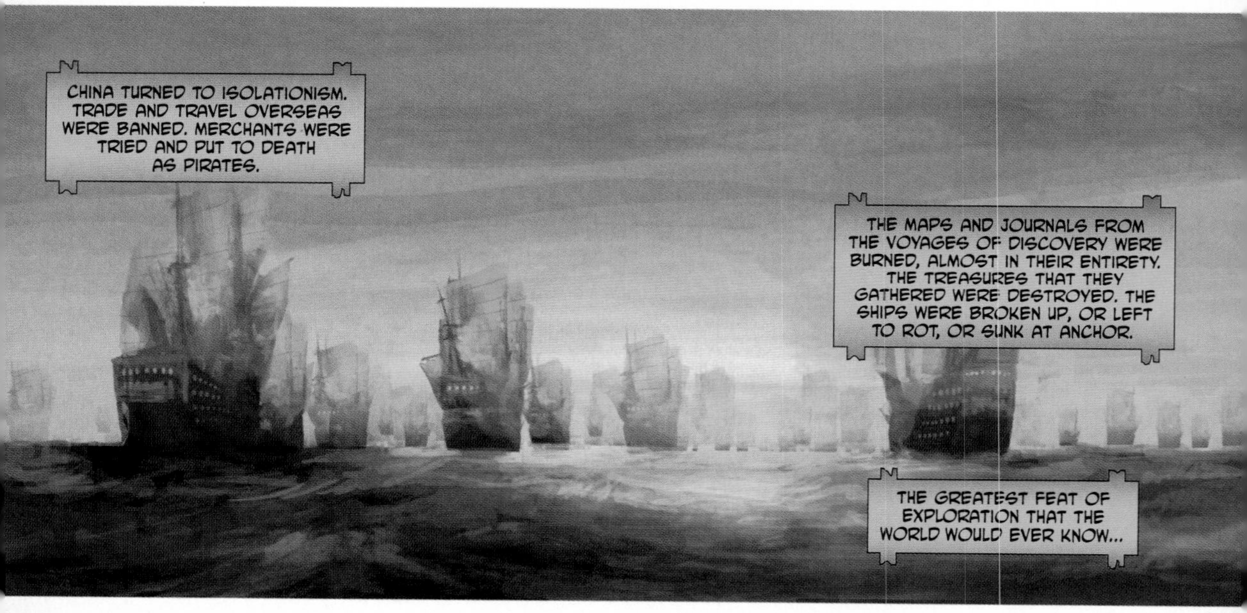
CHINA TURNED TO ISOLATIONISM. TRADE AND TRAVEL OVERSEAS WERE BANNED. MERCHANTS WERE TRIED AND PUT TO DEATH AS PIRATES.
THE MAPS AND JOURNALS FROM THE VOYAGES OF DISCOVERY WERE BURNED, ALMOST IN THEIR ENTIRETY. THE TREASURES THAT THEY GATHERED WERE DESTROYED. THE SHIPS WERE BROKEN UP, OR LEFT TO ROT, OR SUNK AT ANCHOR.
THE GREATEST FEAT OF EXPLORATION THAT THE WORLD WOULD EVER KNOW...

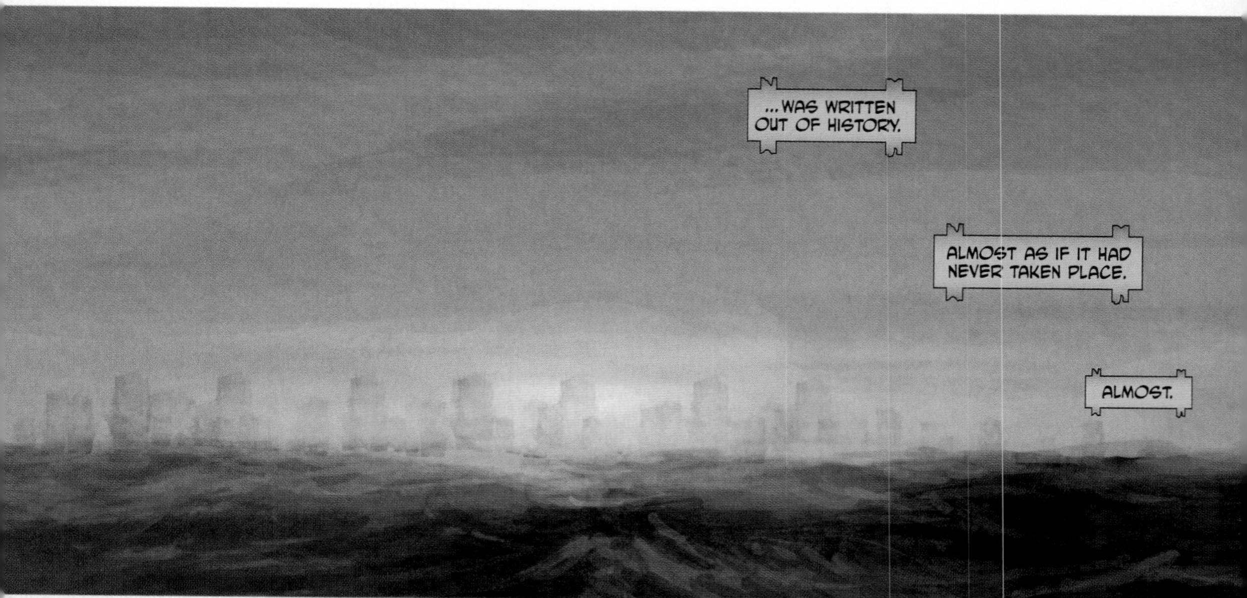
...WAS WRITTEN OUT OF HISTORY.
ALMOST AS IF IT HAD NEVER TAKEN PLACE.
ALMOST.

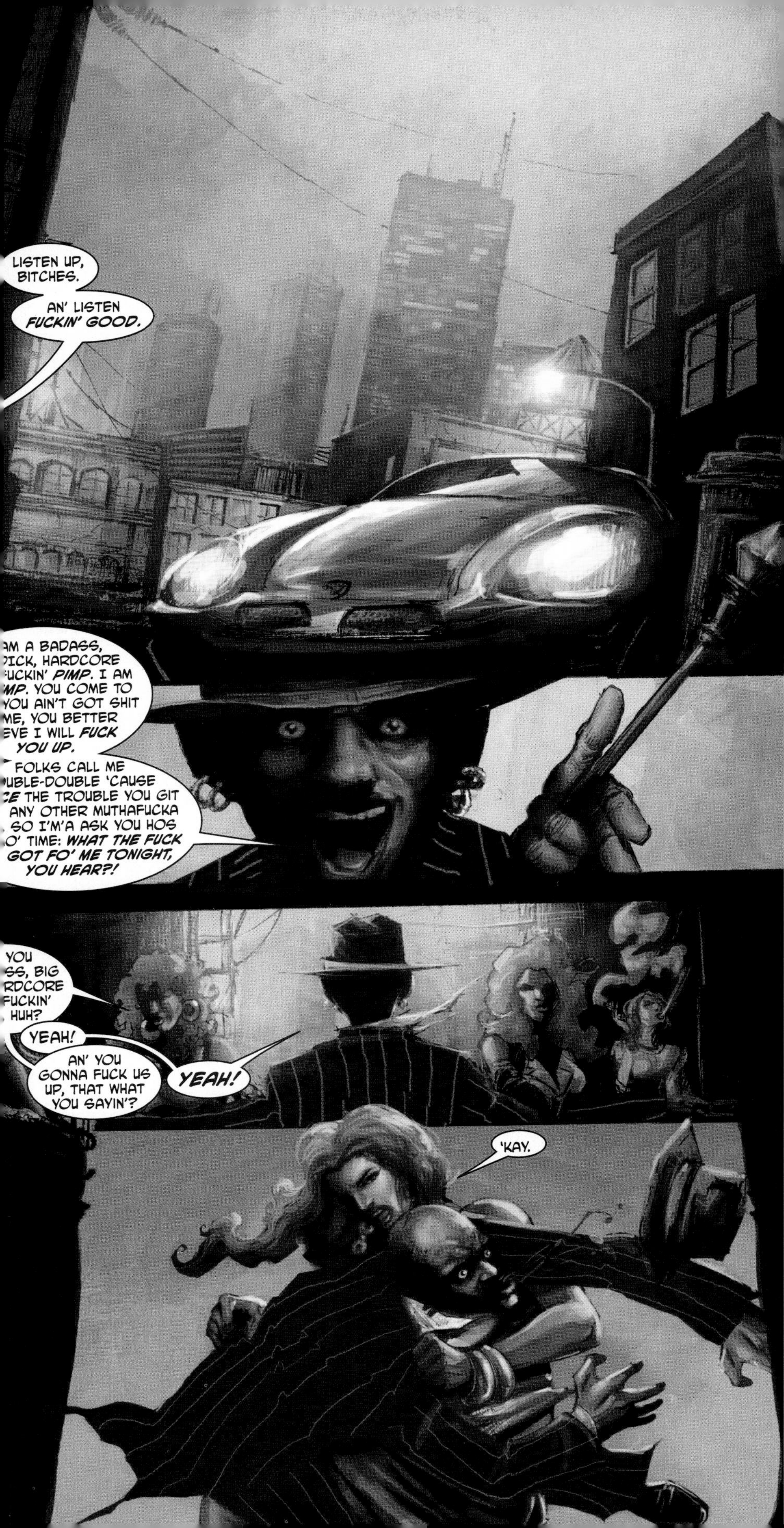
LISTEN UP, BITCHES.
AN' LISTEN FUCKIN' GOOD.
AM A BADASS, ICK, HARDCORE UCKIN' PIMP. I AM MP. YOU COME TO YOU AIN'T GOT SHIT ME, YOU BETTER EVE I WILL FUCK YOU UP.
FOLKS CALL ME UBLE-DOUBLE 'CAUSE THE TROUBLE YOU GIT ANY OTHER MUTHAFUCKA SO I'M'A ASK YOU HOS O' TIME: WHAT THE FUCK GOT FO' ME TONIGHT, YOU HEAR?!
YOU SS, BIG RDCORE FUCKIN' HUH?
YEAH!
AN' YOU GONNA FUCK US UP, THAT WHAT YOU SAYIN'?
YEAH!
'KAY.

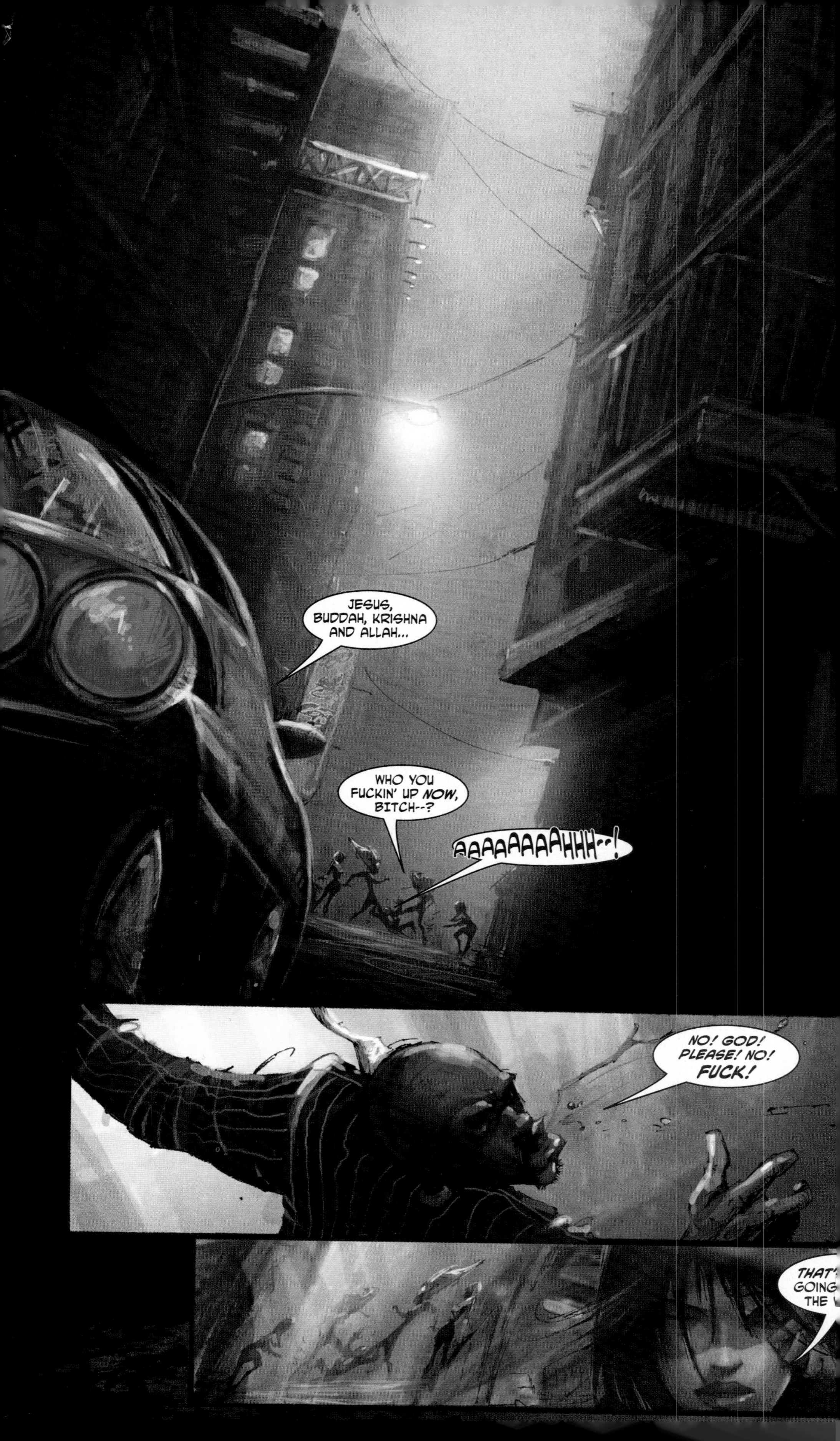
JESUS, BUDDAH, KRISHNA AND ALLAH...
WHO YOU FUCKIN' UP *NOW*, BITCH--?
AAAAAAAAHHH--!
NO! GOD! PLEASE! NO! **FUCK!**
THAT' GOING THE

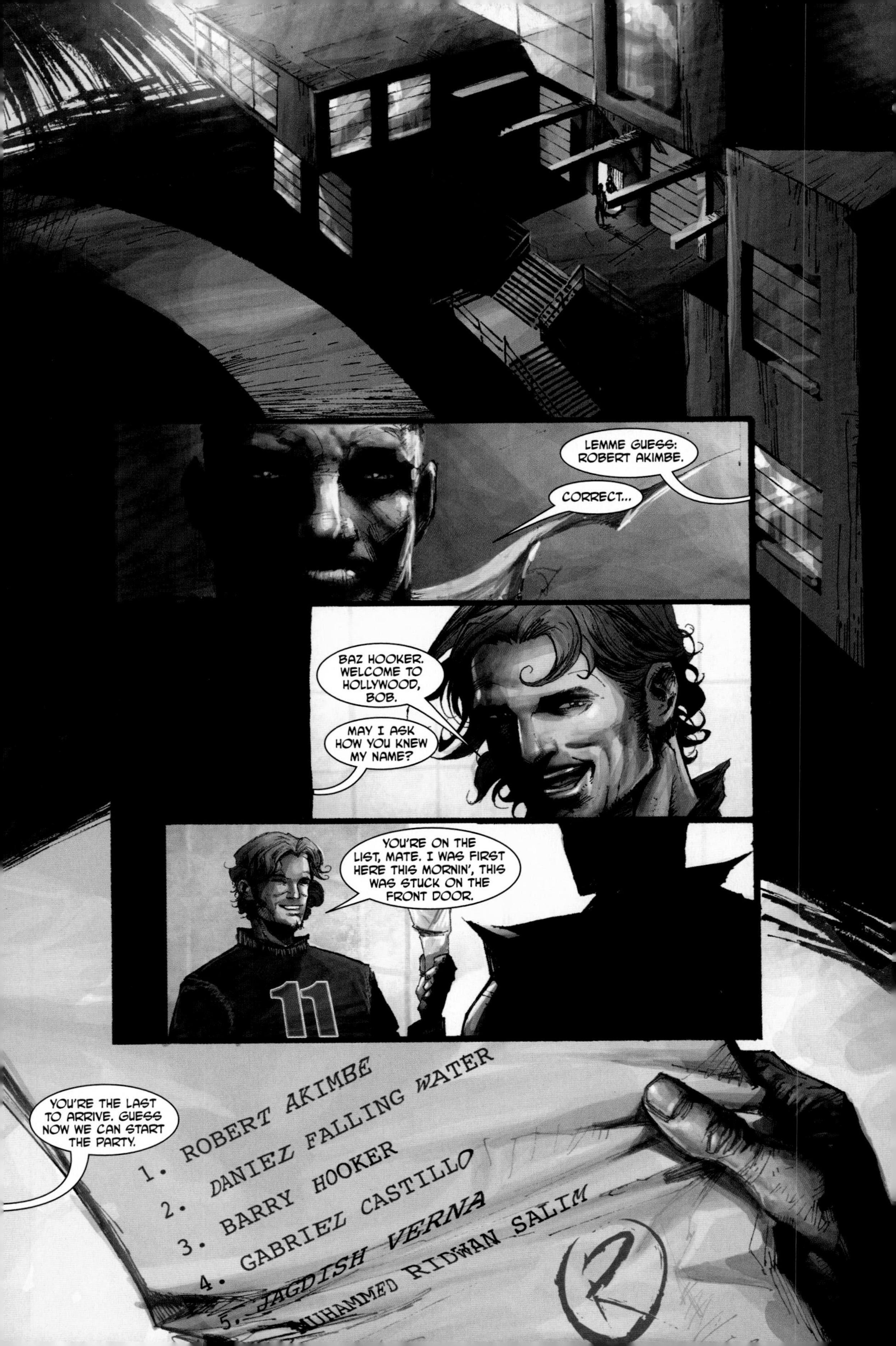
LEMME GUESS: ROBERT AKIMBE.
CORRECT...
BAZ HOOKER. WELCOME TO HOLLYWOOD, BOB.
MAY I ASK HOW YOU KNEW MY NAME?
YOU'RE ON THE LIST, MATE. I WAS FIRST HERE THIS MORNIN', THIS WAS STUCK ON THE FRONT DOOR.
YOU'RE THE LAST TO ARRIVE. GUESS NOW WE CAN START THE PARTY.
1. ROBERT AKIMBE
DANIEL FALLING WATER
2. BARRY HOOKER
3. GABRIEL CASTILLO
4. JAGDISH VERNA
5. MUHAMMED RIDWAN SALIM

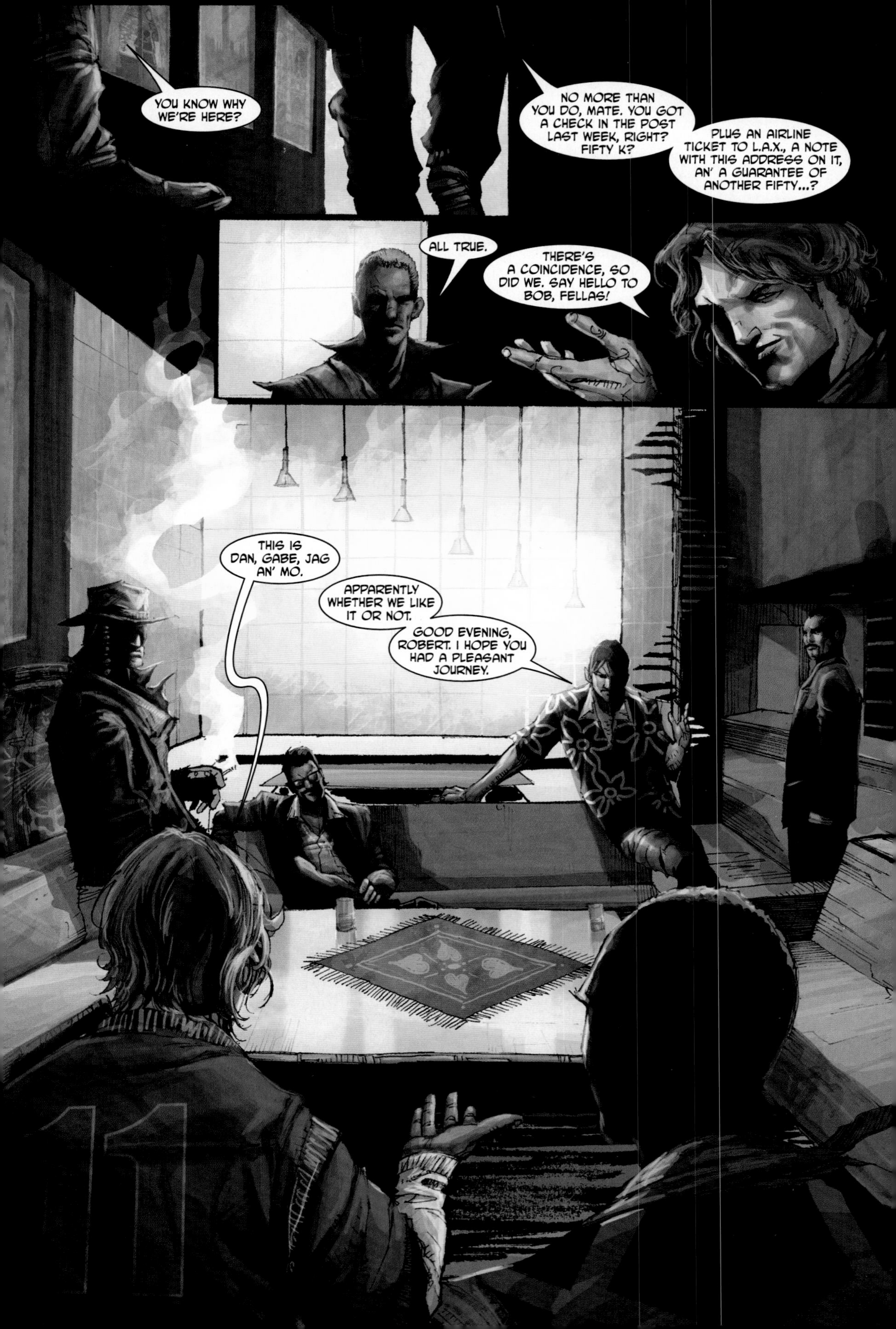
YOU KNOW WHY WE'RE HERE?
NO MORE THAN YOU DO, MATE. YOU GOT A CHECK IN THE POST LAST WEEK, RIGHT? FIFTY K?
PLUS AN AIRLINE TICKET TO L.A.X., A NOTE WITH THIS ADDRESS ON IT, AN' A GUARANTEE OF ANOTHER FIFTY...?
ALL TRUE.
THERE'S A COINCIDENCE, SO DID WE. SAY HELLO TO BOB, FELLAS!
THIS IS DAN, GABE, JAG AN' MO.
APPARENTLY WHETHER WE LIKE IT OR NOT.
GOOD EVENING, ROBERT. I HOPE YOU HAD A PLEASANT JOURNEY.
11

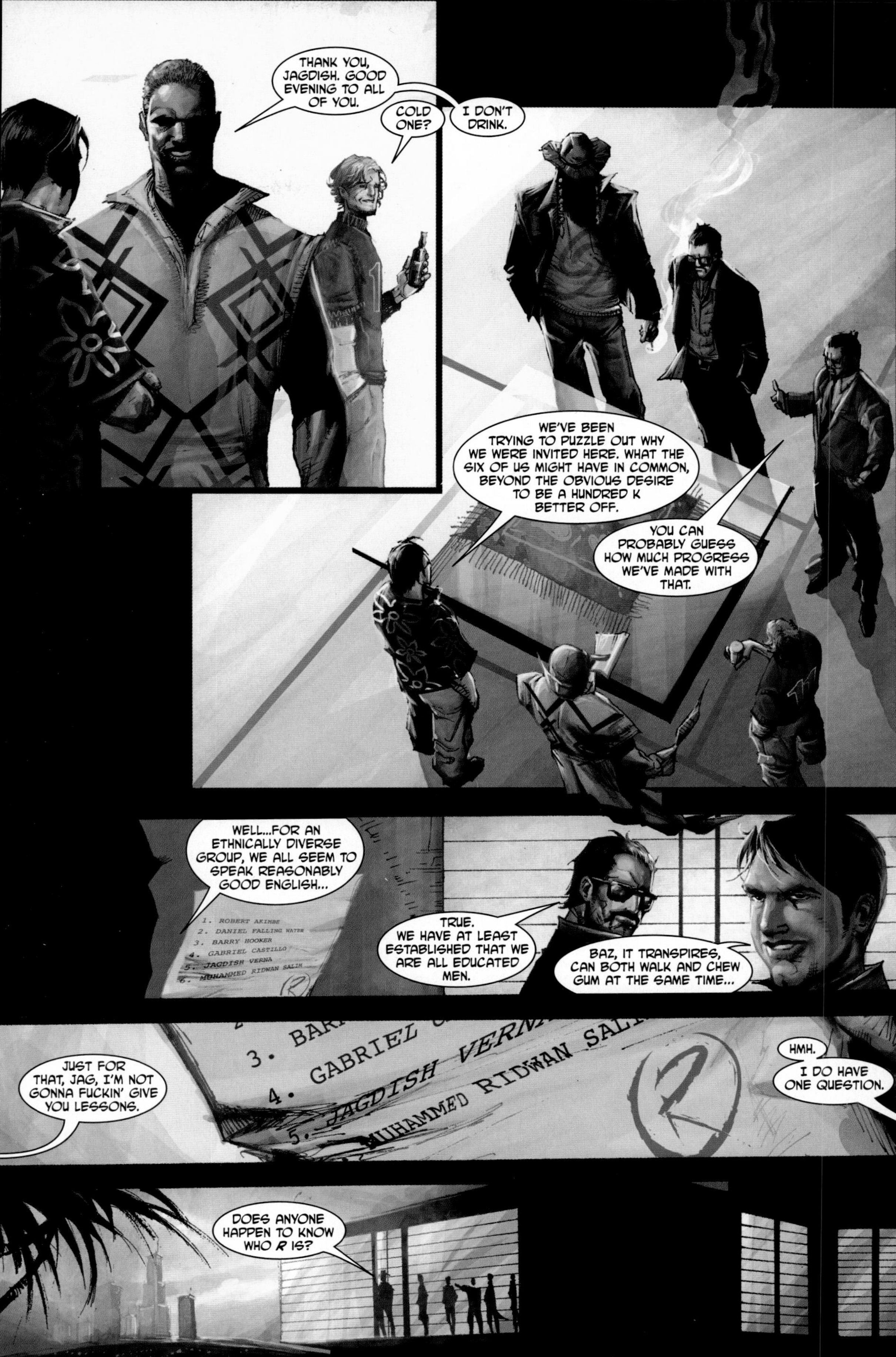
THANK YOU, JAGDISH. GOOD EVENING TO ALL OF YOU.
COLD ONE?
I DON'T DRINK.
WE'VE BEEN TRYING TO PUZZLE OUT WHY WE WERE INVITED HERE. WHAT THE SIX OF US MIGHT HAVE IN COMMON, BEYOND THE OBVIOUS DESIRE TO BE A HUNDRED K BETTER OFF.
YOU CAN PROBABLY GUESS HOW MUCH PROGRESS WE'VE MADE WITH THAT.
WELL...FOR AN ETHNICALLY DIVERSE GROUP, WE ALL SEEM TO SPEAK REASONABLY GOOD ENGLISH...
1. ROBERT AKIMBE
2. DANIEL FALLING WATER
3. BARRY HOOKER
4. GABRIEL CASTILLO
5. JAGDISH VERNA
6. MUHAMMED RIDWAN SALIM
TRUE. WE HAVE AT LEAST ESTABLISHED THAT WE ARE ALL EDUCATED MEN.
BAZ, IT TRANSPIRES, CAN BOTH WALK AND CHEW GUM AT THE SAME TIME...
JUST FOR THAT, JAG, I'M NOT GONNA FUCKIN' GIVE YOU LESSONS.
3. BAR
4. GABRIEL C
5. JAGDISH VERN
MUHAMMED RIDWAN SAL
HMH.
I DO HAVE ONE QUESTION.
DOES ANYONE HAPPEN TO KNOW WHO *R* IS?

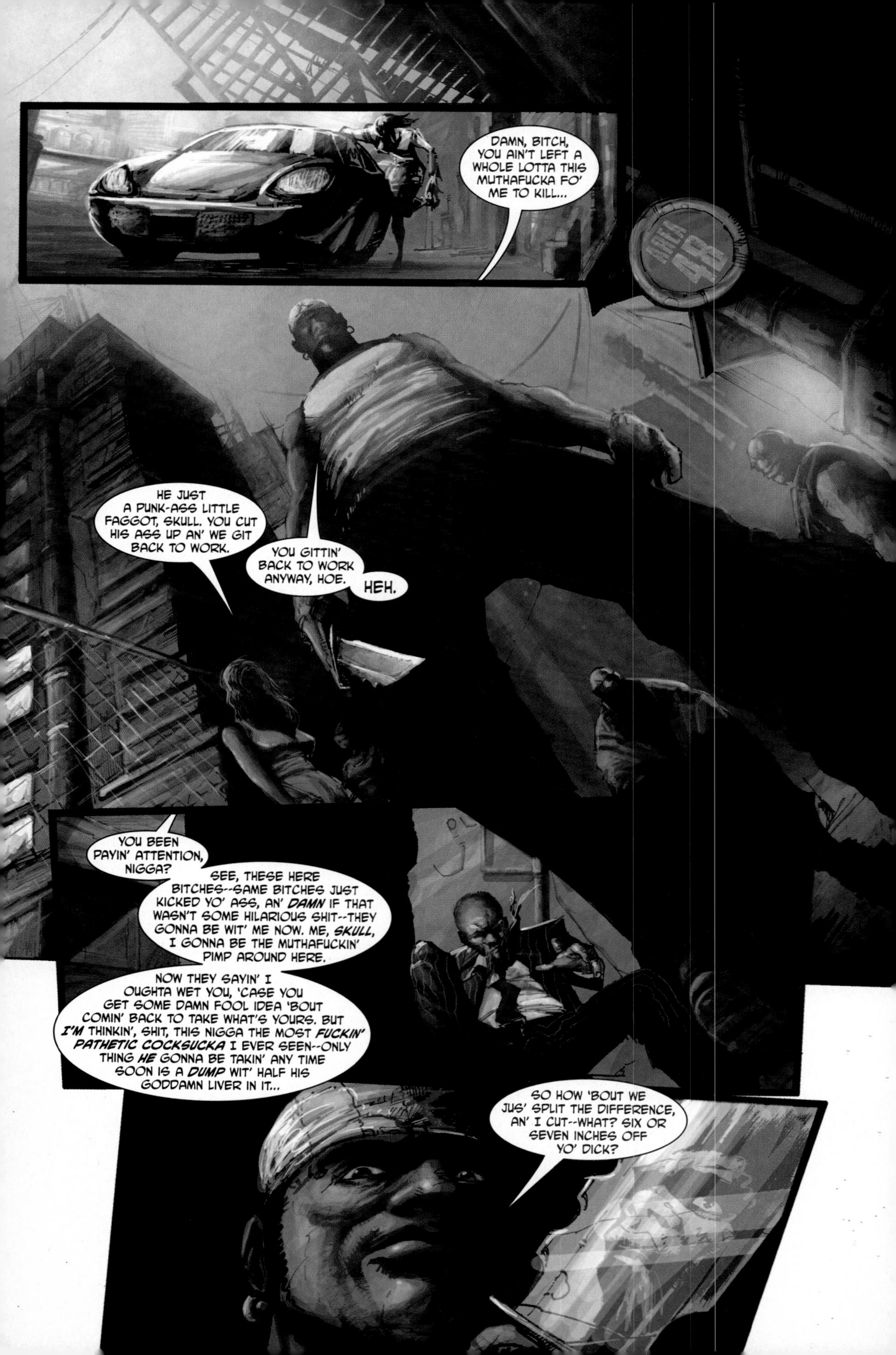
DAMN, BITCH, YOU AIN'T LEFT A WHOLE LOTTA THIS MUTHAFUCKA FO' ME TO KILL...
HE JUST A PUNK-ASS LITTLE FAGGOT, SKULL. YOU CUT HIS ASS UP AN' WE GIT BACK TO WORK.
YOU GITTIN' BACK TO WORK ANYWAY, HOE.
HEH.
YOU BEEN PAYIN' ATTENTION, NIGGA?
SEE, THESE HERE BITCHES--SAME BITCHES JUST KICKED YO' ASS, AN' DAMN IF THAT WASN'T SOME HILARIOUS SHIT--THEY GONNA BE WIT' ME NOW. ME, SKULL, I GONNA BE THE MUTHAFUCKIN' PIMP AROUND HERE.
NOW THEY SAYIN' I OUGHTA WET YOU, 'CASE YOU GET SOME DAMN FOOL IDEA 'BOUT COMIN' BACK TO TAKE WHAT'S YOURS. BUT I'M THINKIN', SHIT, THIS NIGGA THE MOST FUCKIN' PATHETIC COCKSUCKA I EVER SEEN--ONLY THING HE GONNA BE TAKIN' ANY TIME SOON IS A DUMP WIT' HALF HIS GODDAMN LIVER IN IT...
SO HOW 'BOUT WE JUS' SPLIT THE DIFFERENCE, AN' I CUT--WHAT? SIX OR SEVEN INCHES OFF YO' DICK?

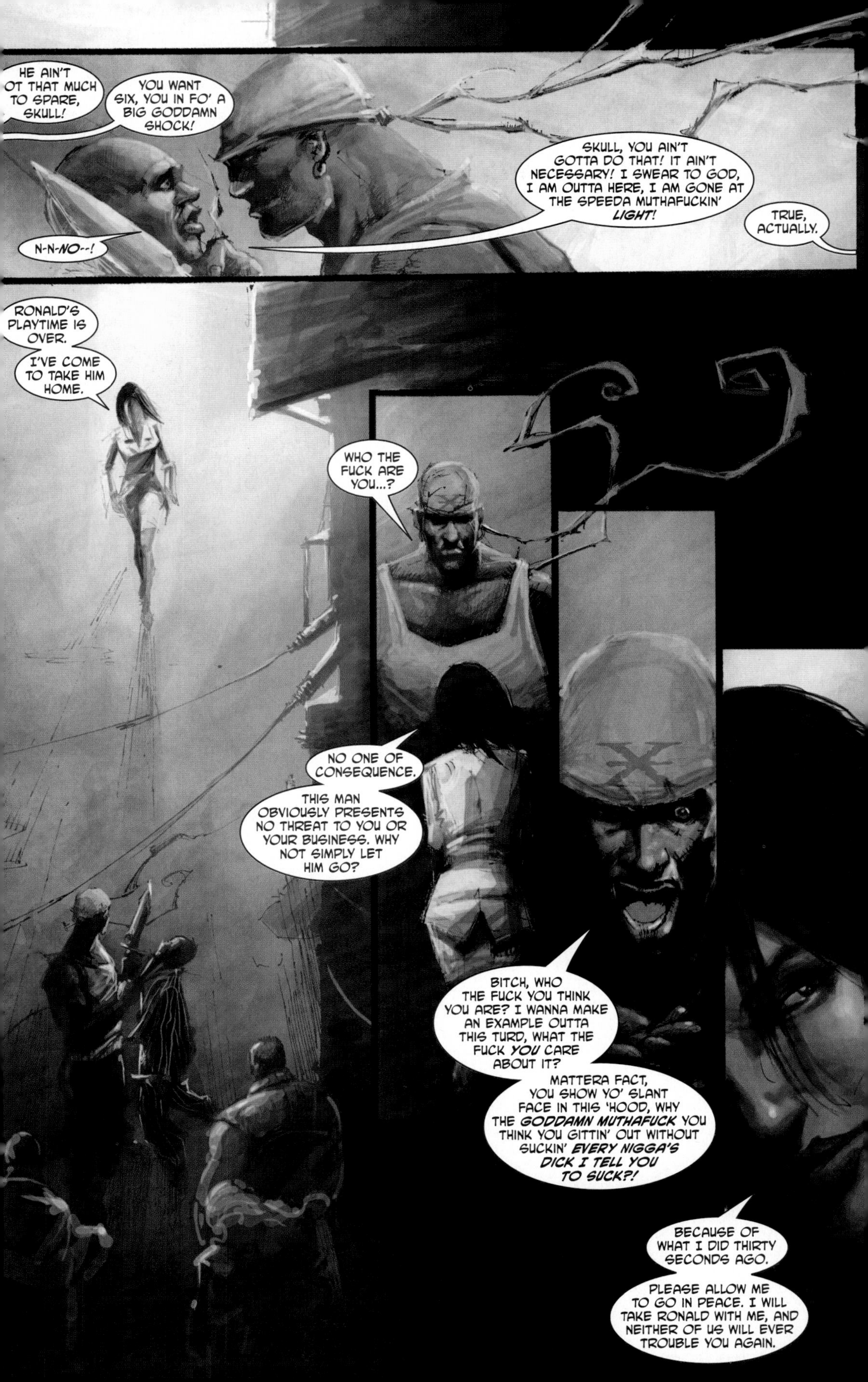
HE AIN'T OT THAT MUCH TO SPARE, SKULL!
YOU WANT SIX, YOU IN FO' A BIG GODDAMN SHOCK!
N-N-NO--!
SKULL, YOU AIN'T GOTTA DO THAT! IT AIN'T NECESSARY! I SWEAR TO GOD, I AM OUTTA HERE, I AM GONE AT THE SPEEDA MUTHAFUCKIN' LIGHT!
TRUE, ACTUALLY.
RONALD'S PLAYTIME IS OVER.
I'VE COME TO TAKE HIM HOME.
WHO THE FUCK ARE YOU...?
NO ONE OF CONSEQUENCE.
THIS MAN OBVIOUSLY PRESENTS NO THREAT TO YOU OR YOUR BUSINESS. WHY NOT SIMPLY LET HIM GO?
BITCH, WHO THE FUCK YOU THINK YOU ARE? I WANNA MAKE AN EXAMPLE OUTTA THIS TURD, WHAT THE FUCK YOU CARE ABOUT IT?
MATTERA FACT, YOU SHOW YO' SLANT FACE IN THIS 'HOOD, WHY THE GODDAMN MUTHAFUCK YOU THINK YOU GITTIN' OUT WITHOUT SUCKIN' EVERY NIGGA'S DICK I TELL YOU TO SUCK?!
BECAUSE OF WHAT I DID THIRTY SECONDS AGO.
PLEASE ALLOW ME TO GO IN PEACE. I WILL TAKE RONALD WITH ME, AND NEITHER OF US WILL EVER TROUBLE YOU AGAIN.

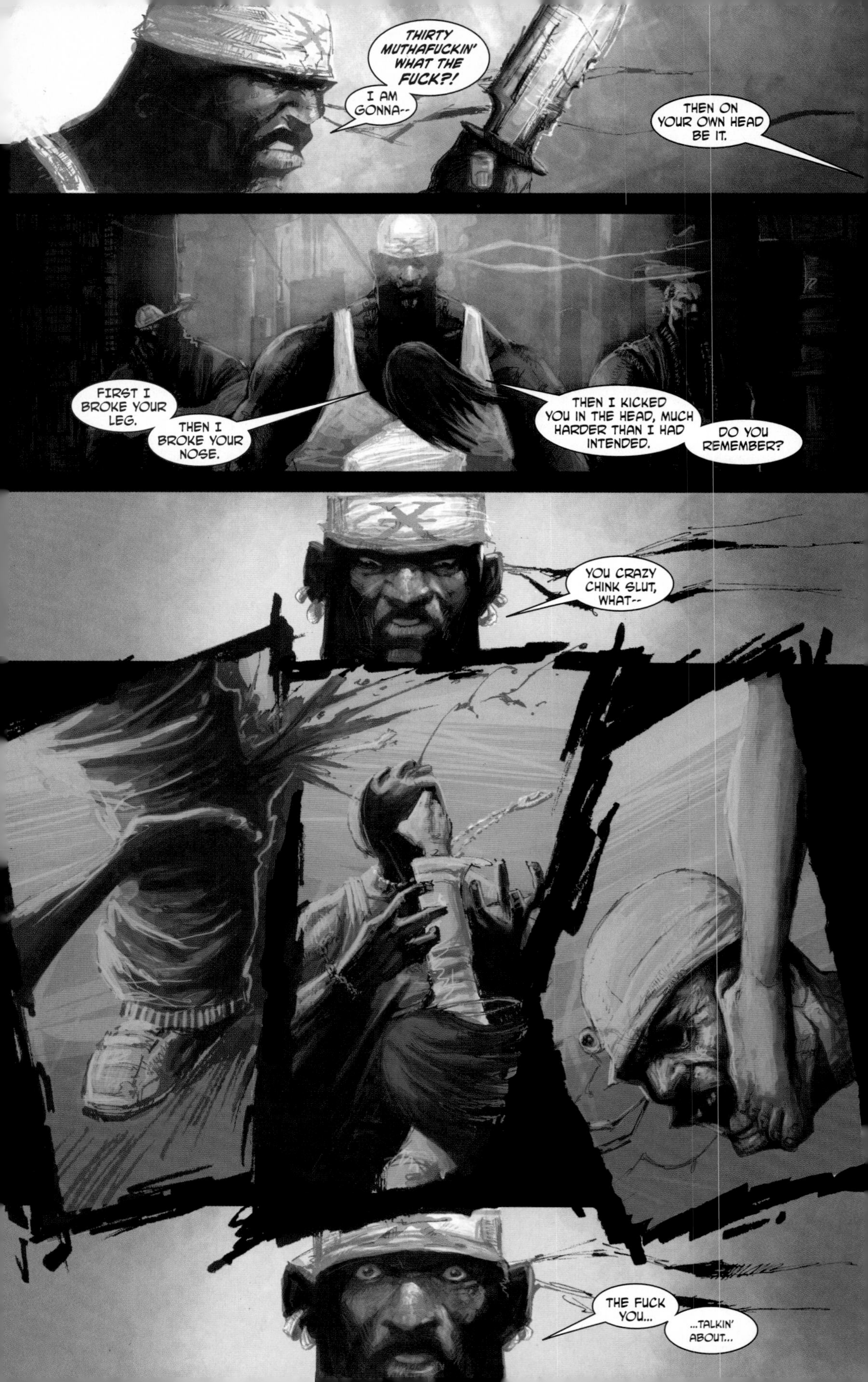
THIRTY MUTHAFUCKIN' WHAT THE FUCK?!
I AM GONNA--
THEN ON YOUR OWN HEAD BE IT.
FIRST I BROKE YOUR LEG.
THEN I BROKE YOUR NOSE.
THEN I KICKED YOU IN THE HEAD, MUCH HARDER THAN I HAD INTENDED.
DO YOU REMEMBER?
YOU CRAZY CHINK SLUT, WHAT--
THE FUCK YOU...
...TALKIN' ABOUT...

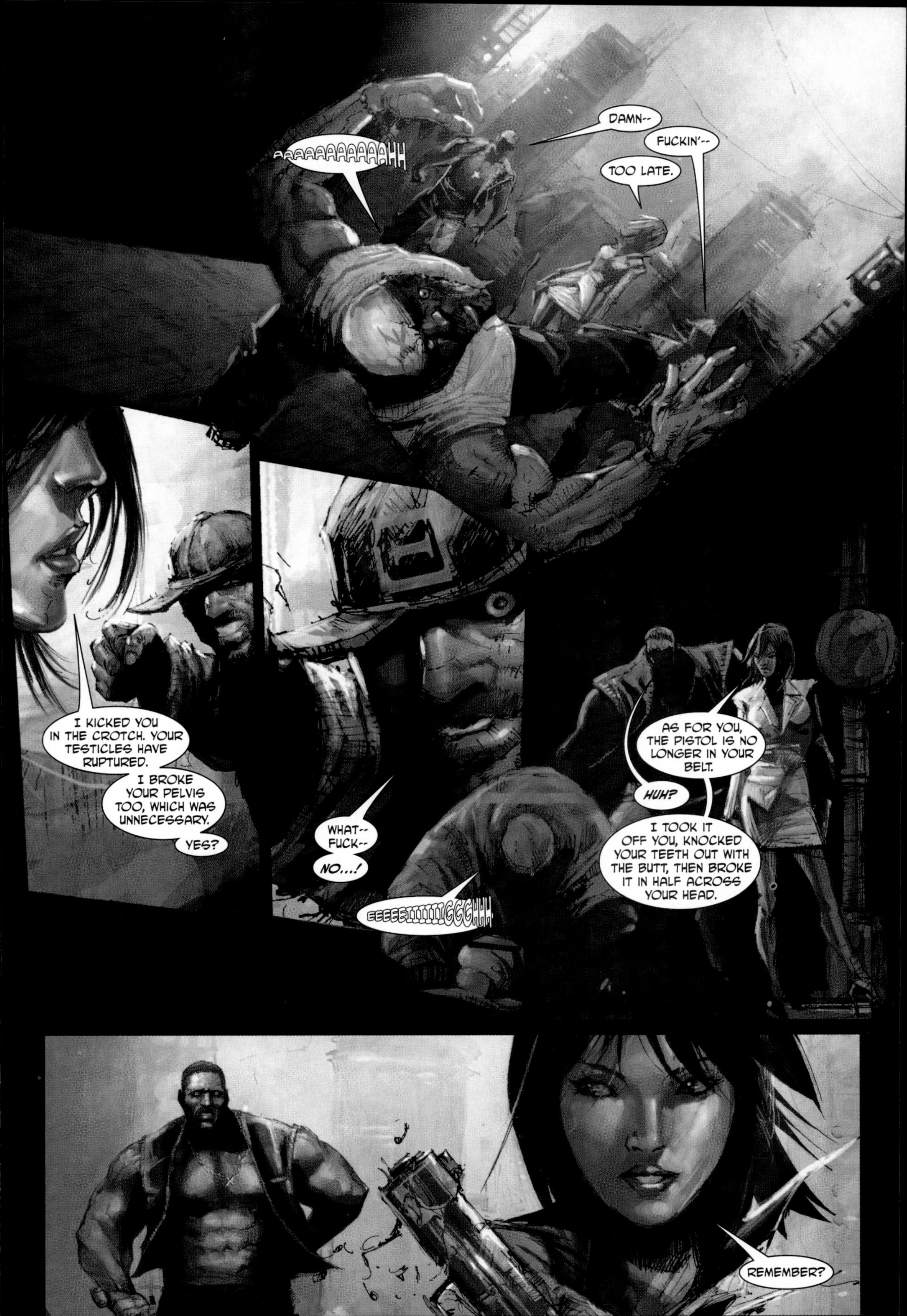

AAAAAAAAAAAAHH
DAMN--
FUCKIN'--
TOO LATE.
I KICKED YOU IN THE CROTCH. YOUR TESTICLES HAVE RUPTURED.
I BROKE YOUR PELVIS TOO, WHICH WAS UNNECESSARY.
YES?
WHAT-- FUCK--
NO...!
EEEEEIIIIIIGGGHHH
AS FOR YOU, THE PISTOL IS NO LONGER IN YOUR BELT.
HUH?
I TOOK IT OFF YOU, KNOCKED YOUR TEETH OUT WITH THE BUTT, THEN BROKE IT IN HALF ACROSS YOUR HEAD.
REMEMBER?

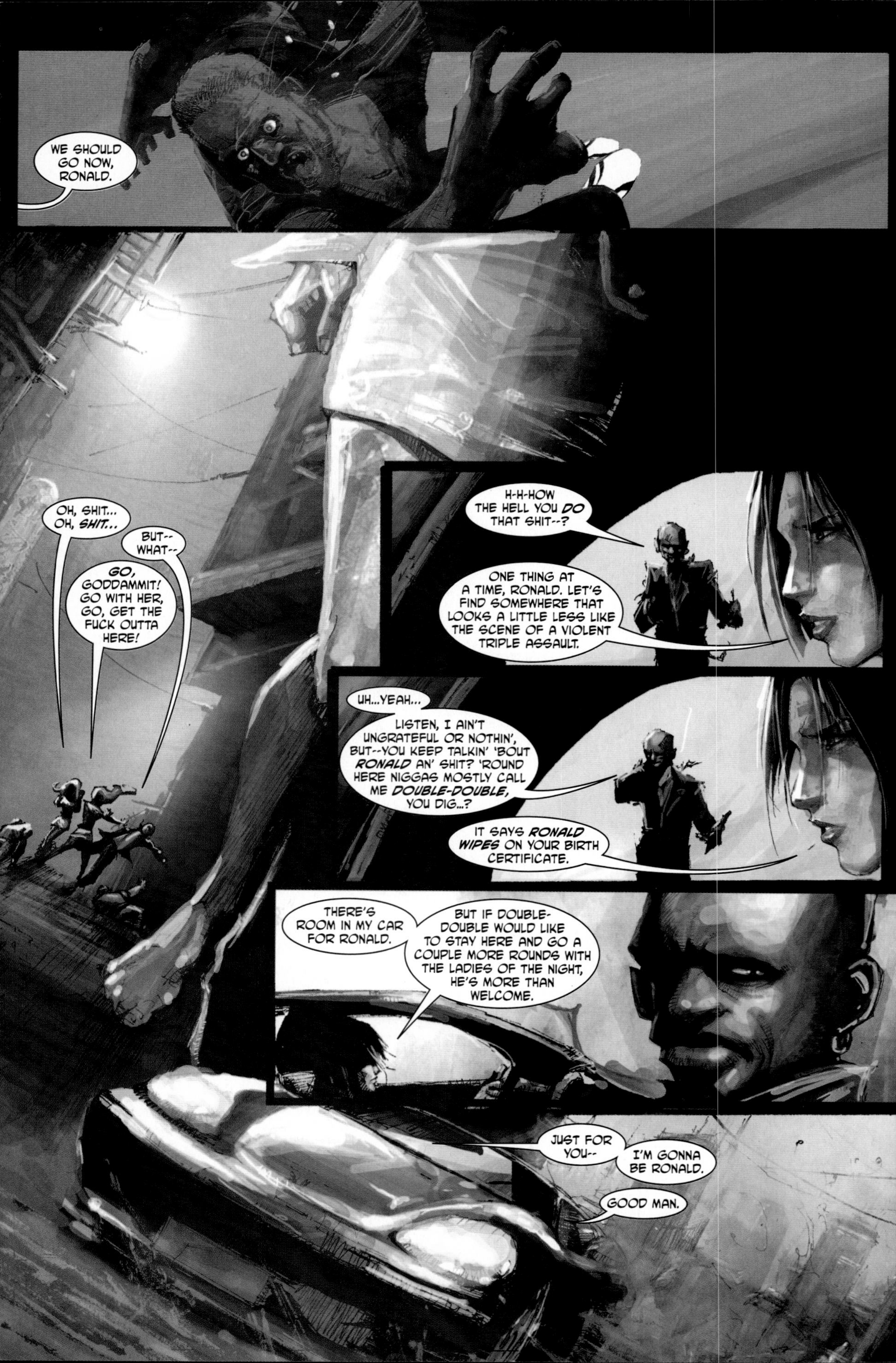
WE SHOULD GO NOW, RONALD.
OH, SHIT... OH, SHIT...
BUT-- WHAT--
GO, GODDAMMIT! GO WITH HER, GO, GET THE FUCK OUTTA HERE!
H-H-HOW THE HELL YOU DO THAT SHIT--?
ONE THING AT A TIME, RONALD. LET'S FIND SOMEWHERE THAT LOOKS A LITTLE LESS LIKE THE SCENE OF A VIOLENT TRIPLE ASSAULT.
UH...YEAH...
LISTEN, I AIN'T UNGRATEFUL OR NOTHIN', BUT--YOU KEEP TALKIN' 'BOUT RONALD AN' SHIT? 'ROUND HERE NIGGAS MOSTLY CALL ME DOUBLE-DOUBLE, YOU DIG...?
IT SAYS RONALD WIPES ON YOUR BIRTH CERTIFICATE.
THERE'S ROOM IN MY CAR FOR RONALD.
BUT IF DOUBLE-DOUBLE WOULD LIKE TO STAY HERE AND GO A COUPLE MORE ROUNDS WITH THE LADIES OF THE NIGHT, HE'S MORE THAN WELCOME.
JUST FOR YOU--
I'M GONNA BE RONALD.
GOOD MAN.

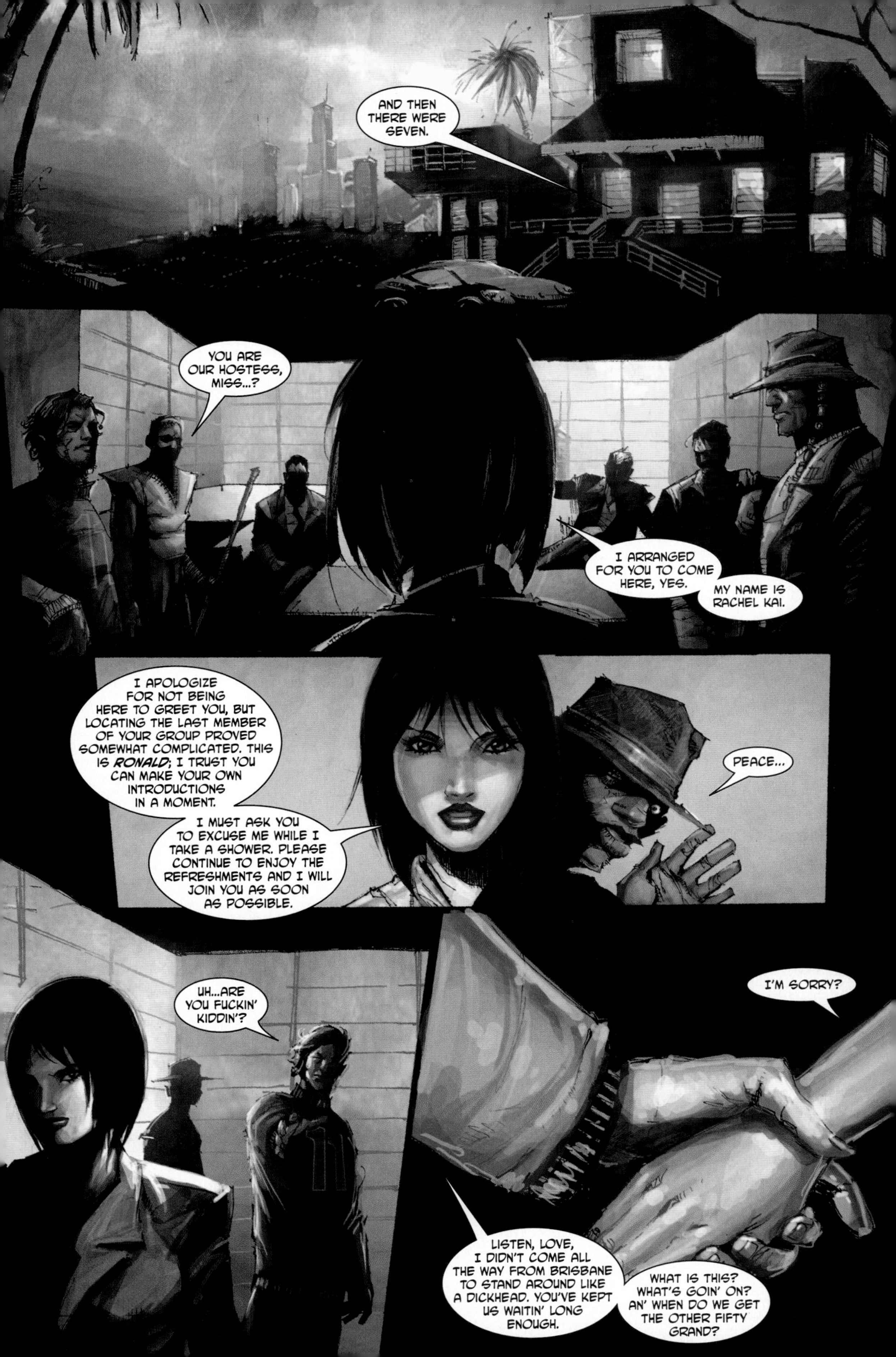

AND THEN THERE WERE SEVEN.
YOU ARE OUR HOSTESS, MISS...?
I ARRANGED FOR YOU TO COME HERE, YES.
MY NAME IS RACHEL KAI.
I APOLOGIZE FOR NOT BEING HERE TO GREET YOU, BUT LOCATING THE LAST MEMBER OF YOUR GROUP PROVED SOMEWHAT COMPLICATED. THIS IS *RONALD*; I TRUST YOU CAN MAKE YOUR OWN INTRODUCTIONS IN A MOMENT.
PEACE...
I MUST ASK YOU TO EXCUSE ME WHILE I TAKE A SHOWER. PLEASE CONTINUE TO ENJOY THE REFRESHMENTS AND I WILL JOIN YOU AS SOON AS POSSIBLE.
UH...ARE YOU FUCKIN' KIDDIN'?
I'M SORRY?
LISTEN, LOVE, I DIDN'T COME ALL THE WAY FROM BRISBANE TO STAND AROUND LIKE A DICKHEAD. YOU'VE KEPT US WAITIN' LONG ENOUGH.
WHAT IS THIS? WHAT'S GOIN' ON? AN' WHEN DO WE GET THE OTHER FIFTY GRAND?

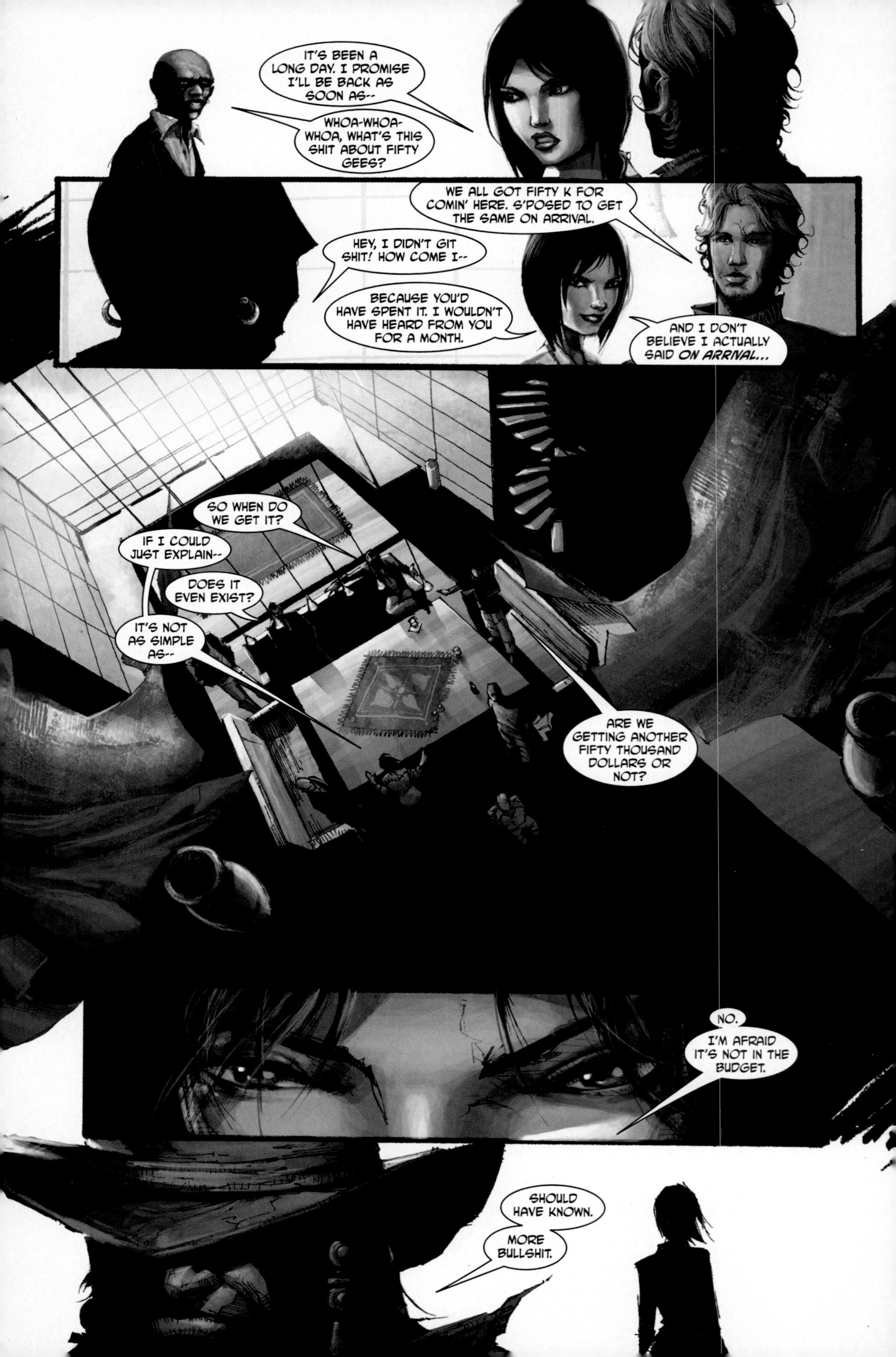
IT'S BEEN A LONG DAY. I PROMISE I'LL BE BACK AS SOON AS--
WHOA-WHOA-WHOA, WHAT'S THIS SHIT ABOUT FIFTY GEES?
WE ALL GOT FIFTY K FOR COMIN' HERE. S'POSED TO GET THE SAME ON ARRIVAL.
HEY, I DIDN'T GIT SHIT! HOW COME I--
BECAUSE YOU'D HAVE SPENT IT. I WOULDN'T HAVE HEARD FROM YOU FOR A MONTH.
AND I DON'T BELIEVE I ACTUALLY SAID *ON ARRIVAL...*
SO WHEN DO WE GET IT?
IF I COULD JUST EXPLAIN--
DOES IT EVEN EXIST?
IT'S NOT AS SIMPLE AS--
ARE WE GETTING ANOTHER FIFTY THOUSAND DOLLARS OR NOT?
NO.
I'M AFRAID IT'S NOT IN THE BUDGET.
SHOULD HAVE KNOWN.
MORE BULLSHIT.

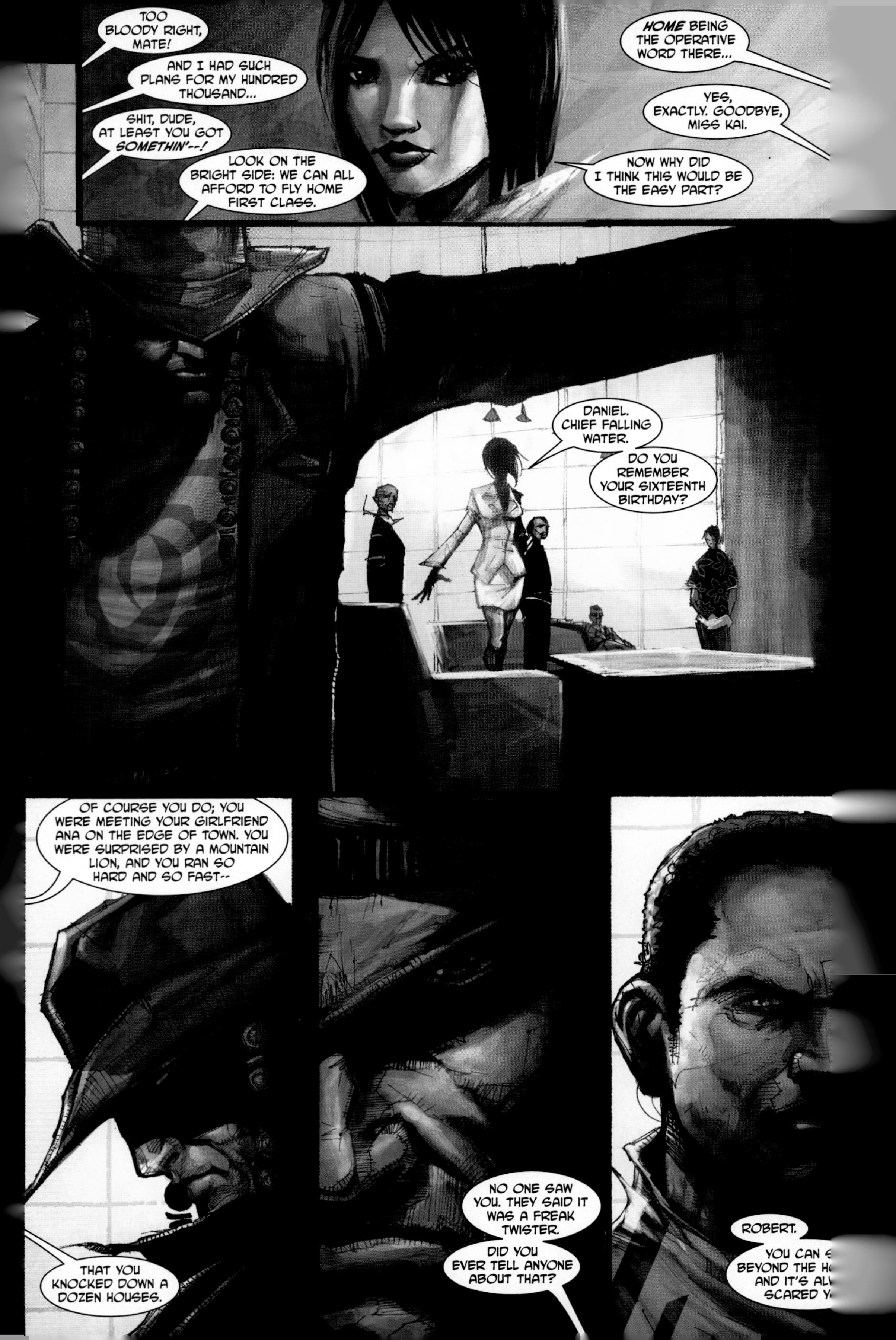
TOO BLOODY RIGHT, MATE!
AND I HAD SUCH PLANS FOR MY HUNDRED THOUSAND...
SHIT, DUDE, AT LEAST YOU GOT *SOMETHIN'*--!
LOOK ON THE BRIGHT SIDE: WE CAN ALL AFFORD TO FLY HOME FIRST CLASS.
HOME BEING THE OPERATIVE WORD THERE...
YES, EXACTLY. GOODBYE, MISS KAI.
NOW WHY DID I THINK THIS WOULD BE THE EASY PART?
DANIEL. CHIEF FALLING WATER.
DO YOU REMEMBER YOUR SIXTEENTH BIRTHDAY?
OF COURSE YOU DO; YOU WERE MEETING YOUR GIRLFRIEND ANA ON THE EDGE OF TOWN. YOU WERE SURPRISED BY A MOUNTAIN LION, AND YOU RAN SO HARD AND SO FAST--
THAT YOU KNOCKED DOWN A DOZEN HOUSES.
NO ONE SAW YOU. THEY SAID IT WAS A FREAK TWISTER.
DID YOU EVER TELL ANYONE ABOUT THAT?
ROBERT.

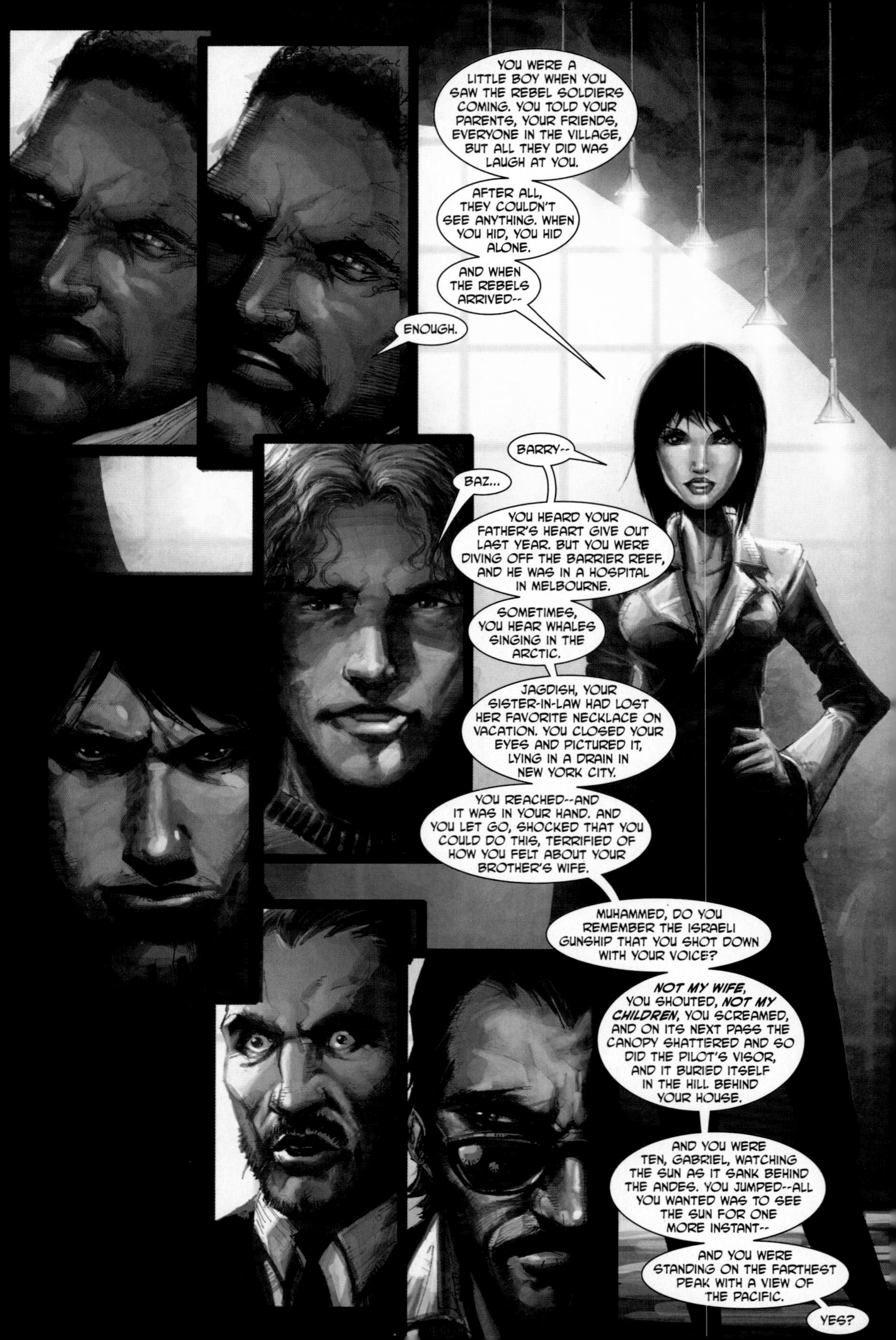
YOU WERE A LITTLE BOY WHEN YOU SAW THE REBEL SOLDIERS COMING. YOU TOLD YOUR PARENTS, YOUR FRIENDS, EVERYONE IN THE VILLAGE, BUT ALL THEY DID WAS LAUGH AT YOU.
AFTER ALL, THEY COULDN'T SEE ANYTHING. WHEN YOU HID, YOU HID ALONE.
AND WHEN THE REBELS ARRIVED--
ENOUGH.
BARRY--
BAZ...
YOU HEARD YOUR FATHER'S HEART GIVE OUT LAST YEAR. BUT YOU WERE DIVING OFF THE BARRIER REEF, AND HE WAS IN A HOSPITAL IN MELBOURNE.
SOMETIMES, YOU HEAR WHALES SINGING IN THE ARCTIC.
JAGDISH, YOUR SISTER-IN-LAW HAD LOST HER FAVORITE NECKLACE ON VACATION. YOU CLOSED YOUR EYES AND PICTURED IT, LYING IN A DRAIN IN NEW YORK CITY.
YOU REACHED--AND IT WAS IN YOUR HAND. AND YOU LET GO, SHOCKED THAT YOU COULD DO THIS, TERRIFIED OF HOW YOU FELT ABOUT YOUR BROTHER'S WIFE.
MUHAMMED, DO YOU REMEMBER THE ISRAELI GUNSHIP THAT YOU SHOT DOWN WITH YOUR VOICE?
NOT MY WIFE, YOU SHOUTED, *NOT MY CHILDREN*, YOU SCREAMED, AND ON ITS NEXT PASS THE CANOPY SHATTERED AND SO DID THE PILOT'S VISOR, AND IT BURIED ITSELF IN THE HILL BEHIND YOUR HOUSE.
AND YOU WERE TEN, GABRIEL, WATCHING THE SUN AS IT SANK BEHIND THE ANDES. YOU JUMPED--ALL YOU WANTED WAS TO SEE THE SUN FOR ONE MORE INSTANT--
AND YOU WERE STANDING ON THE FARTHEST PEAK WITH A VIEW OF THE PACIFIC.
YES?

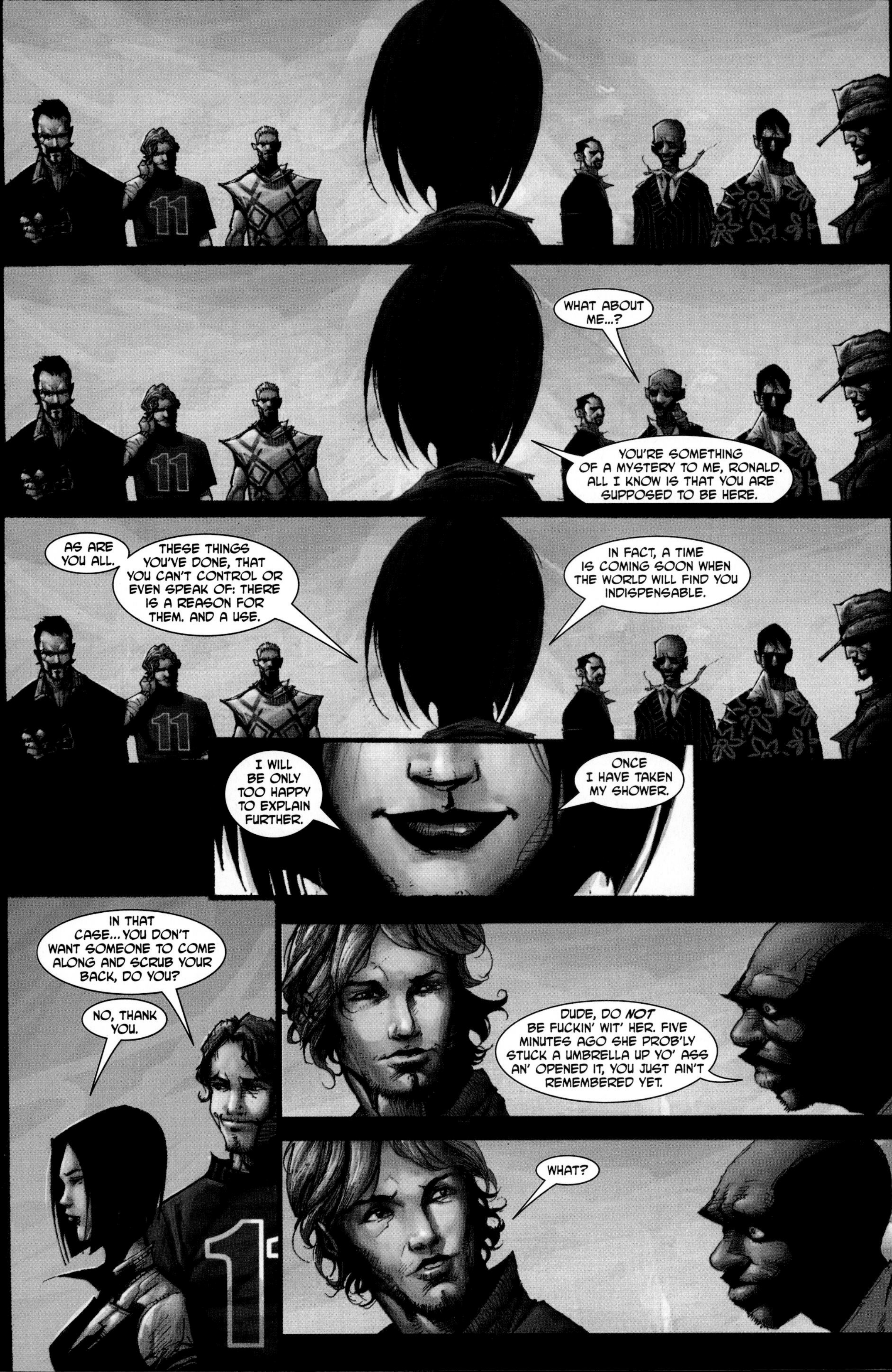
WHAT ABOUT ME...?
YOU'RE SOMETHING OF A MYSTERY TO ME, RONALD. ALL I KNOW IS THAT YOU ARE SUPPOSED TO BE HERE.
AS ARE YOU ALL.
THESE THINGS YOU'VE DONE, THAT YOU CAN'T CONTROL OR EVEN SPEAK OF: THERE IS A REASON FOR THEM. AND A USE.
IN FACT, A TIME IS COMING SOON WHEN THE WORLD WILL FIND YOU INDISPENSABLE.
I WILL BE ONLY TOO HAPPY TO EXPLAIN FURTHER.
ONCE I HAVE TAKEN MY SHOWER.
IN THAT CASE...YOU DON'T WANT SOMEONE TO COME ALONG AND SCRUB YOUR BACK, DO YOU?
NO, THANK YOU.
DUDE, DO NOT BE FUCKIN' WIT' HER. FIVE MINUTES AGO SHE PROB'LY STUCK A UMBRELLA UP YO' ASS AN' OPENED IT, YOU JUST AIN'T REMEMBERED YET.
WHAT?

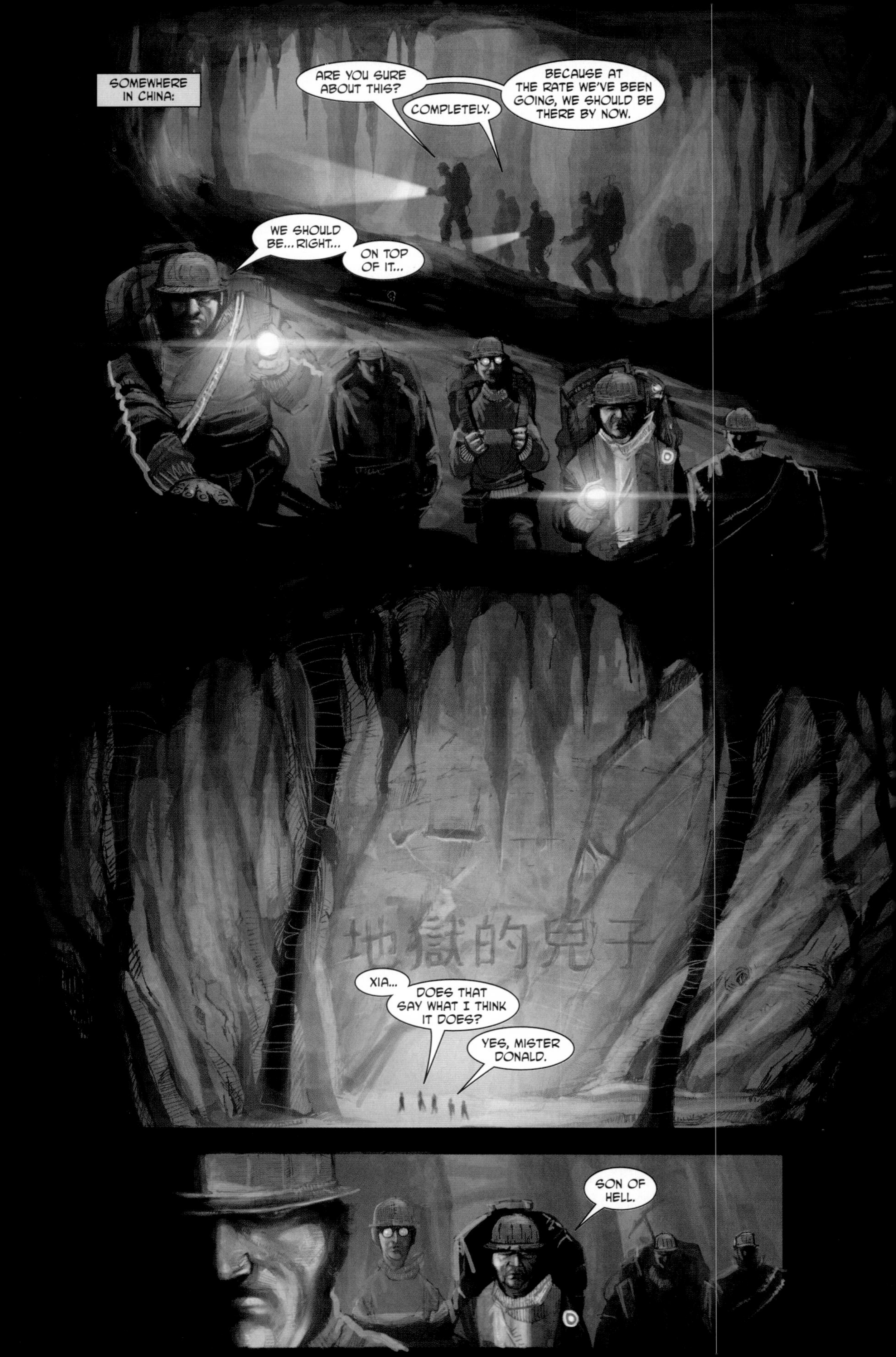
SOMEWHERE IN CHINA:
ARE YOU SURE ABOUT THIS?
BECAUSE AT THE RATE WE'VE BEEN GOING, WE SHOULD BE THERE BY NOW.
COMPLETELY.
WE SHOULD BE... RIGHT...
ON TOP OF IT...
地獄的兒子
XIA...
DOES THAT SAY WHAT I THINK IT DOES?
YES, MISTER DONALD.
SON OF HELL.

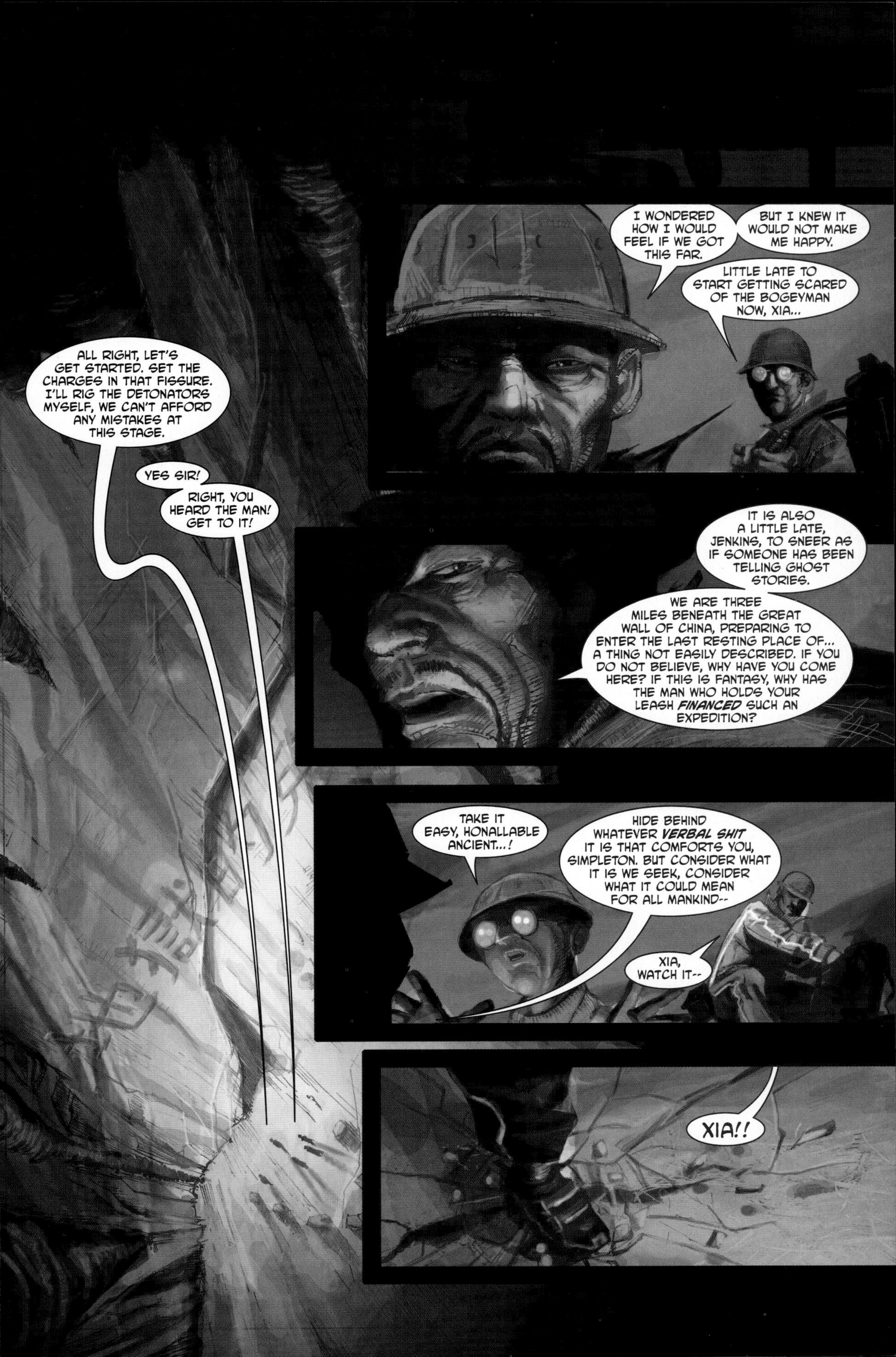
I WONDERED HOW I WOULD FEEL IF WE GOT THIS FAR.
BUT I KNEW IT WOULD NOT MAKE ME HAPPY.
LITTLE LATE TO START GETTING SCARED OF THE BOGEYMAN NOW, XIA...
ALL RIGHT, LET'S GET STARTED. SET THE CHARGES IN THAT FISSURE. I'LL RIG THE DETONATORS MYSELF, WE CAN'T AFFORD ANY MISTAKES AT THIS STAGE.
YES SIR!
RIGHT, YOU HEARD THE MAN! GET TO IT!
IT IS ALSO A LITTLE LATE, JENKINS, TO SNEER AS IF SOMEONE HAS BEEN TELLING GHOST STORIES.
WE ARE THREE MILES BENEATH THE GREAT WALL OF CHINA, PREPARING TO ENTER THE LAST RESTING PLACE OF... A THING NOT EASILY DESCRIBED. IF YOU DO NOT BELIEVE, WHY HAVE YOU COME HERE? IF THIS IS FANTASY, WHY HAS THE MAN WHO HOLDS YOUR LEASH *FINANCED* SUCH AN EXPEDITION?
TAKE IT EASY, HONALLABLE ANCIENT...!
HIDE BEHIND WHATEVER *VERBAL SHIT* IT IS THAT COMFORTS YOU, SIMPLETON. BUT CONSIDER WHAT IT IS WE SEEK, CONSIDER WHAT IT COULD MEAN FOR ALL MANKIND--
XIA, WATCH IT--
XIA!!

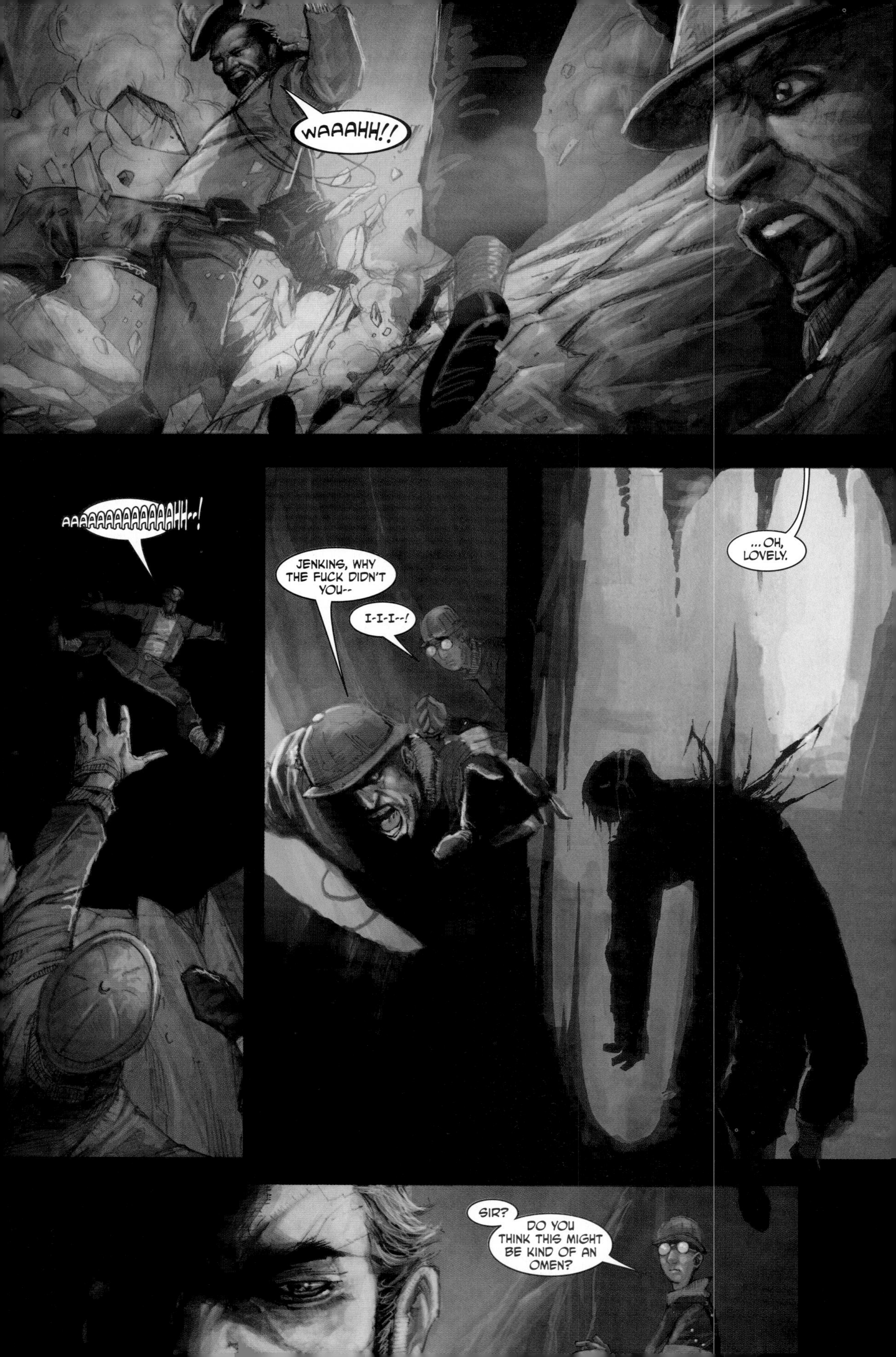
WAAAHH!!
AAAAAAAAAAAAAAAHH--!
JENKINS, WHY THE FUCK DIDN'T YOU--
I-I-I--!
...OH, LOVELY.
SIR?
DO YOU THINK THIS MIGHT BE KIND OF AN OMEN?

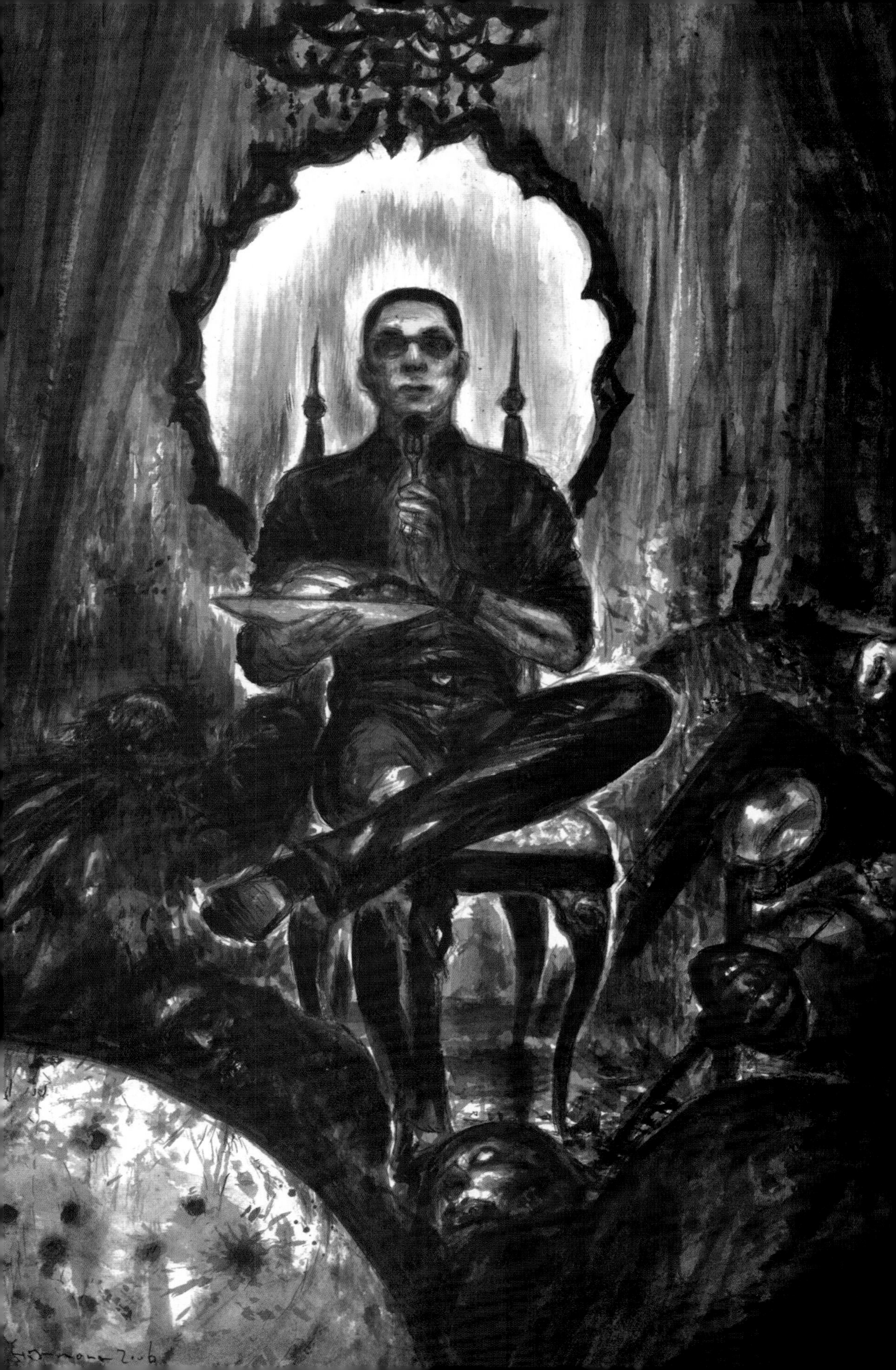

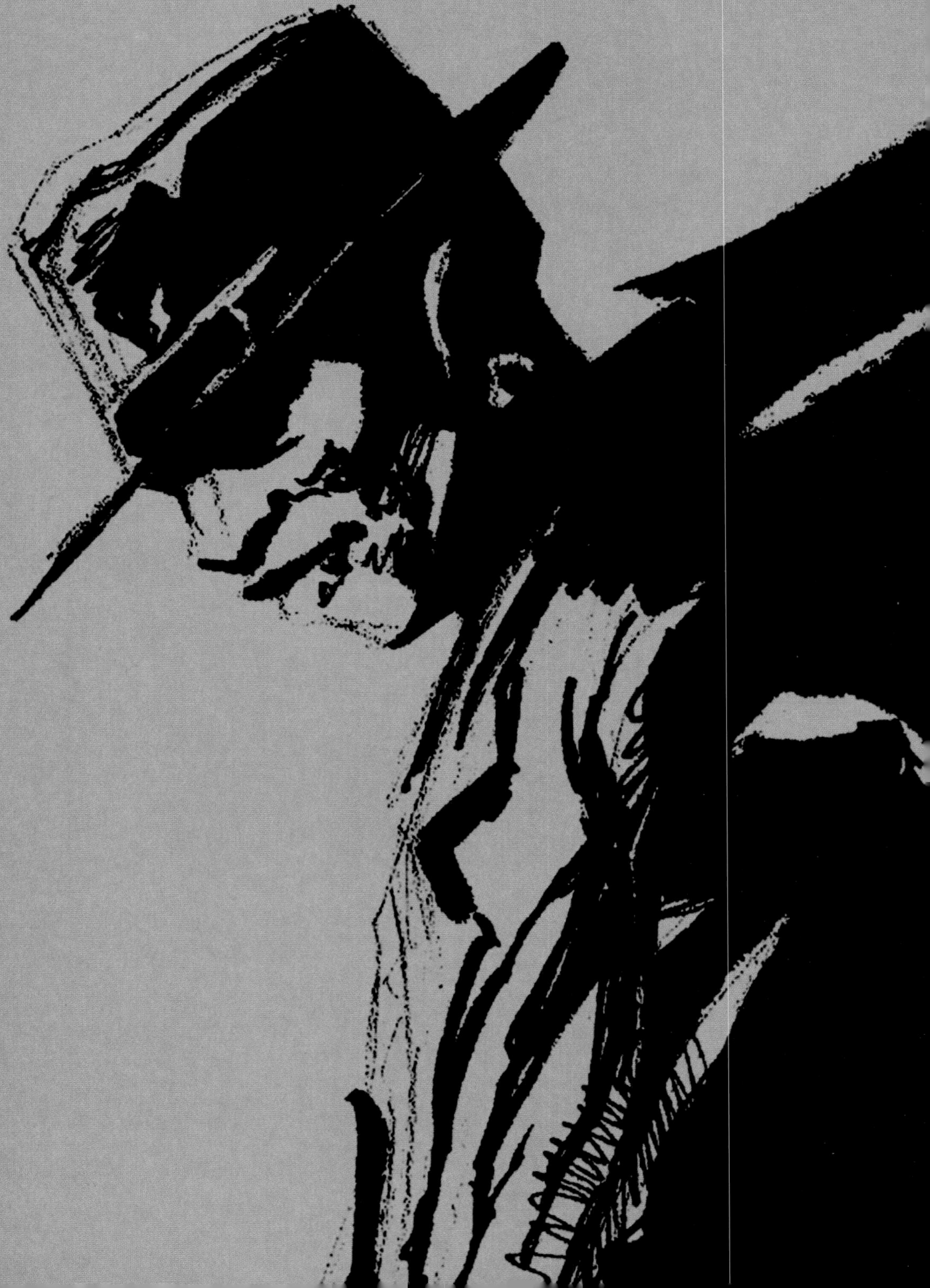

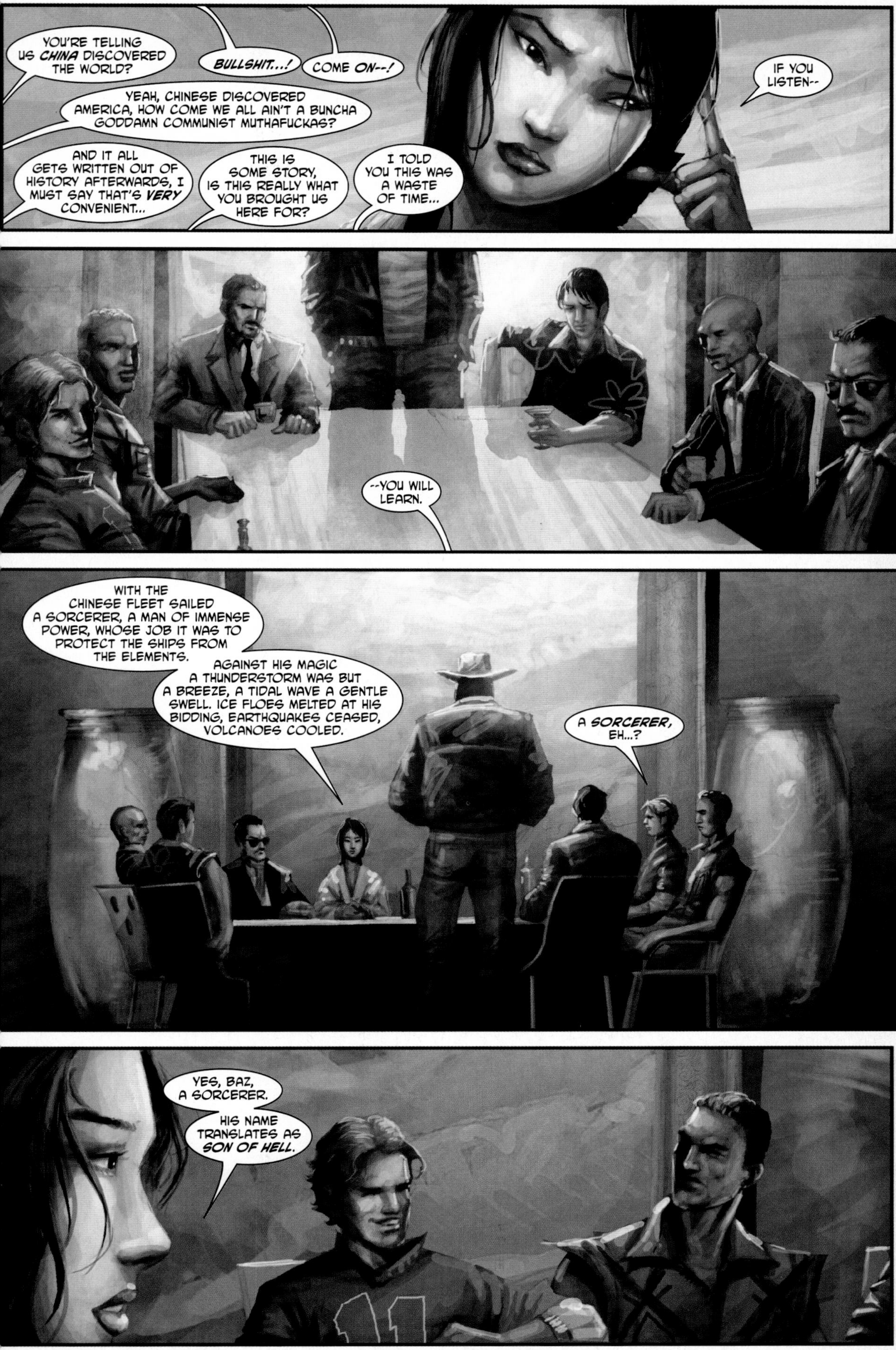
YOU'RE TELLING US *CHINA* DISCOVERED THE WORLD?
BULLSHIT...!
COME *ON--!*
YEAH, CHINESE DISCOVERED AMERICA, HOW COME WE ALL AIN'T A BUNCHA GODDAMN COMMUNIST MUTHAFUCKAS?
AND IT ALL GETS WRITTEN OUT OF HISTORY AFTERWARDS, I MUST SAY THAT'S *VERY* CONVENIENT...
THIS IS SOME STORY, IS THIS REALLY WHAT YOU BROUGHT US HERE FOR?
I TOLD YOU THIS WAS A WASTE OF TIME...
IF YOU LISTEN--
--YOU WILL LEARN.
WITH THE CHINESE FLEET SAILED A SORCERER, A MAN OF IMMENSE POWER, WHOSE JOB IT WAS TO PROTECT THE SHIPS FROM THE ELEMENTS.
AGAINST HIS MAGIC A THUNDERSTORM WAS BUT A BREEZE, A TIDAL WAVE A GENTLE SWELL. ICE FLOES MELTED AT HIS BIDDING, EARTHQUAKES CEASED, VOLCANOES COOLED.
A *SORCERER,* EH...?
YES, BAZ, A SORCERER.
HIS NAME TRANSLATES AS *SON OF HELL.*

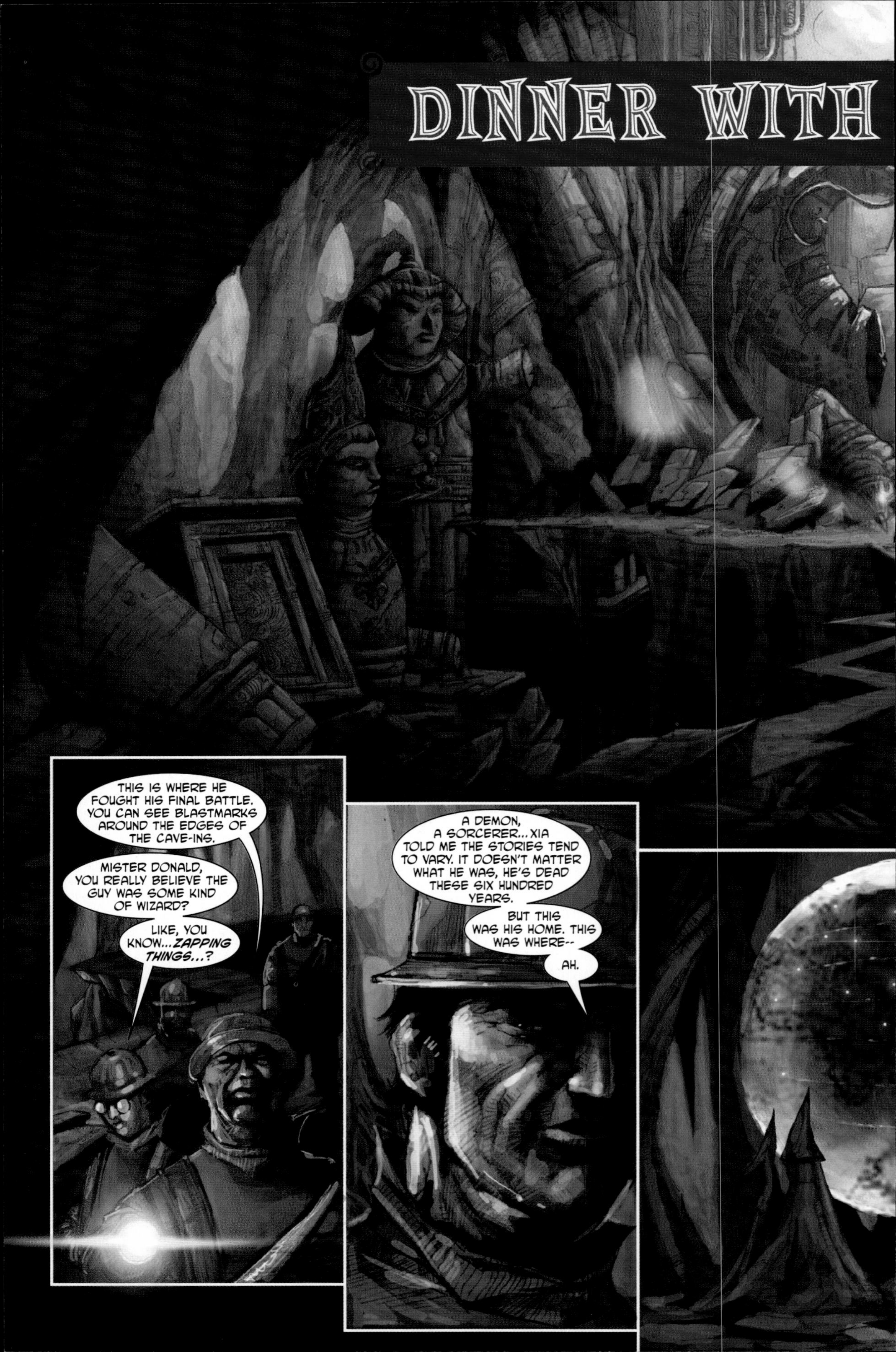
DINNER WITH
THIS IS WHERE HE FOUGHT HIS FINAL BATTLE. YOU CAN SEE BLASTMARKS AROUND THE EDGES OF THE CAVE-INS.
MISTER DONALD, YOU REALLY BELIEVE THE GUY WAS SOME KIND OF WIZARD?
LIKE, YOU KNOW...*ZAPPING THINGS...?*
A DEMON, A SORCERER... XIA TOLD ME THE STORIES TEND TO VARY. IT DOESN'T MATTER WHAT HE WAS, HE'S DEAD THESE SIX HUNDRED YEARS.
BUT THIS WAS HIS HOME. THIS WAS WHERE--
AH.

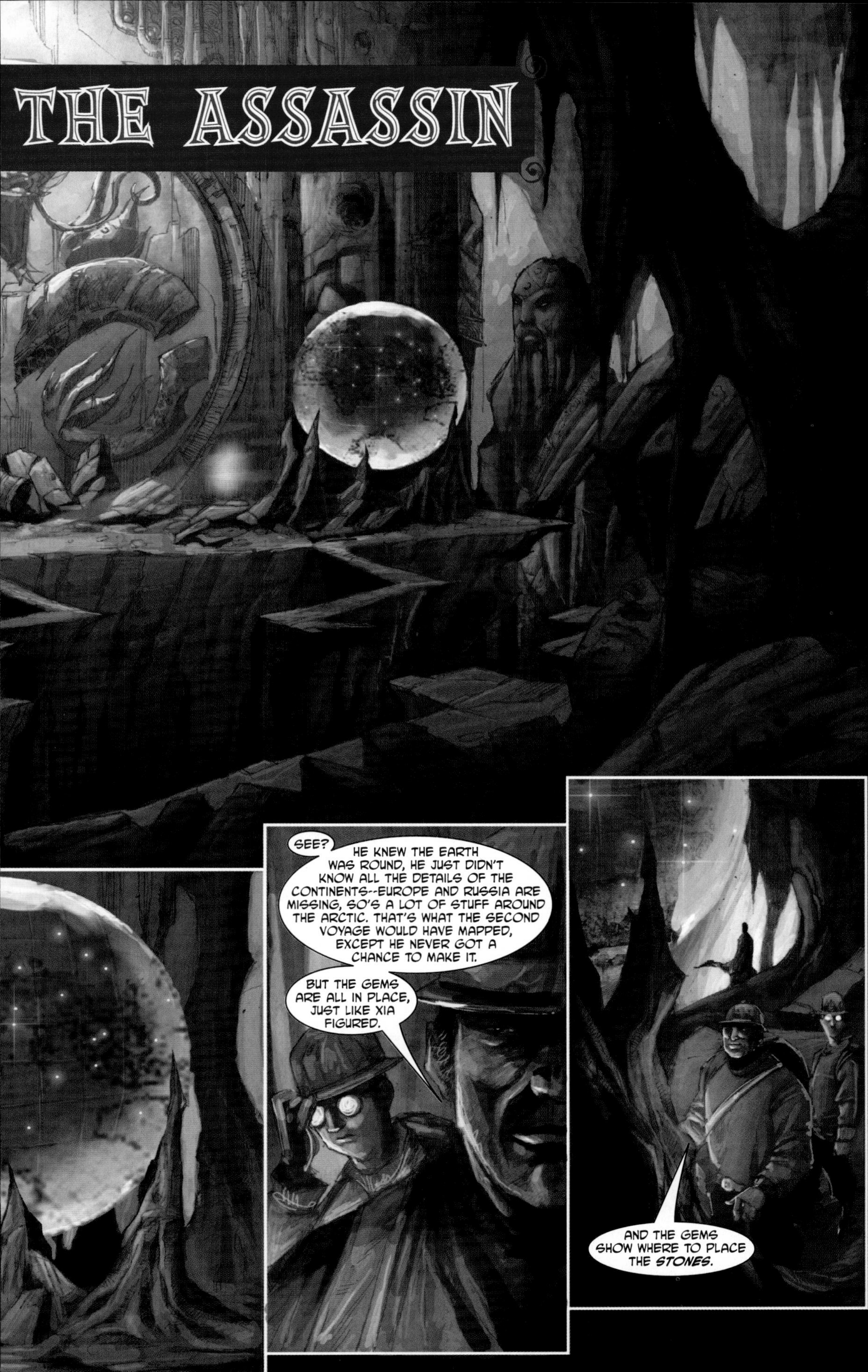
THE ASSASSIN
SEE?
HE KNEW THE EARTH WAS ROUND, HE JUST DIDN'T KNOW ALL THE DETAILS OF THE CONTINENTS--EUROPE AND RUSSIA ARE MISSING, SO'S A LOT OF STUFF AROUND THE ARCTIC. THAT'S WHAT THE SECOND VOYAGE WOULD HAVE MAPPED, EXCEPT HE NEVER GOT A CHANCE TO MAKE IT.
BUT THE GEMS ARE ALL IN PLACE, JUST LIKE XIA FIGURED.
AND THE GEMS SHOW WHERE TO PLACE THE *STONES*.

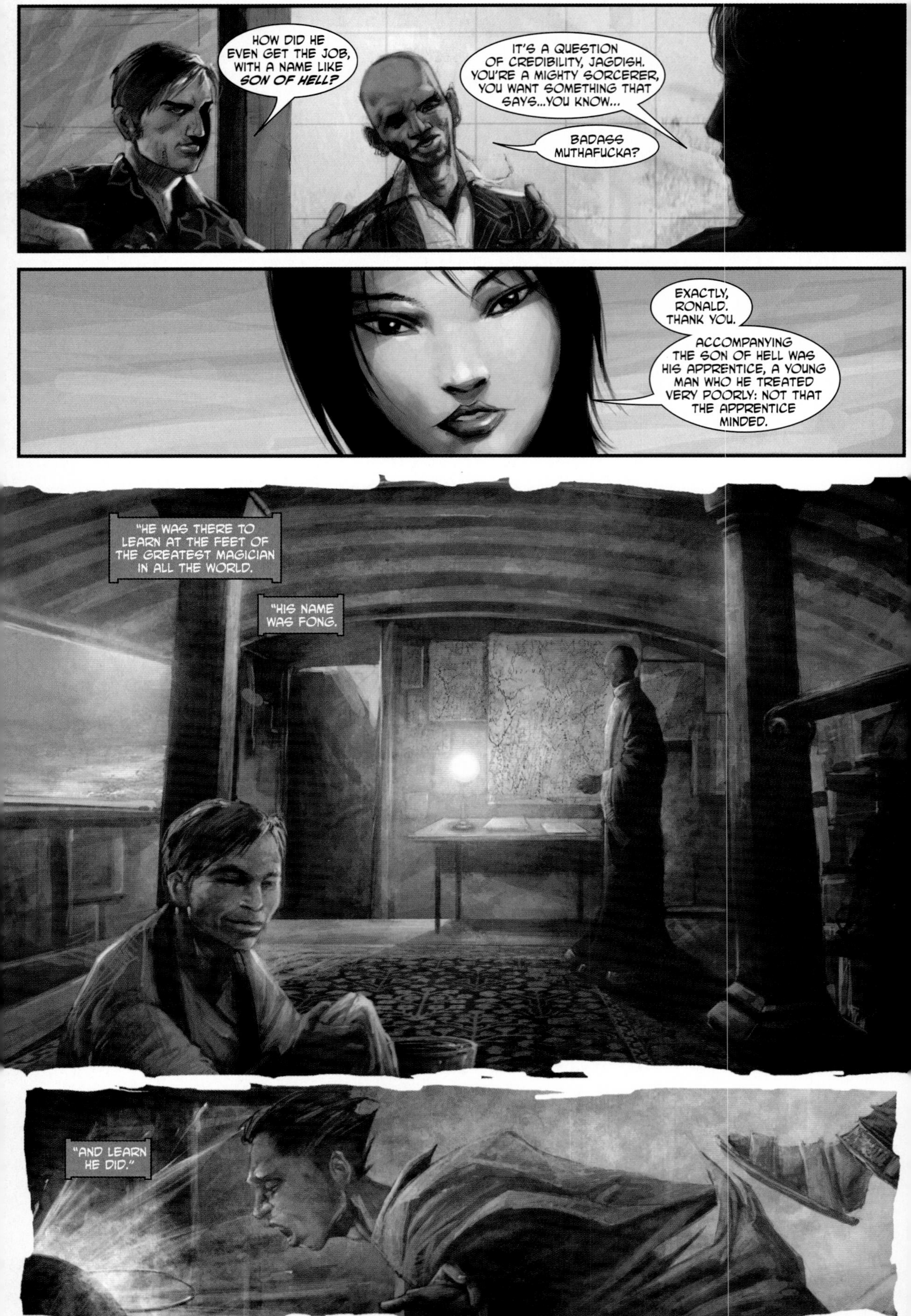

HOW DID HE EVEN GET THE JOB, WITH A NAME LIKE *SON OF HELL?*
IT'S A QUESTION OF CREDIBILITY, JAGDISH. YOU'RE A MIGHTY SORCERER, YOU WANT SOMETHING THAT SAYS...YOU KNOW...
BADASS MUTHAFUCKA?
EXACTLY, RONALD. THANK YOU.
ACCOMPANYING THE SON OF HELL WAS HIS APPRENTICE, A YOUNG MAN WHO HE TREATED VERY POORLY: NOT THAT THE APPRENTICE MINDED.
"HE WAS THERE TO LEARN AT THE FEET OF THE GREATEST MAGICIAN IN ALL THE WORLD.
"HIS NAME WAS FONG.
"AND LEARN HE DID."

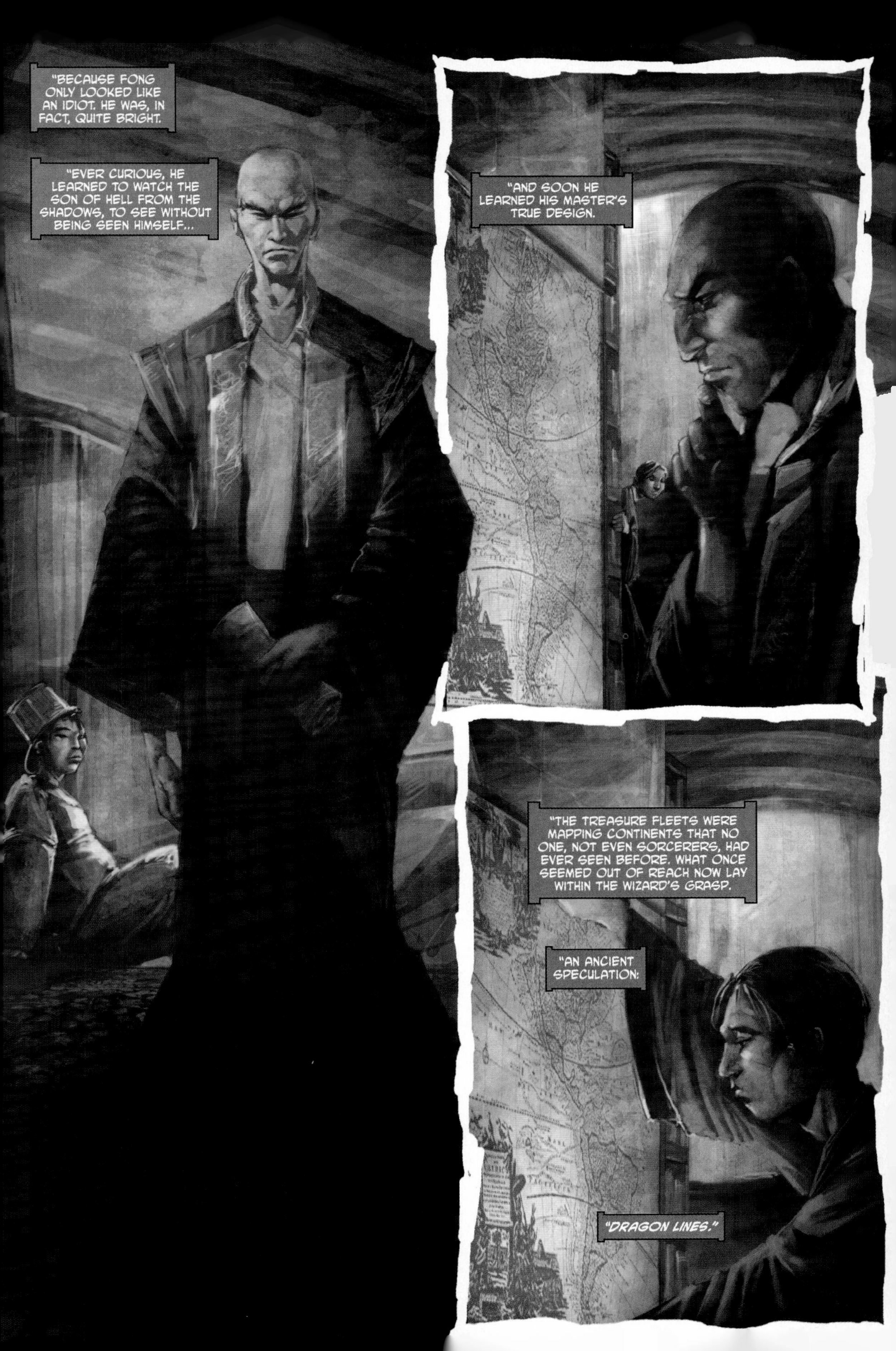
"BECAUSE FONG ONLY LOOKED LIKE AN IDIOT. HE WAS, IN FACT, QUITE BRIGHT.
"EVER CURIOUS, HE LEARNED TO WATCH THE SON OF HELL FROM THE SHADOWS, TO SEE WITHOUT BEING SEEN HIMSELF...
"AND SOON HE LEARNED HIS MASTER'S TRUE DESIGN.
"THE TREASURE FLEETS WERE MAPPING CONTINENTS THAT NO ONE, NOT EVEN SORCERERS, HAD EVER SEEN BEFORE. WHAT ONCE SEEMED OUT OF REACH NOW LAY WITHIN THE WIZARD'S GRASP.
"AN ANCIENT SPECULATION:
"DRAGON LINES."

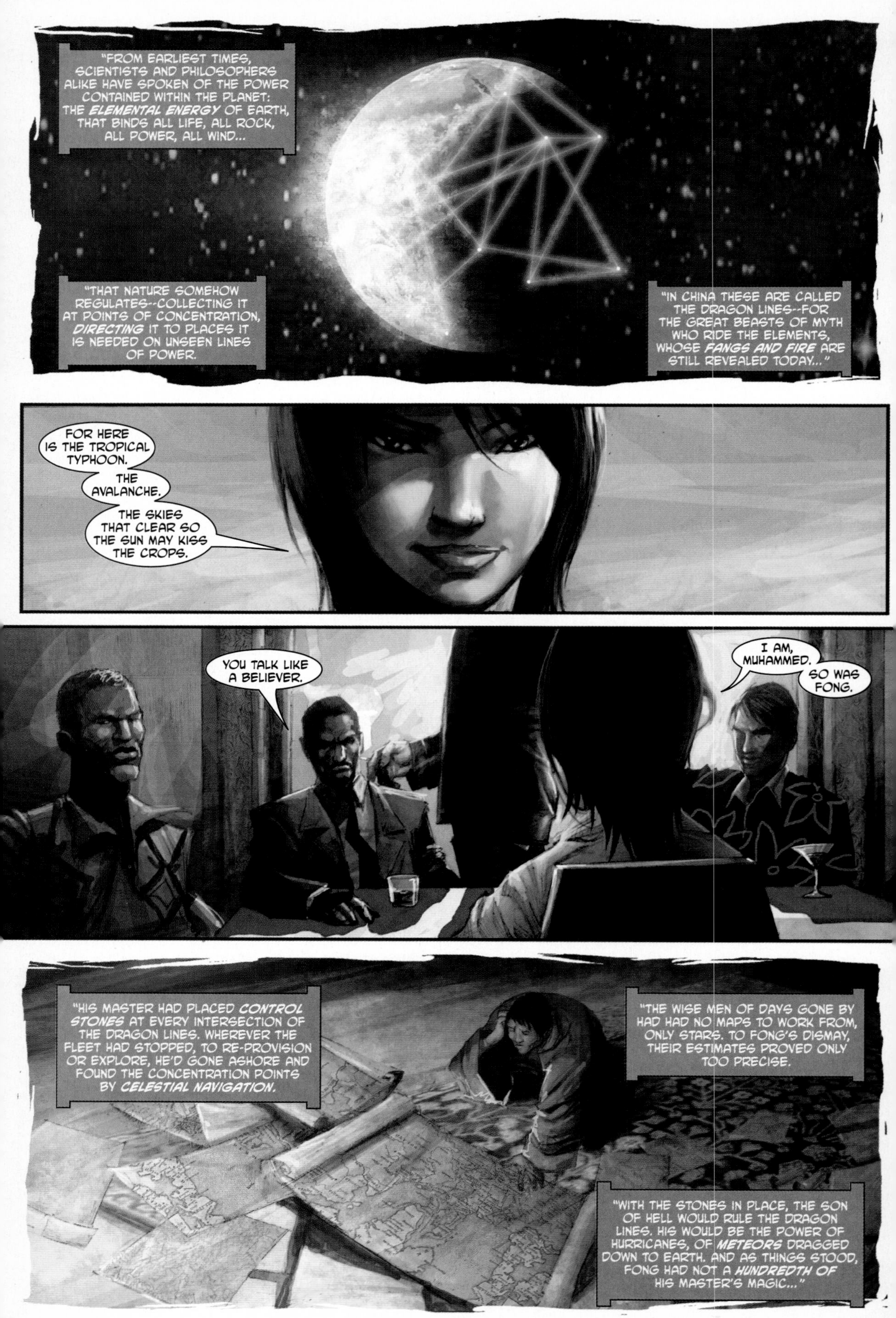
"FROM EARLIEST TIMES, SCIENTISTS AND PHILOSOPHERS ALIKE HAVE SPOKEN OF THE POWER CONTAINED WITHIN THE PLANET: THE *ELEMENTAL ENERGY* OF EARTH, THAT BINDS ALL LIFE, ALL ROCK, ALL POWER, ALL WIND...
"THAT NATURE SOMEHOW REGULATES--COLLECTING IT AT POINTS OF CONCENTRATION, *DIRECTING* IT TO PLACES IT IS NEEDED ON UNSEEN LINES OF POWER.
"IN CHINA THESE ARE CALLED THE DRAGON LINES--FOR THE GREAT BEASTS OF MYTH WHO RIDE THE ELEMENTS, WHOSE *FANGS AND FIRE* ARE STILL REVEALED TODAY..."
FOR HERE IS THE TROPICAL TYPHOON.
THE AVALANCHE.
THE SKIES THAT CLEAR SO THE SUN MAY KISS THE CROPS.
YOU TALK LIKE A BELIEVER.
I AM, MUHAMMED.
SO WAS FONG.
"HIS MASTER HAD PLACED *CONTROL STONES* AT EVERY INTERSECTION OF THE DRAGON LINES. WHEREVER THE FLEET HAD STOPPED, TO RE-PROVISION OR EXPLORE, HE'D GONE ASHORE AND FOUND THE CONCENTRATION POINTS BY *CELESTIAL NAVIGATION.*
"THE WISE MEN OF DAYS GONE BY HAD HAD NO MAPS TO WORK FROM, ONLY STARS. TO FONG'S DISMAY, THEIR ESTIMATES PROVED ONLY TOO PRECISE.
"WITH THE STONES IN PLACE, THE SON OF HELL WOULD RULE THE DRAGON LINES. HIS WOULD BE THE POWER OF HURRICANES, OF *METEORS* DRAGGED DOWN TO EARTH. AND AS THINGS STOOD, FONG HAD NOT A *HUNDREDTH OF* HIS MASTER'S MAGIC..."

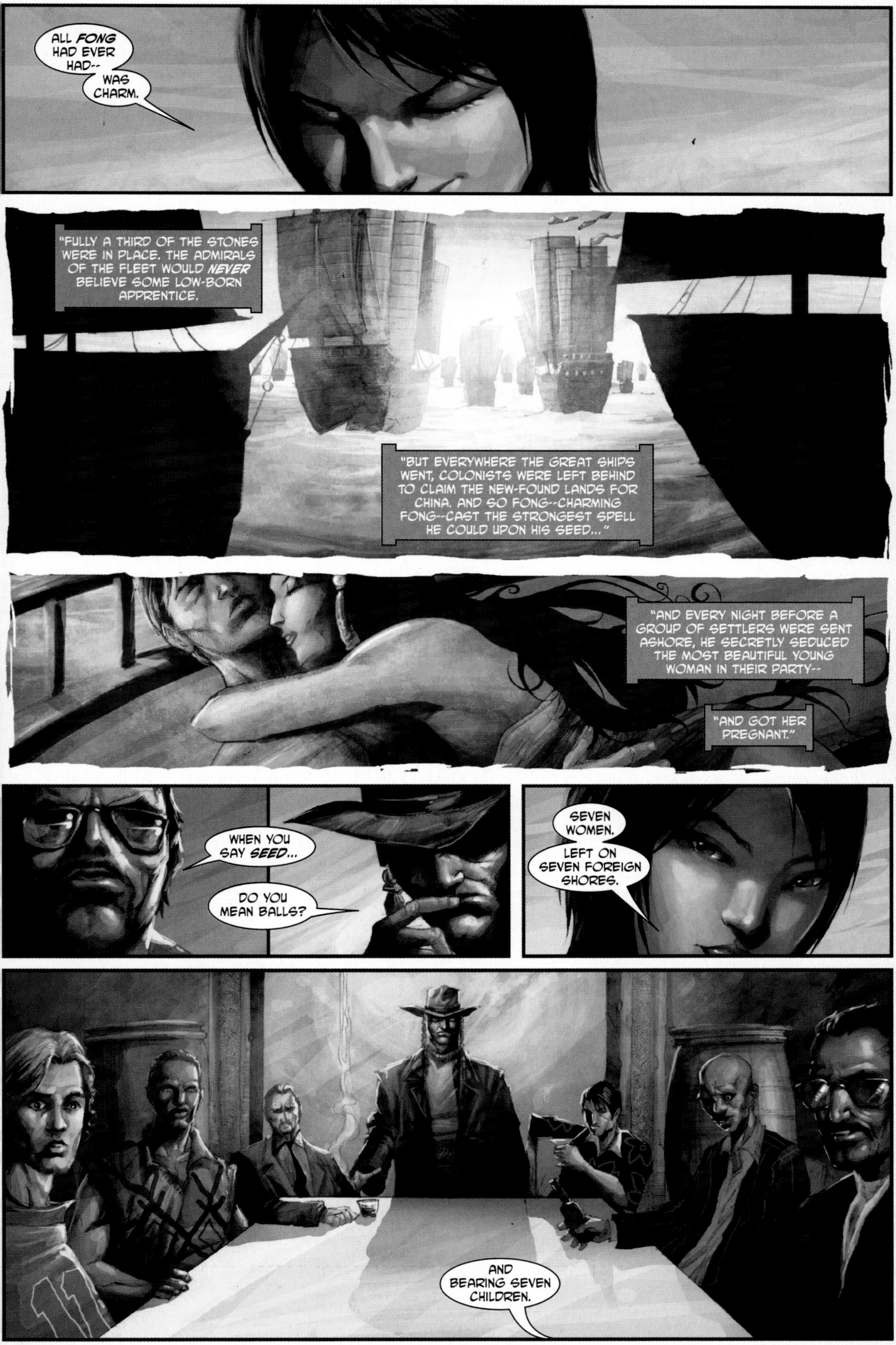
ALL *FONG* HAD EVER HAD--
WAS CHARM.
"FULLY A THIRD OF THE STONES WERE IN PLACE. THE ADMIRALS OF THE FLEET WOULD *NEVER* BELIEVE SOME LOW-BORN APPRENTICE.
"BUT EVERYWHERE THE GREAT SHIPS WENT, COLONISTS WERE LEFT BEHIND TO CLAIM THE NEW-FOUND LANDS FOR CHINA. AND SO FONG--CHARMING FONG--CAST THE STRONGEST SPELL HE COULD UPON HIS SEED..."
"AND EVERY NIGHT BEFORE A GROUP OF SETTLERS WERE SENT ASHORE, HE SECRETLY SEDUCED THE MOST BEAUTIFUL YOUNG WOMAN IN THEIR PARTY--
"AND GOT HER PREGNANT."
WHEN YOU SAY *SEED*...
DO YOU MEAN BALLS?
SEVEN WOMEN.
LEFT ON SEVEN FOREIGN SHORES.
AND BEARING SEVEN CHILDREN.

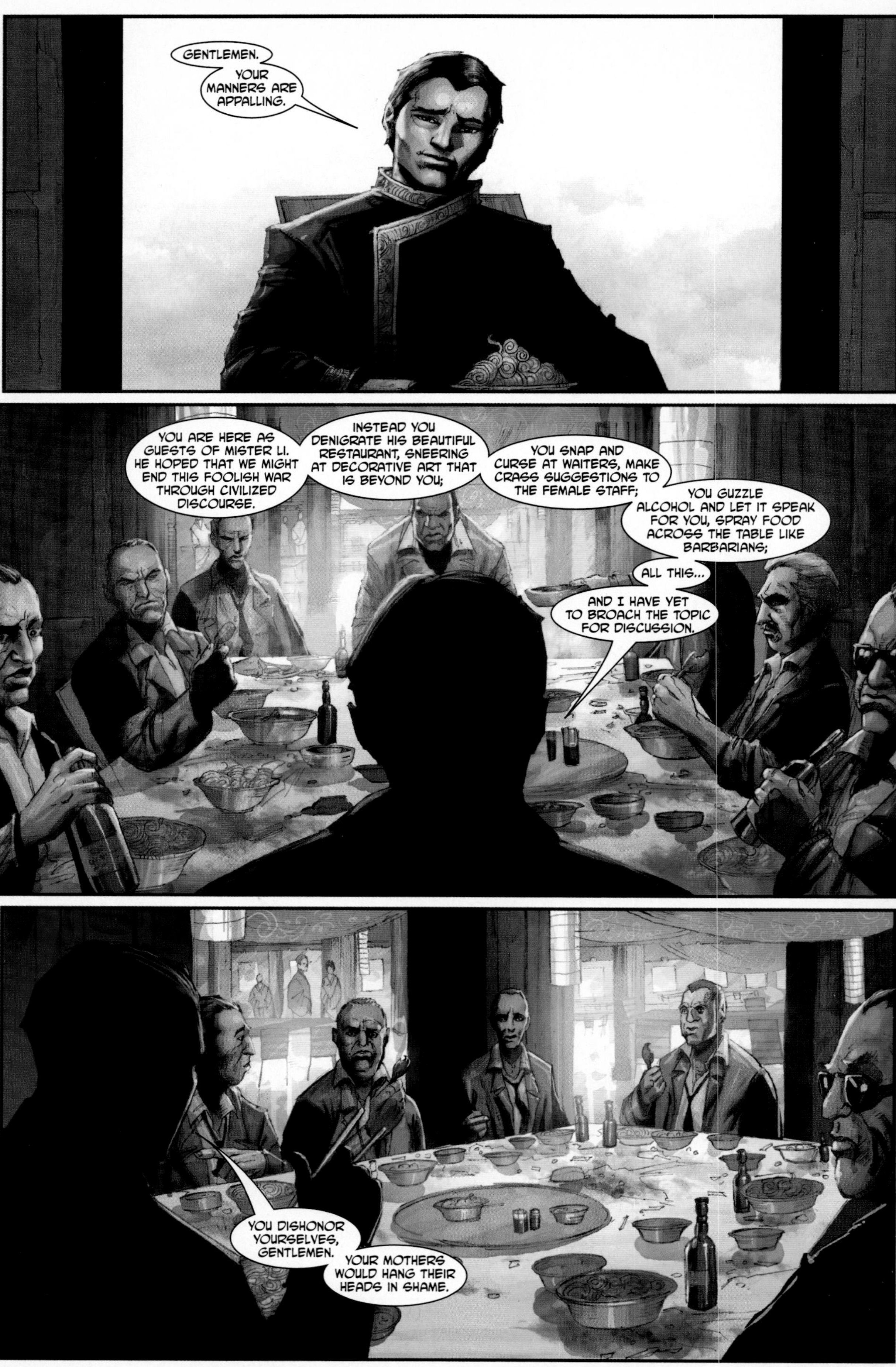
GENTLEMEN.
YOUR MANNERS ARE APPALLING.
YOU ARE HERE AS GUESTS OF MISTER LI. HE HOPED THAT WE MIGHT END THIS FOOLISH WAR THROUGH CIVILIZED DISCOURSE.
INSTEAD YOU DENIGRATE HIS BEAUTIFUL RESTAURANT, SNEERING AT DECORATIVE ART THAT IS BEYOND YOU;
YOU SNAP AND CURSE AT WAITERS, MAKE CRASS SUGGESTIONS TO THE FEMALE STAFF;
YOU GUZZLE ALCOHOL AND LET IT SPEAK FOR YOU, SPRAY FOOD ACROSS THE TABLE LIKE BARBARIANS;
ALL THIS...
AND I HAVE YET TO BROACH THE TOPIC FOR DISCUSSION.
YOU DISHONOR YOURSELVES, GENTLEMEN.
YOUR MOTHERS WOULD HANG THEIR HEADS IN SHAME.

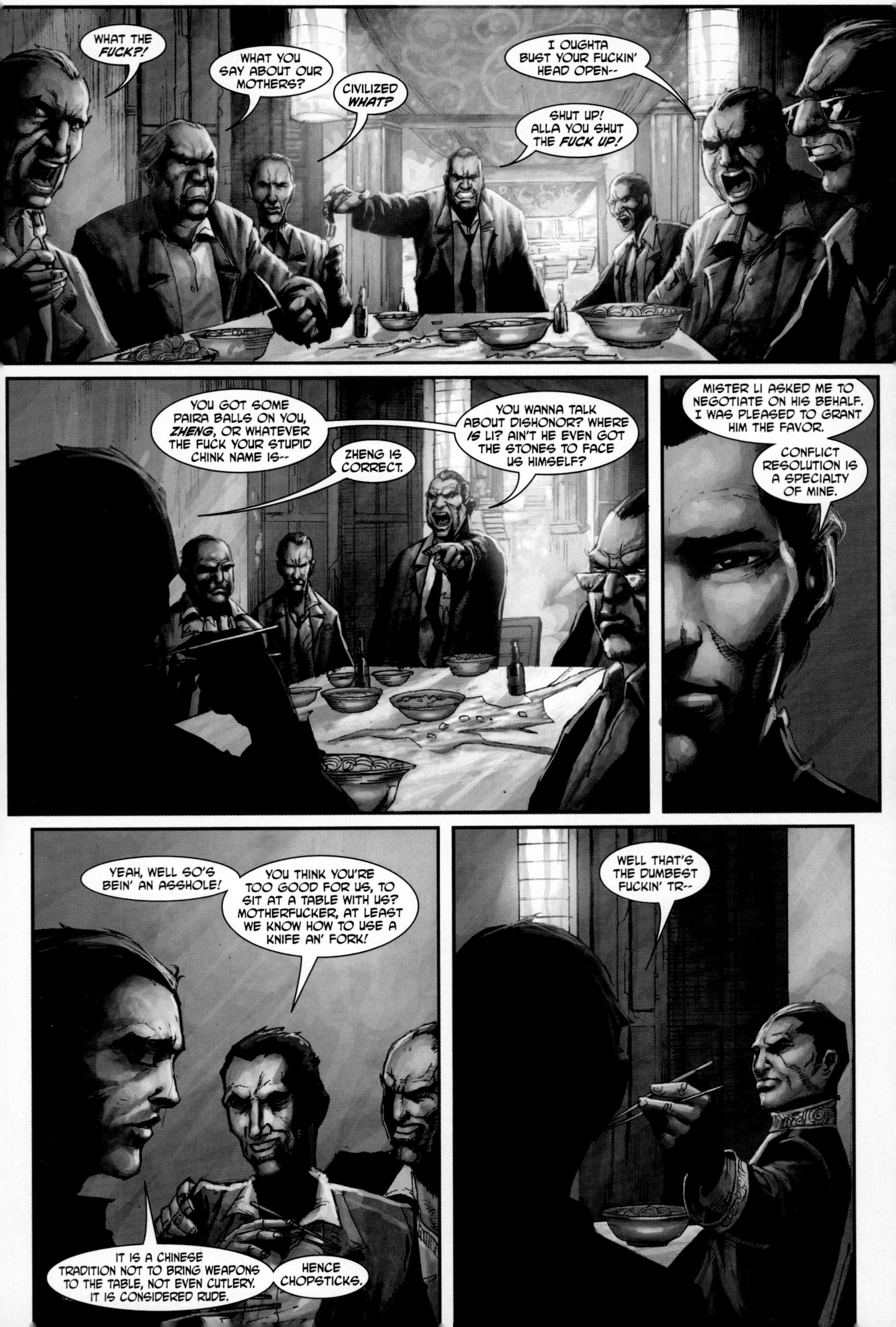
WHAT THE FUCK?!
WHAT YOU SAY ABOUT OUR MOTHERS?
CIVILIZED WHAT?
I OUGHTA BUST YOUR FUCKIN' HEAD OPEN--
SHUT UP! ALLA YOU SHUT THE FUCK UP!
YOU GOT SOME PAIRA BALLS ON YOU, ZHENG, OR WHATEVER THE FUCK YOUR STUPID CHINK NAME IS--
ZHENG IS CORRECT.
YOU WANNA TALK ABOUT DISHONOR? WHERE IS LI? AIN'T HE EVEN GOT THE STONES TO FACE US HIMSELF?
MISTER LI ASKED ME TO NEGOTIATE ON HIS BEHALF. I WAS PLEASED TO GRANT HIM THE FAVOR.
CONFLICT RESOLUTION IS A SPECIALTY OF MINE.
YEAH, WELL SO'S BEIN' AN ASSHOLE!
YOU THINK YOU'RE TOO GOOD FOR US, TO SIT AT A TABLE WITH US? MOTHERFUCKER, AT LEAST WE KNOW HOW TO USE A KNIFE AN' FORK!
IT IS A CHINESE TRADITION NOT TO BRING WEAPONS TO THE TABLE, NOT EVEN CUTLERY. IT IS CONSIDERED RUDE.
HENCE CHOPSTICKS.
WELL THAT'S THE DUMBEST FUCKIN' TR--

WH-- WH--

YOUR WIVES ARE DEAD.

YOUR CHILDREN TAKEN.

MISTER LI'S TERRITORY NOW EXTENDS THE LENGTH OF MOTT STREET. LITTLE ITALY EXISTS IN NAME ONLY. YOU WILL CEASE YOUR RECENT IDIOCY AND PAY TRIBUTE ON A WEEKLY BASIS.

ONE DAY, PERHAPS, YOUR CHILDREN WILL BE RETURNED TO YOU.

BULLSHIT--!

YOU COULDN'T HAVE--

YOU CROSSED THE LINE WITH THAT SHIT, I'M GONNA FUCKIN'--

I VISITED YOUR HOMES THIS AFTERNOON. THE LAST AN HOUR BEFORE I CAME HERE.

WE GOT PEOPLE, COCKSUCKER, THEY'DA CALLED US IF YOU CAME NEAR OUR--

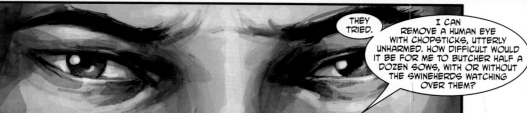

THEY TRIED.

I CAN REMOVE A HUMAN EYE WITH CHOPSTICKS, UTTERLY UNHARMED. HOW DIFFICULT WOULD IT BE FOR ME TO BUTCHER HALF A DOZEN SOWS, WITH OR WITHOUT THE SWINEHERDS WATCHING OVER THEM?

SONS AND DAUGHTERS.

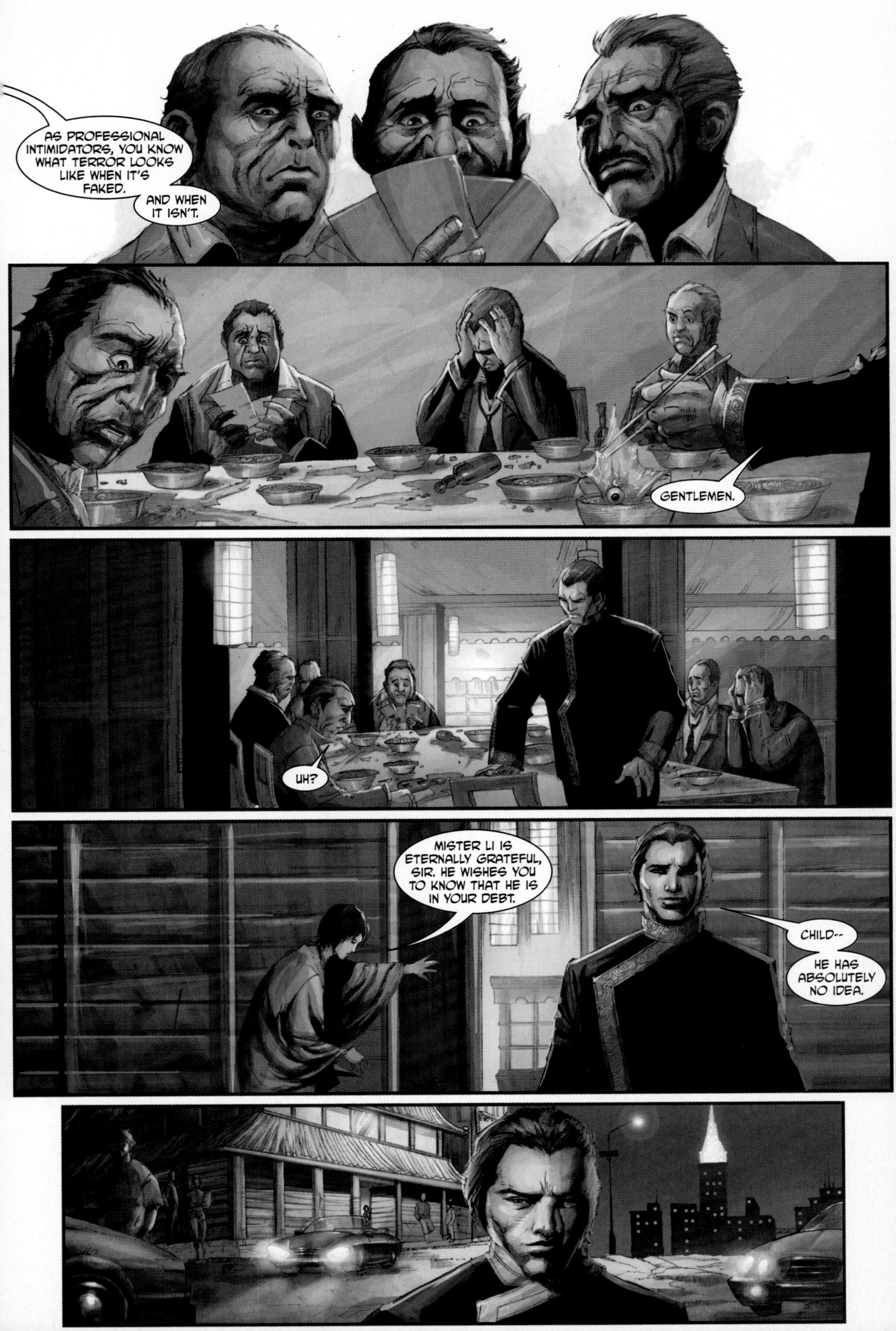
AS PROFESSIONAL INTIMIDATORS, YOU KNOW WHAT TERROR LOOKS LIKE WHEN IT'S FAKED.
AND WHEN IT ISN'T.
GENTLEMEN.
UH?
MISTER LI IS ETERNALLY GRATEFUL, SIR. HE WISHES YOU TO KNOW THAT HE IS IN YOUR DEBT.
CHILD--
HE HAS ABSOLUTELY NO IDEA.

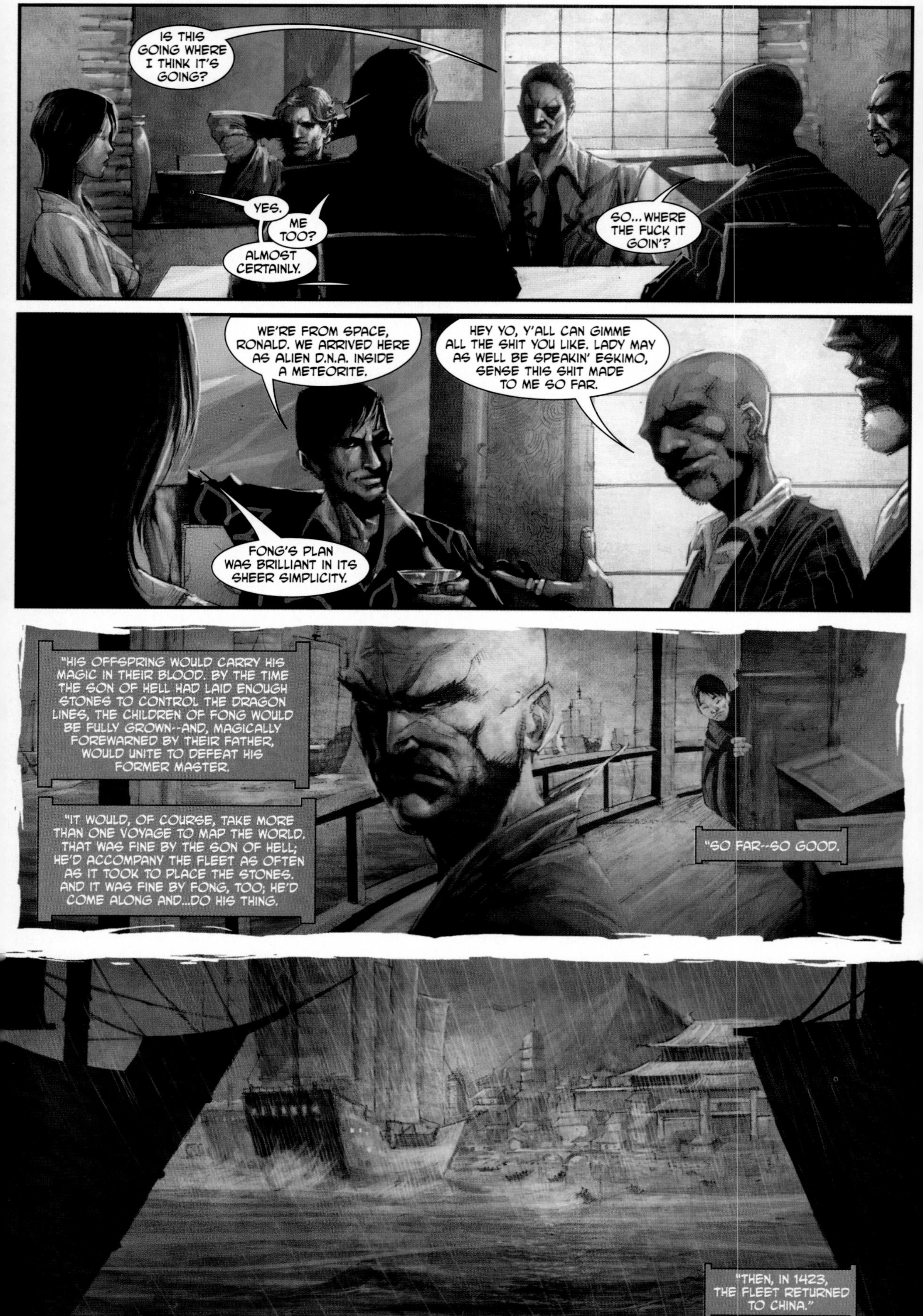

IS THIS GOING WHERE I THINK IT'S GOING?
YES.
ME TOO?
ALMOST CERTAINLY.
SO...WHERE THE FUCK IT GOIN'?
WE'RE FROM SPACE, RONALD. WE ARRIVED HERE AS ALIEN D.N.A. INSIDE A METEORITE.
HEY YO, Y'ALL CAN GIMME ALL THE SHIT YOU LIKE. LADY MAY AS WELL BE SPEAKIN' ESKIMO, SENSE THIS SHIT MADE TO ME SO FAR.
FONG'S PLAN WAS BRILLIANT IN ITS SHEER SIMPLICITY.
"HIS OFFSPRING WOULD CARRY HIS MAGIC IN THEIR BLOOD. BY THE TIME THE SON OF HELL HAD LAID ENOUGH STONES TO CONTROL THE DRAGON LINES, THE CHILDREN OF FONG WOULD BE FULLY GROWN--AND, MAGICALLY FOREWARNED BY THEIR FATHER, WOULD UNITE TO DEFEAT HIS FORMER MASTER.
"IT WOULD, OF COURSE, TAKE MORE THAN ONE VOYAGE TO MAP THE WORLD. THAT WAS FINE BY THE SON OF HELL; HE'D ACCOMPANY THE FLEET AS OFTEN AS IT TOOK TO PLACE THE STONES. AND IT WAS FINE BY FONG, TOO; HE'D COME ALONG AND...DO HIS THING.
"SO FAR--SO GOOD.
"THEN, IN 1423, THE FLEET RETURNED TO CHINA."

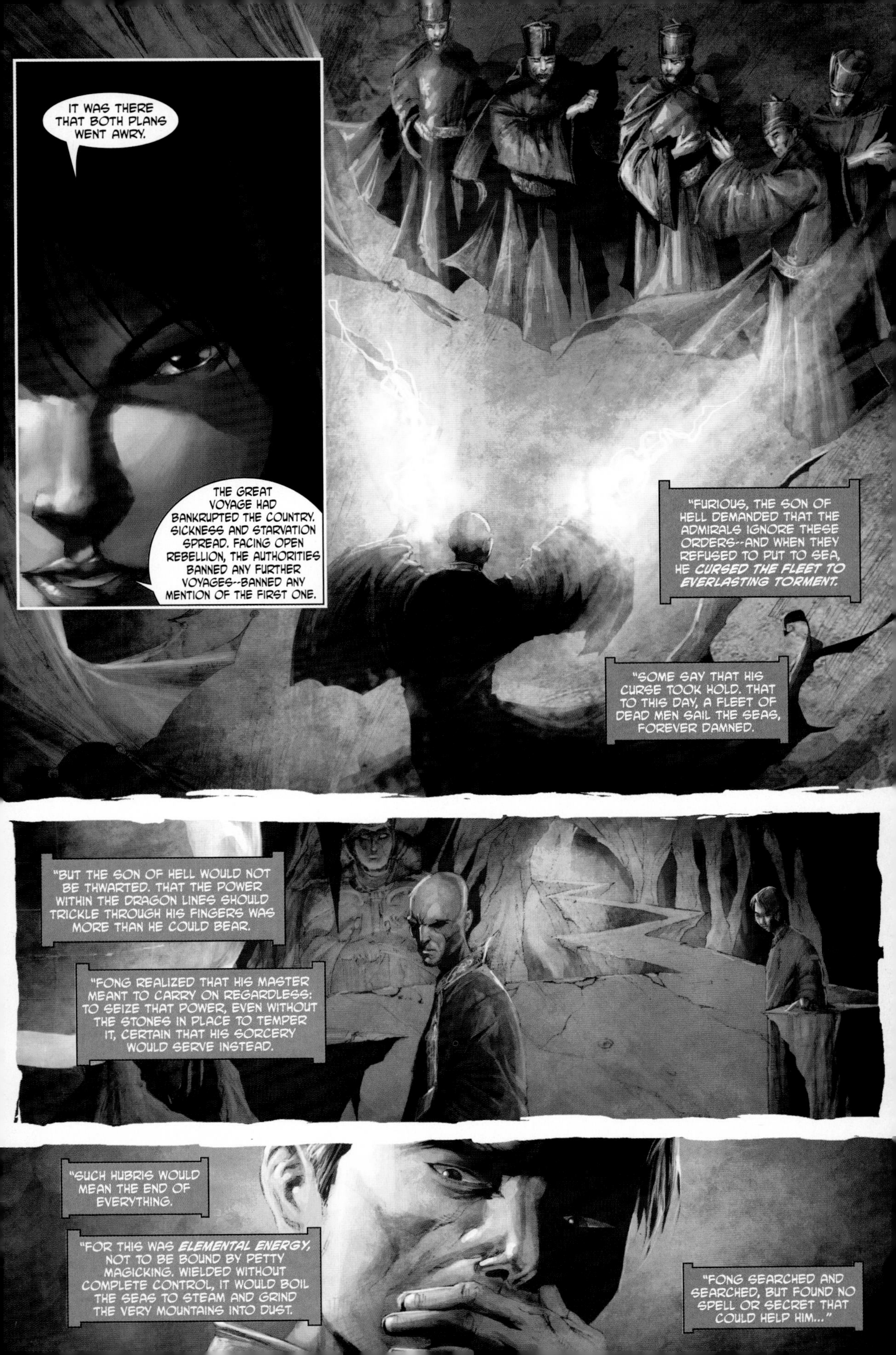
IT WAS THERE THAT BOTH PLANS WENT AWRY.
THE GREAT VOYAGE HAD BANKRUPTED THE COUNTRY. SICKNESS AND STARVATION SPREAD. FACING OPEN REBELLION, THE AUTHORITIES BANNED ANY FURTHER VOYAGES--BANNED ANY MENTION OF THE FIRST ONE.
"FURIOUS, THE SON OF HELL DEMANDED THAT THE ADMIRALS IGNORE THESE ORDERS--AND WHEN THEY REFUSED TO PUT TO SEA, HE *CURSED THE FLEET TO EVERLASTING TORMENT.*
"SOME SAY THAT HIS CURSE TOOK HOLD. THAT TO THIS DAY, A FLEET OF DEAD MEN SAIL THE SEAS, FOREVER DAMNED.
"BUT THE SON OF HELL WOULD NOT BE THWARTED. THAT THE POWER WITHIN THE DRAGON LINES SHOULD TRICKLE THROUGH HIS FINGERS WAS MORE THAN HE COULD BEAR.
"FONG REALIZED THAT HIS MASTER MEANT TO CARRY ON REGARDLESS: TO SEIZE THAT POWER, EVEN WITHOUT THE STONES IN PLACE TO TEMPER IT, CERTAIN THAT HIS SORCERY WOULD SERVE INSTEAD.
"SUCH HUBRIS WOULD MEAN THE END OF EVERYTHING.
"FOR THIS WAS *ELEMENTAL ENERGY,* NOT TO BE BOUND BY PETTY MAGICKING. WIELDED WITHOUT COMPLETE CONTROL, IT WOULD BOIL THE SEAS TO STEAM AND GRIND THE VERY MOUNTAINS INTO DUST.
"FONG SEARCHED AND SEARCHED, BUT FOUND NO SPELL OR SECRET THAT COULD HELP HIM..."

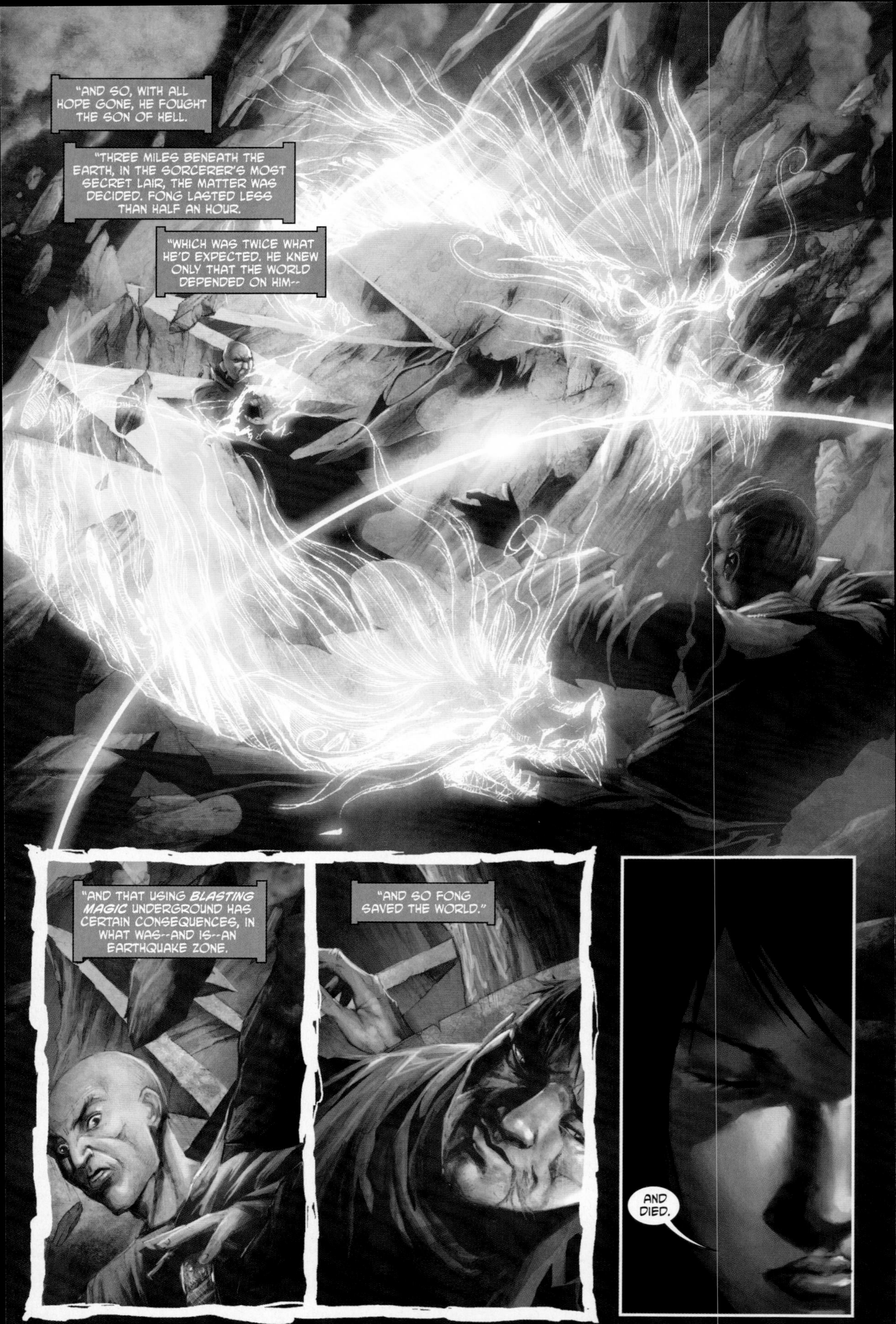
"AND SO, WITH ALL HOPE GONE, HE FOUGHT THE SON OF HELL.
"THREE MILES BENEATH THE EARTH, IN THE SORCERER'S MOST SECRET LAIR, THE MATTER WAS DECIDED. FONG LASTED LESS THAN HALF AN HOUR.
"WHICH WAS TWICE WHAT HE'D EXPECTED. HE KNEW ONLY THAT THE WORLD DEPENDED ON HIM--
"AND THAT USING *BLASTING MAGIC* UNDERGROUND HAS CERTAIN CONSEQUENCES, IN WHAT WAS--AND IS--AN EARTHQUAKE ZONE.
"AND SO FONG SAVED THE WORLD."
AND DIED.

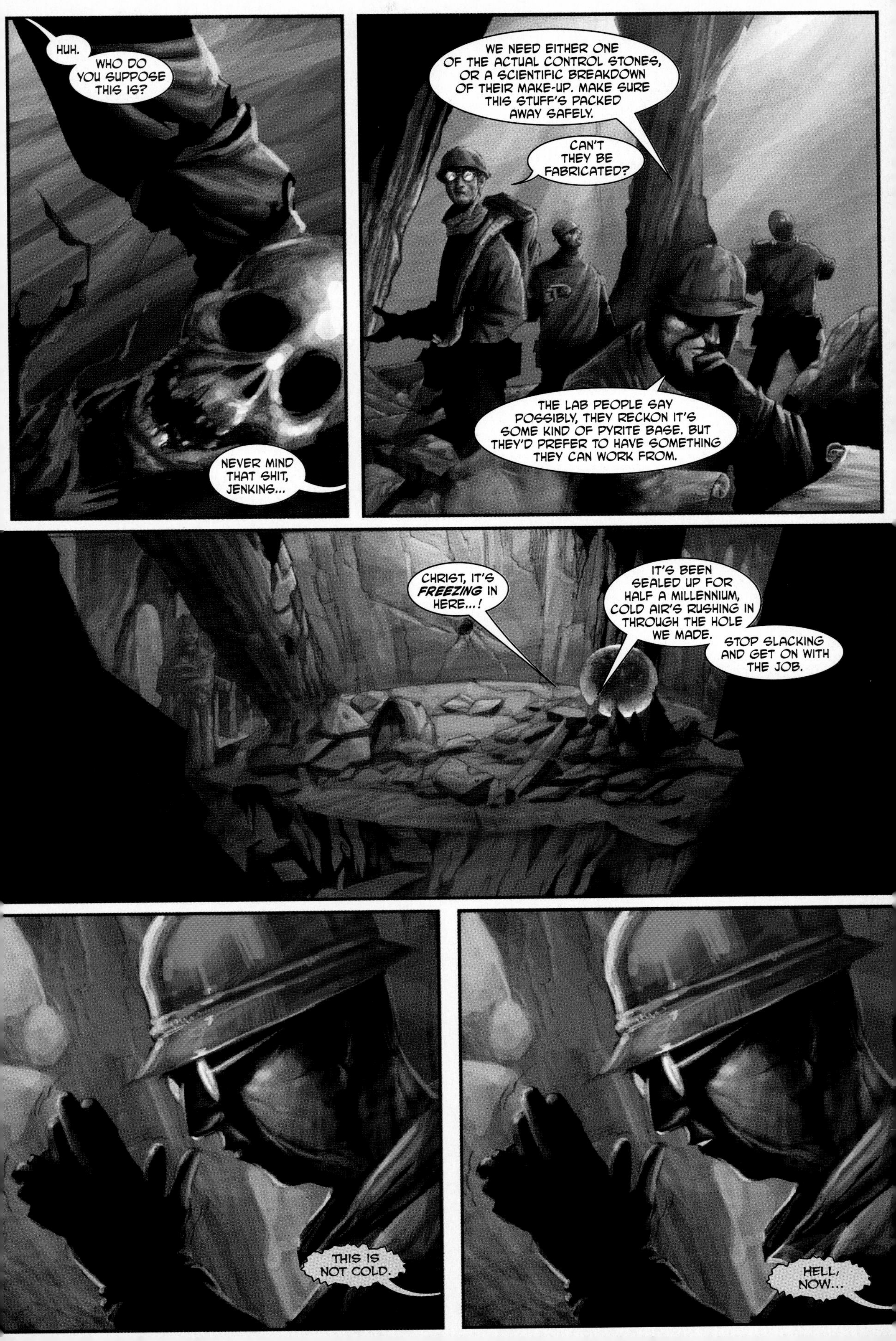
HUH.
WHO DO YOU SUPPOSE THIS IS?
NEVER MIND THAT SHIT, JENKINS...
WE NEED EITHER ONE OF THE ACTUAL CONTROL STONES, OR A SCIENTIFIC BREAKDOWN OF THEIR MAKE-UP. MAKE SURE THIS STUFF'S PACKED AWAY SAFELY.
CAN'T THEY BE FABRICATED?
THE LAB PEOPLE SAY POSSIBLY, THEY RECKON IT'S SOME KIND OF PYRITE BASE. BUT THEY'D PREFER TO HAVE SOMETHING THEY CAN WORK FROM.
CHRIST, IT'S *FREEZING* IN HERE...!
IT'S BEEN SEALED UP FOR HALF A MILLENNIUM, COLD AIR'S RUSHING IN THROUGH THE HOLE WE MADE.
STOP SLACKING AND GET ON WITH THE JOB.
THIS IS NOT COLD.
HELL, NOW...

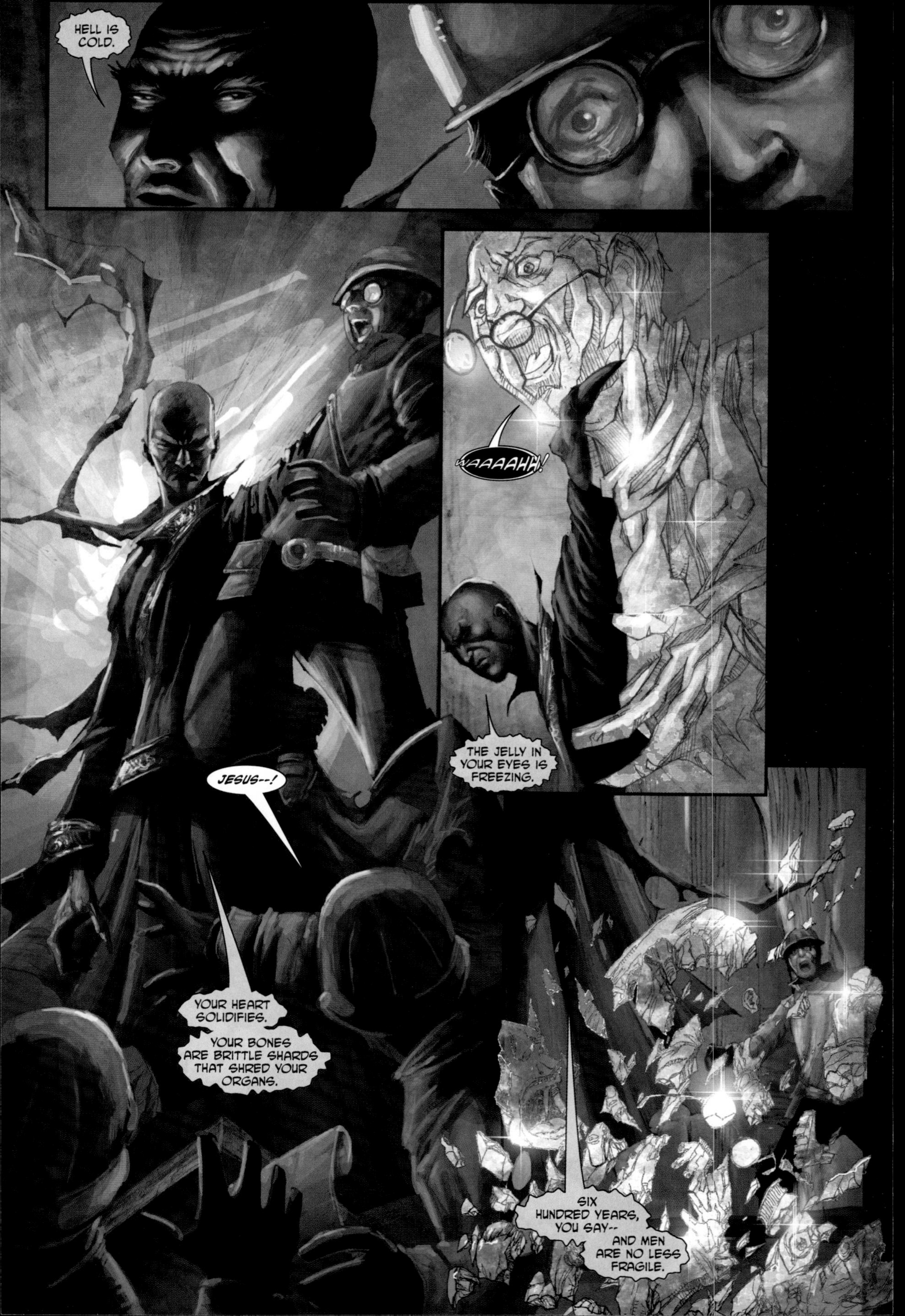
HELL IS COLD.
WAAAAHH!
THE JELLY IN YOUR EYES IS FREEZING.
JESUS--!
YOUR HEART SOLIDIFIES.
YOUR BONES ARE BRITTLE SHARDS THAT SHRED YOUR ORGANS.
SIX HUNDRED YEARS, YOU SAY--
AND MEN ARE NO LESS FRAGILE.

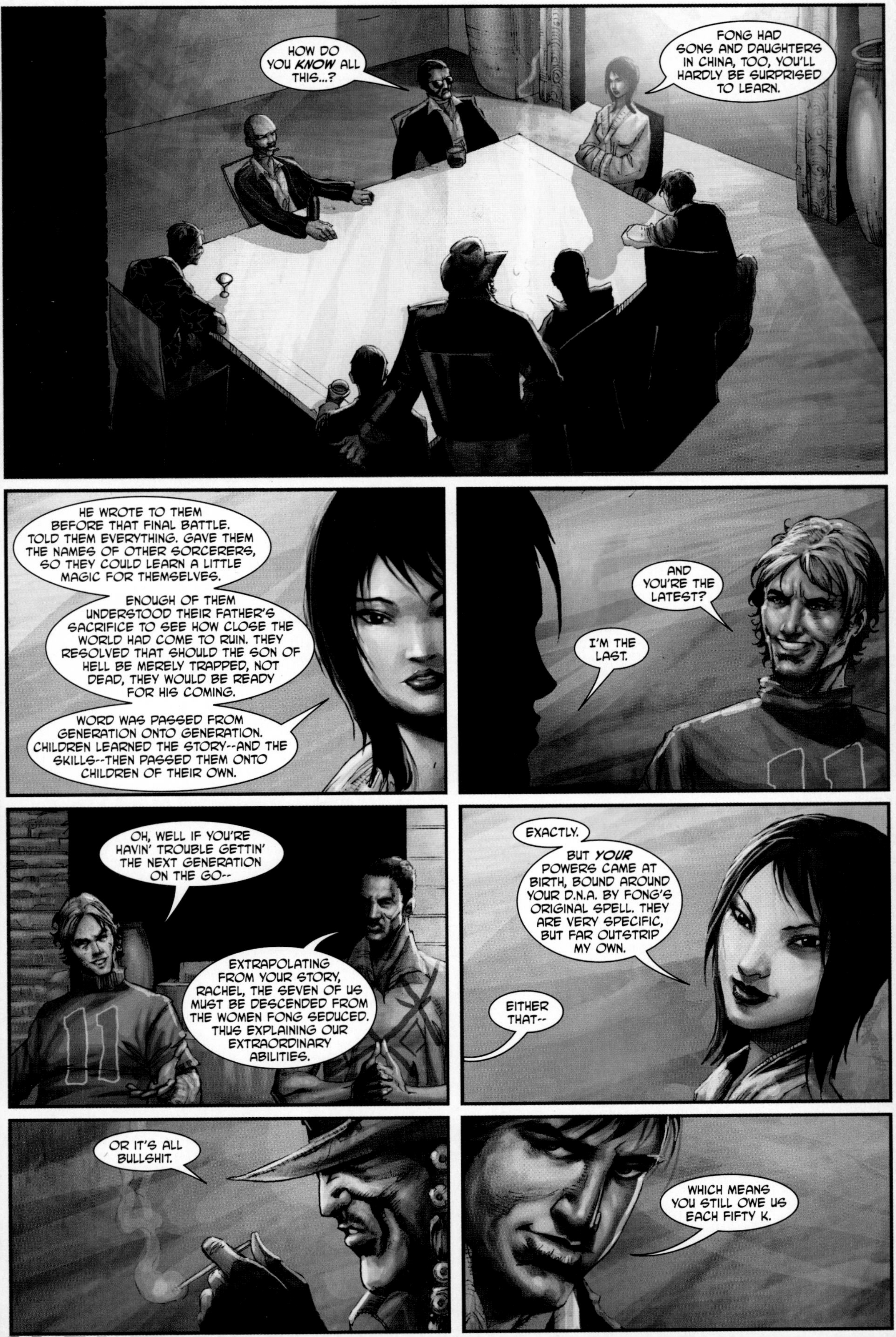
HOW DO YOU *KNOW* ALL THIS...?
FONG HAD SONS AND DAUGHTERS IN CHINA, TOO, YOU'LL HARDLY BE SURPRISED TO LEARN.
HE WROTE TO THEM BEFORE THAT FINAL BATTLE. TOLD THEM EVERYTHING. GAVE THEM THE NAMES OF OTHER SORCERERS, SO THEY COULD LEARN A LITTLE MAGIC FOR THEMSELVES.
ENOUGH OF THEM UNDERSTOOD THEIR FATHER'S SACRIFICE TO SEE HOW CLOSE THE WORLD HAD COME TO RUIN. THEY RESOLVED THAT SHOULD THE SON OF HELL BE MERELY TRAPPED, NOT DEAD, THEY WOULD BE READY FOR HIS COMING.
WORD WAS PASSED FROM GENERATION ONTO GENERATION. CHILDREN LEARNED THE STORY--AND THE SKILLS--THEN PASSED THEM ONTO CHILDREN OF THEIR OWN.
AND YOU'RE THE LATEST?
I'M THE LAST.
OH, WELL IF YOU'RE HAVIN' TROUBLE GETTIN' THE NEXT GENERATION ON THE GO--
EXTRAPOLATING FROM YOUR STORY, RACHEL, THE SEVEN OF US MUST BE DESCENDED FROM THE WOMEN FONG SEDUCED. THUS EXPLAINING OUR EXTRAORDINARY ABILITIES.
EXACTLY.
BUT *YOUR* POWERS CAME AT BIRTH, BOUND AROUND YOUR D.N.A. BY FONG'S ORIGINAL SPELL. THEY ARE VERY SPECIFIC, BUT FAR OUTSTRIP MY OWN.
EITHER THAT--
OR IT'S ALL BULLSHIT.
WHICH MEANS YOU STILL OWE US EACH FIFTY K.

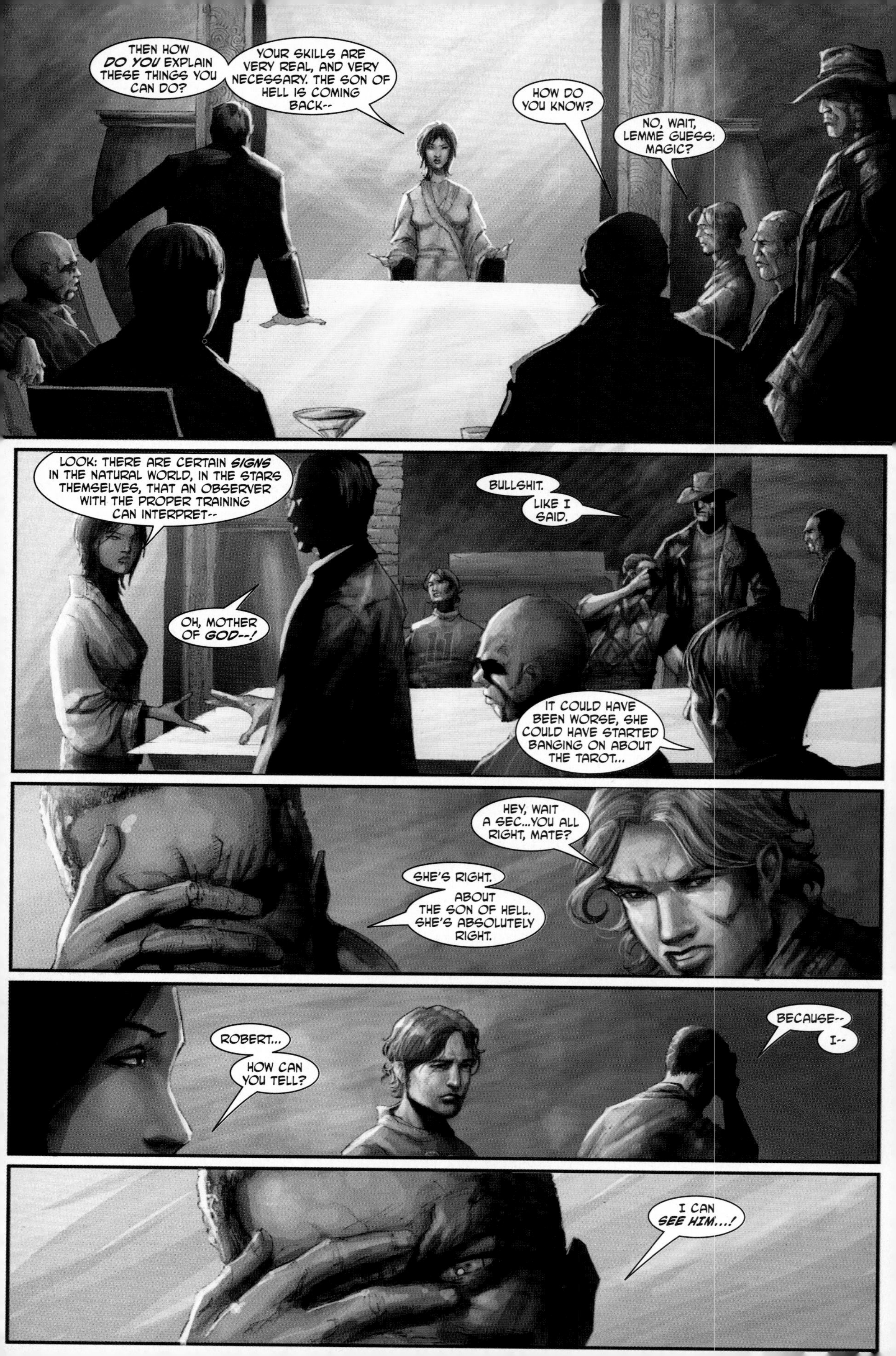
THEN HOW DO YOU EXPLAIN THESE THINGS YOU CAN DO?
YOUR SKILLS ARE VERY REAL, AND VERY NECESSARY. THE SON OF HELL IS COMING BACK--
HOW DO YOU KNOW?
NO, WAIT, LEMME GUESS: MAGIC?
LOOK: THERE ARE CERTAIN SIGNS IN THE NATURAL WORLD, IN THE STARS THEMSELVES, THAT AN OBSERVER WITH THE PROPER TRAINING CAN INTERPRET--
BULLSHIT.
LIKE I SAID.
OH, MOTHER OF GOD--!
IT COULD HAVE BEEN WORSE, SHE COULD HAVE STARTED BANGING ON ABOUT THE TAROT...
HEY, WAIT A SEC...YOU ALL RIGHT, MATE?
SHE'S RIGHT.
ABOUT THE SON OF HELL. SHE'S ABSOLUTELY RIGHT.
ROBERT...
HOW CAN YOU TELL?
BECAUSE--
I--
I CAN SEE HIM...!

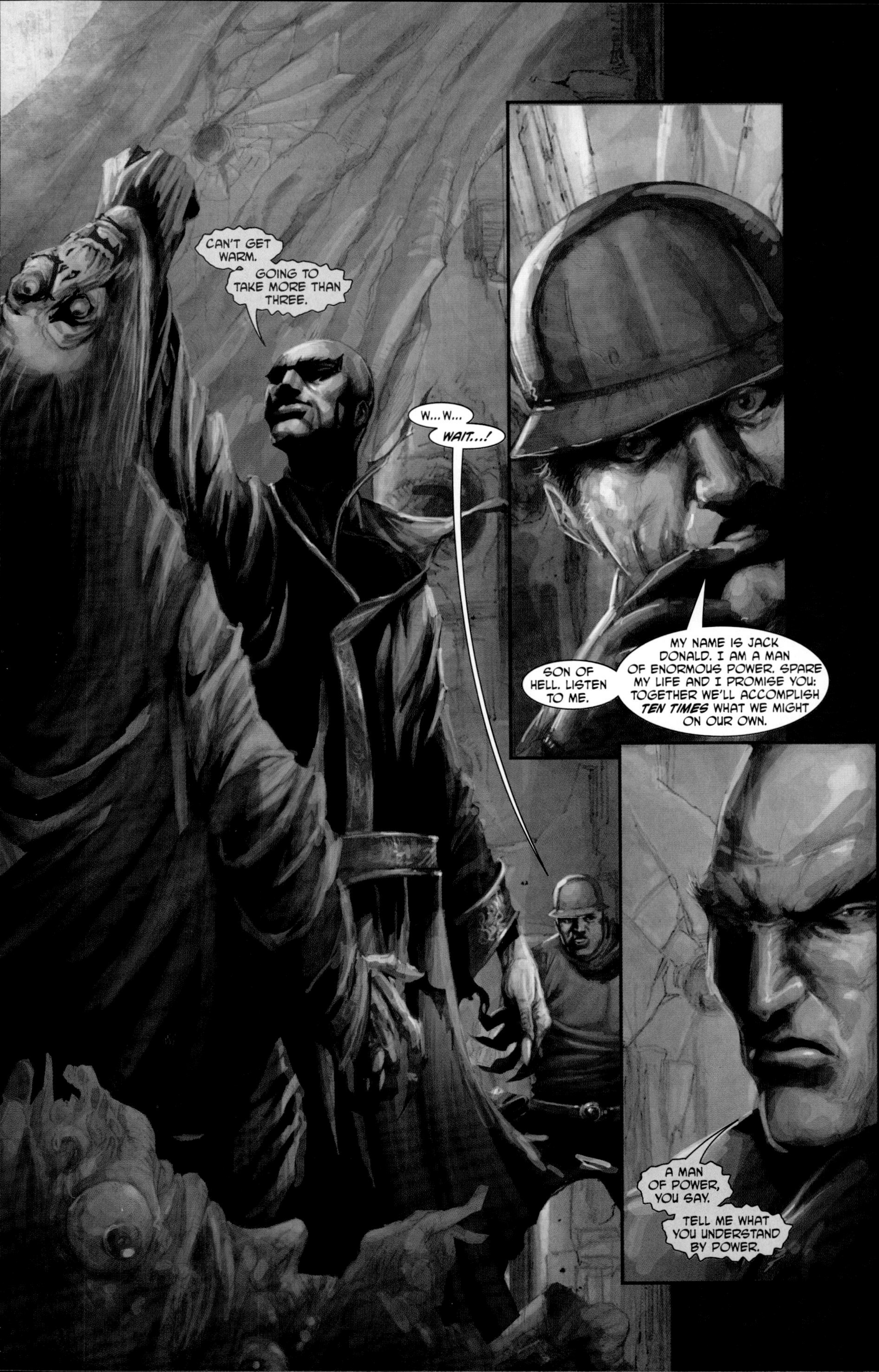
CAN'T GET WARM.
GOING TO TAKE MORE THAN THREE.
W... W...
WAIT...!
SON OF HELL. LISTEN TO ME.
MY NAME IS JACK DONALD. I AM A MAN OF ENORMOUS POWER. SPARE MY LIFE AND I PROMISE YOU: TOGETHER WE'LL ACCOMPLISH TEN TIMES WHAT WE MIGHT ON OUR OWN.
A MAN OF POWER, YOU SAY.
TELL ME WHAT YOU UNDERSTAND BY POWER.

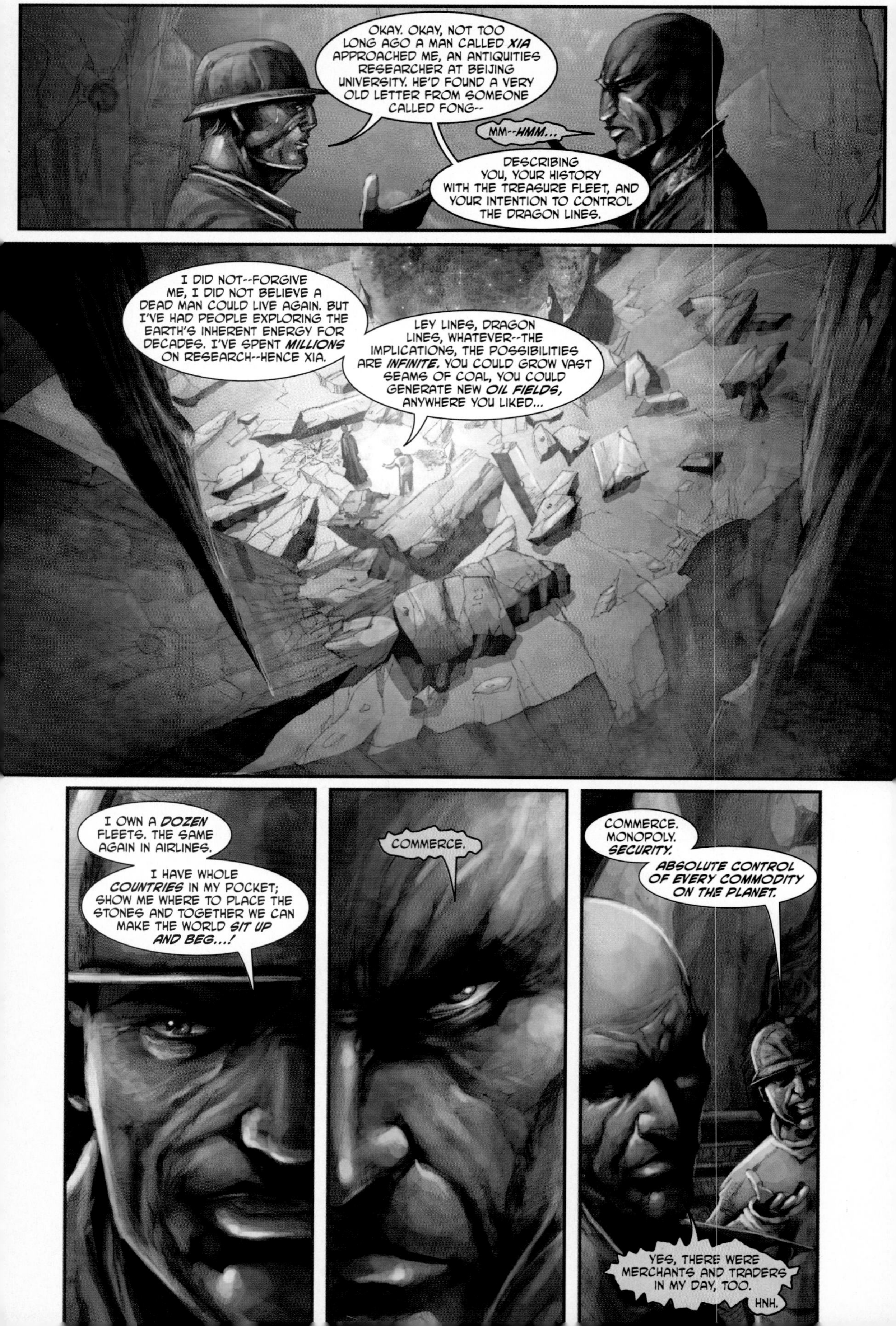
OKAY. OKAY, NOT TOO LONG AGO A MAN CALLED *XIA* APPROACHED ME, AN ANTIQUITIES RESEARCHER AT BEIJING UNIVERSITY. HE'D FOUND A VERY OLD LETTER FROM SOMEONE CALLED FONG--
MM--*HMM...*
DESCRIBING YOU, YOUR HISTORY WITH THE TREASURE FLEET, AND YOUR INTENTION TO CONTROL THE DRAGON LINES.
I DID NOT--FORGIVE ME, I DID NOT BELIEVE A DEAD MAN COULD LIVE AGAIN. BUT I'VE HAD PEOPLE EXPLORING THE EARTH'S INHERENT ENERGY FOR DECADES. I'VE SPENT *MILLIONS* ON RESEARCH--HENCE XIA.
LEY LINES, DRAGON LINES, WHATEVER--THE IMPLICATIONS, THE POSSIBILITIES ARE *INFINITE.* YOU COULD GROW VAST SEAMS OF COAL, YOU COULD GENERATE NEW *OIL FIELDS,* ANYWHERE YOU LIKED...
I OWN A *DOZEN* FLEETS. THE SAME AGAIN IN AIRLINES.
I HAVE WHOLE *COUNTRIES* IN MY POCKET; SHOW ME WHERE TO PLACE THE STONES AND TOGETHER WE CAN MAKE THE WORLD *SIT UP AND BEG...!*
COMMERCE.
COMMERCE. MONOPOLY. *SECURITY.*
ABSOLUTE CONTROL OF EVERY COMMODITY ON THE PLANET.
YES, THERE WERE MERCHANTS AND TRADERS IN MY DAY, TOO.
HNH.

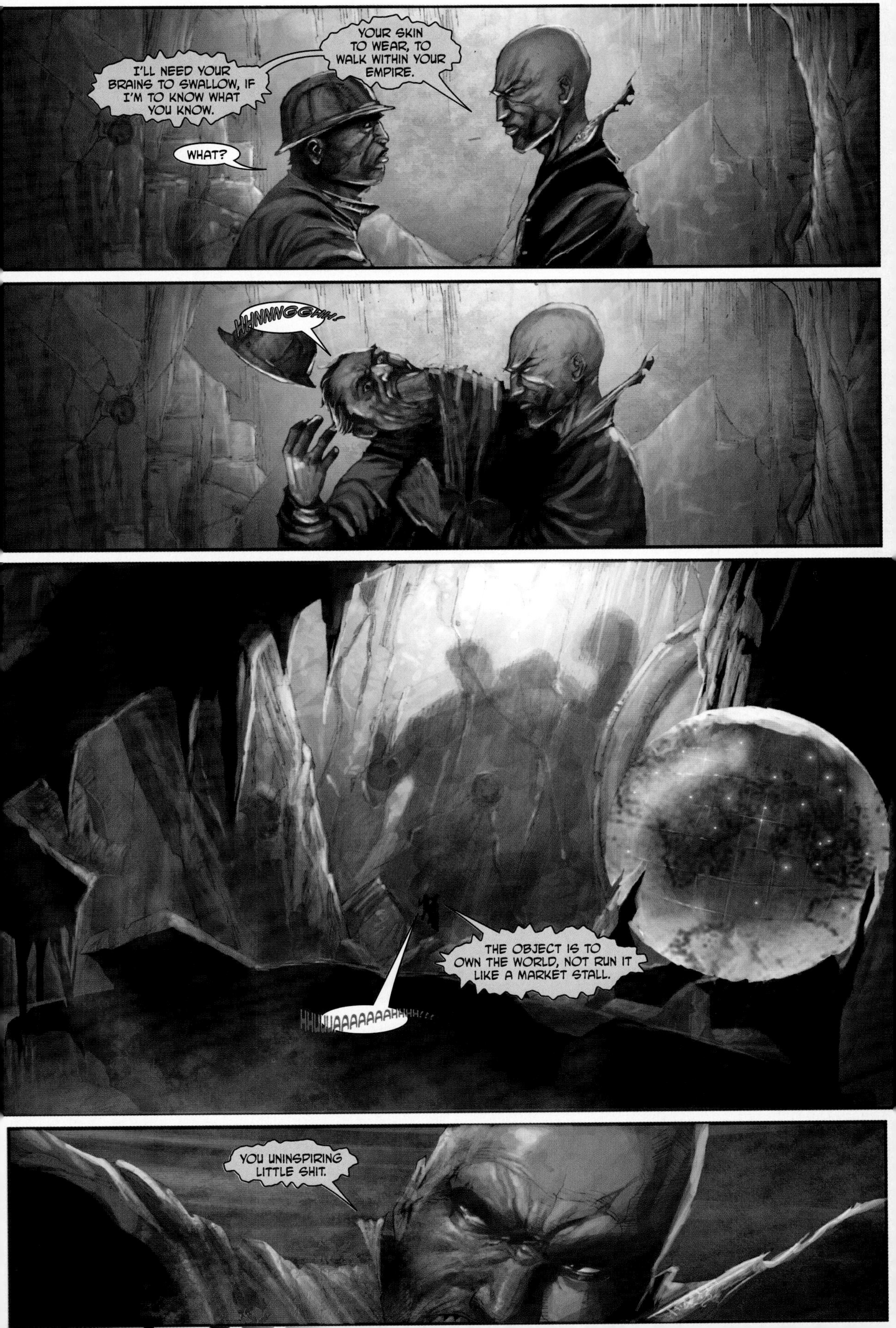
YOUR SKIN TO WEAR, TO WALK WITHIN YOUR EMPIRE.
I'LL NEED YOUR BRAINS TO SWALLOW, IF I'M TO KNOW WHAT YOU KNOW.
WHAT?
HHNNNGGHH!
THE OBJECT IS TO OWN THE WORLD, NOT RUN IT LIKE A MARKET STALL.
HHUUAAAAAAAAHHHH!!!
YOU UNINSPIRING LITTLE SHIT.

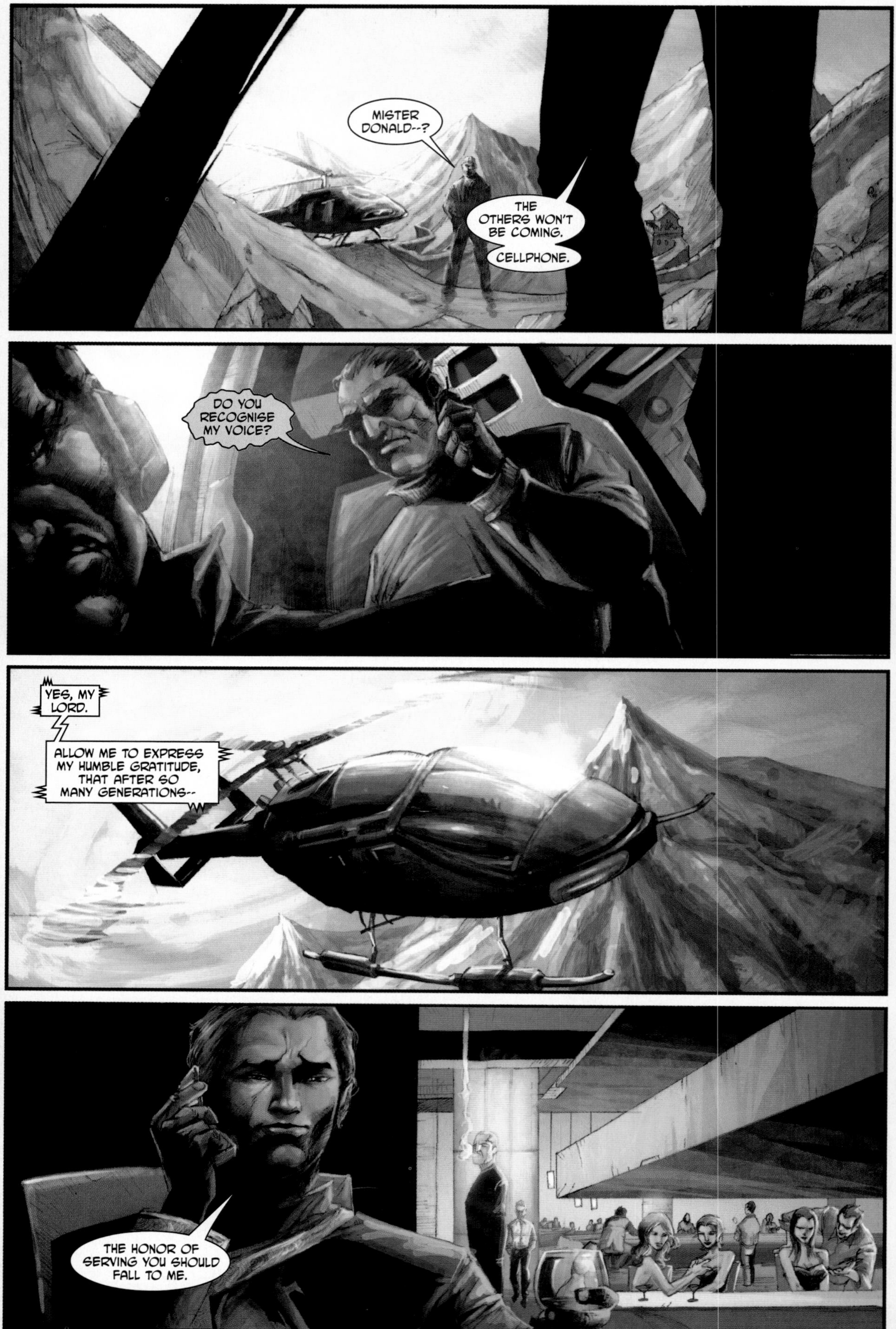
MISTER DONALD--?
THE OTHERS WON'T BE COMING.
CELLPHONE.
DO YOU RECOGNISE MY VOICE?
YES, MY LORD.
ALLOW ME TO EXPRESS MY HUMBLE GRATITUDE, THAT AFTER SO MANY GENERATIONS--
THE HONOR OF SERVING YOU SHOULD FALL TO ME.

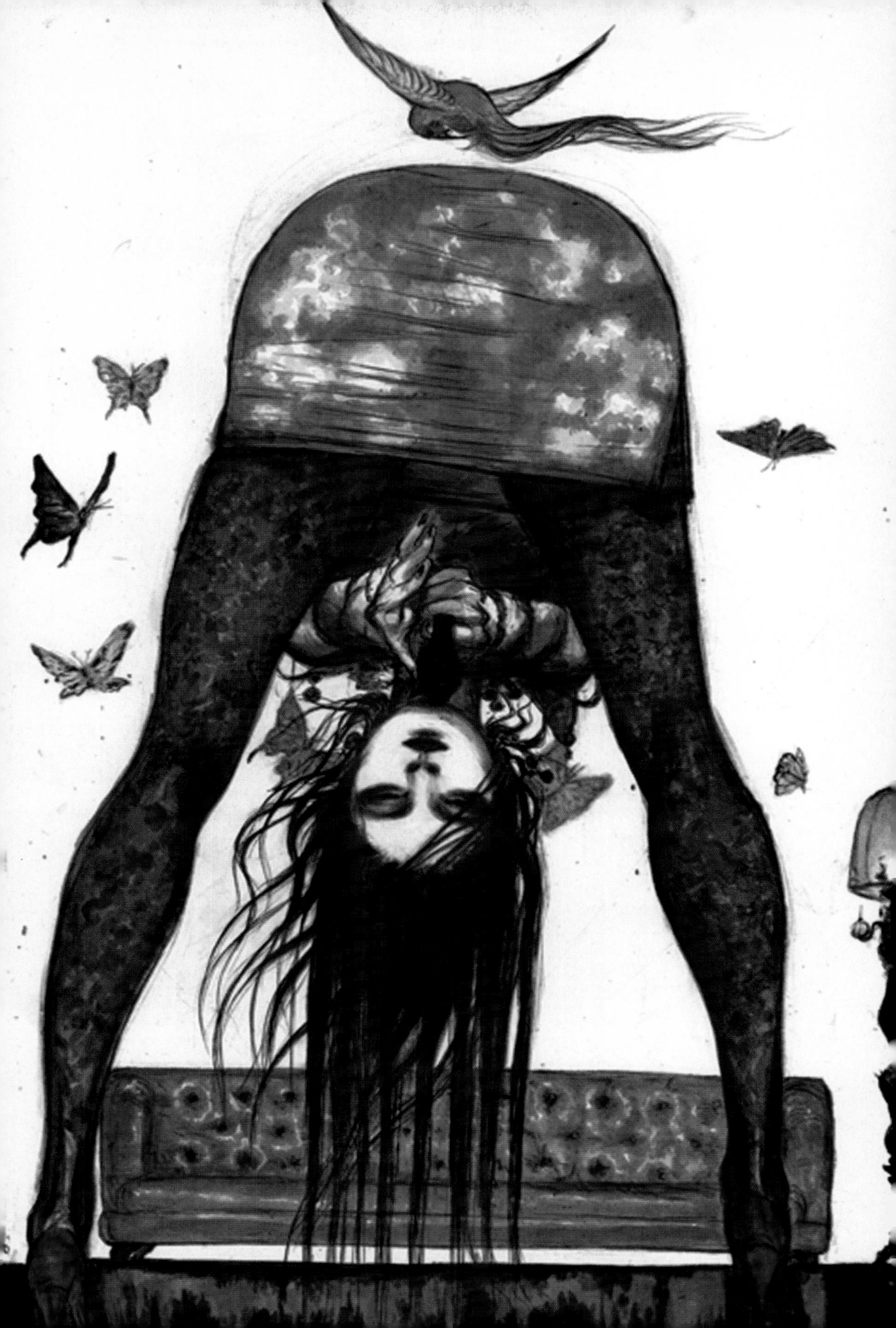

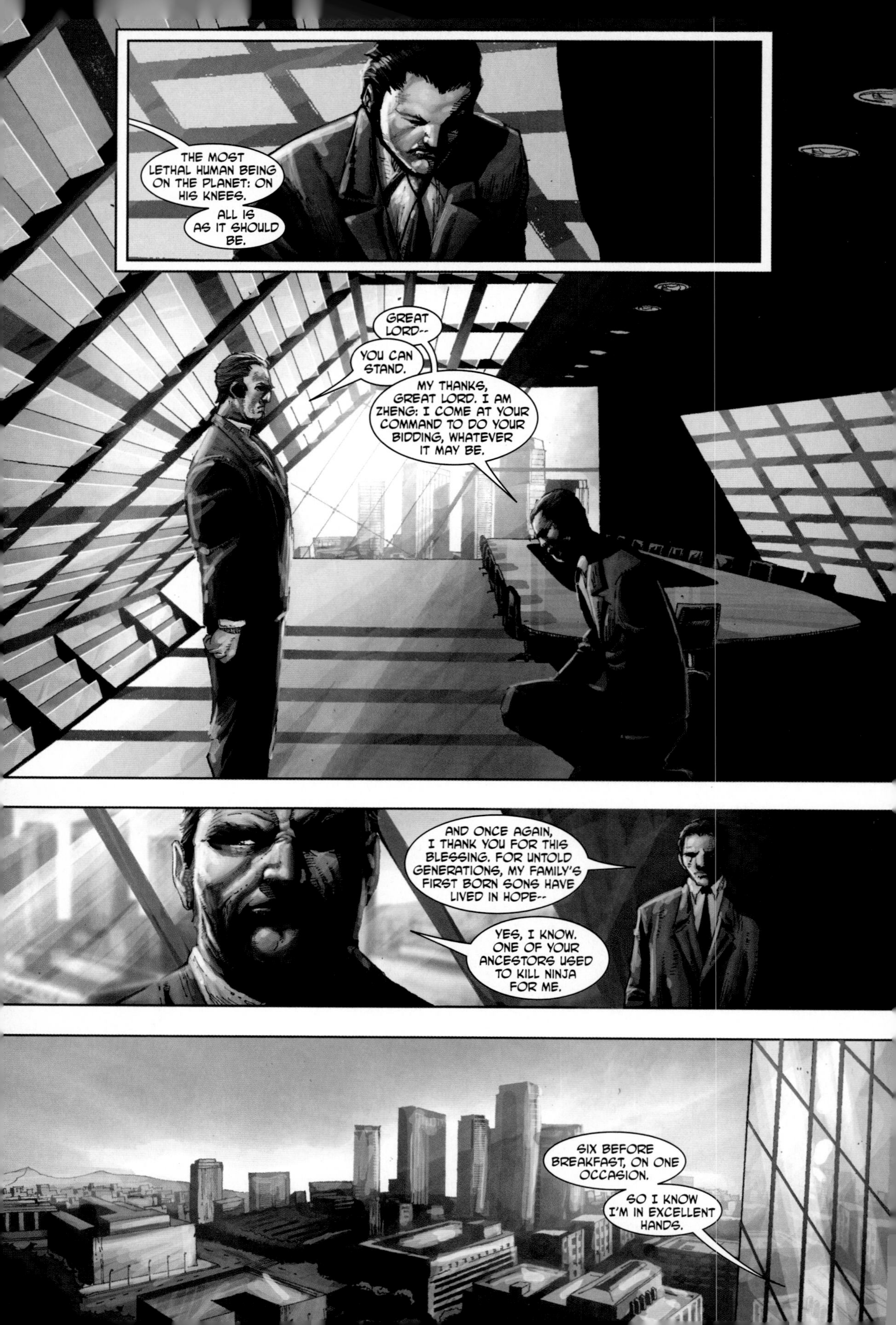
THE MOST LETHAL HUMAN BEING ON THE PLANET: ON HIS KNEES.
ALL IS AS IT SHOULD BE.
GREAT LORD--
YOU CAN STAND.
MY THANKS, GREAT LORD. I AM ZHENG: I COME AT YOUR COMMAND TO DO YOUR BIDDING, WHATEVER IT MAY BE.
AND ONCE AGAIN, I THANK YOU FOR THIS BLESSING. FOR UNTOLD GENERATIONS, MY FAMILY'S FIRST BORN SONS HAVE LIVED IN HOPE--
YES, I KNOW. ONE OF YOUR ANCESTORS USED TO KILL NINJA FOR ME.
SIX BEFORE BREAKFAST, ON ONE OCCASION.
SO I KNOW I'M IN EXCELLENT HANDS.

NOT EXACTLY.

THE TROUBLE WITH USING BLACK AS CAMOUFLAGE IS THAT PEOPLE HAVE A NASTY HABIT OF TURNING THE LIGHT ON.

GREAT LORD, HOW MIGHT I SERVE YOU? HAVE YOU A TARGET FOR ME?

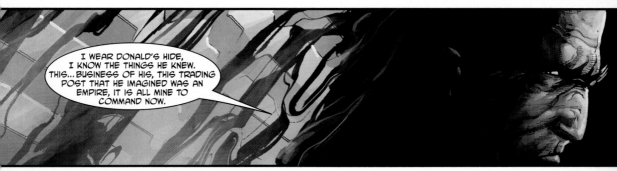

I WEAR DONALD'S HIDE, I KNOW THE THINGS HE KNEW. THIS... BUSINESS OF HIS, THIS TRADING POST THAT HE IMAGINED WAS AN EMPIRE, IT IS ALL MINE TO COMMAND NOW.

THROUGH ITS PEONS, I SHALL ENACT MY OLD DESIGN. EVEN NOW, AIRCRAFT CARRY THE CONTROL STONES TO THEIR PROPER PLACES ON THE DRAGON LINES. SET IN PLACE, EMPOWERED BY MY ENCHANTMENTS, THE STONES WILL MAKE THIS PLANET *MINE*.

WHAT *SHOULD HAVE BEEN* SIX HUNDRED YEARS AGO WILL COME TO PASS--AND THIS TIME, NO SHIT OF AN APPRENTICE, NO MEDDLING INSECT, *NO ONE* WILL ROB ME OF MY HEART'S BLACK DESIRE.

THAT IS WHAT YOU ARE GOING TO MAKE SURE OF.

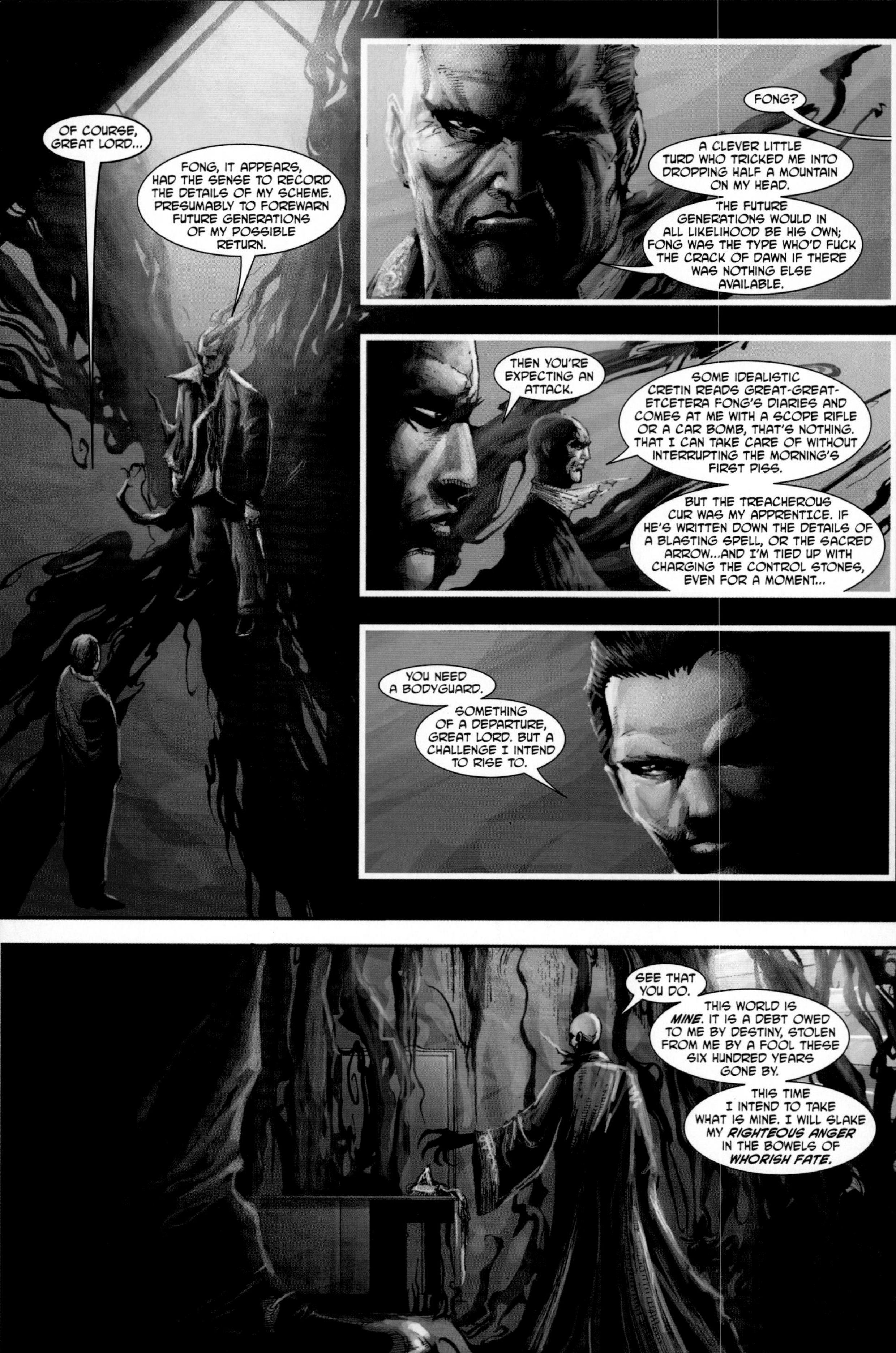
OF COURSE, GREAT LORD...
FONG, IT APPEARS, HAD THE SENSE TO RECORD THE DETAILS OF MY SCHEME. PRESUMABLY TO FOREWARN FUTURE GENERATIONS OF MY POSSIBLE RETURN.
FONG?
A CLEVER LITTLE TURD WHO TRICKED ME INTO DROPPING HALF A MOUNTAIN ON MY HEAD.
THE FUTURE GENERATIONS WOULD IN ALL LIKELIHOOD BE HIS OWN; FONG WAS THE TYPE WHO'D FUCK THE CRACK OF DAWN IF THERE WAS NOTHING ELSE AVAILABLE.
THEN YOU'RE EXPECTING AN ATTACK.
SOME IDEALISTIC CRETIN READS GREAT-GREAT-ETCETERA FONG'S DIARIES AND COMES AT ME WITH A SCOPE RIFLE OR A CAR BOMB, THAT'S NOTHING. THAT I CAN TAKE CARE OF WITHOUT INTERRUPTING THE MORNING'S FIRST PISS.
BUT THE TREACHEROUS CUR WAS MY APPRENTICE. IF HE'S WRITTEN DOWN THE DETAILS OF A BLASTING SPELL, OR THE SACRED ARROW...AND I'M TIED UP WITH CHARGING THE CONTROL STONES, EVEN FOR A MOMENT...
YOU NEED A BODYGUARD.
SOMETHING OF A DEPARTURE, GREAT LORD. BUT A CHALLENGE I INTEND TO RISE TO.
SEE THAT YOU DO.
THIS WORLD IS ***MINE***. IT IS A DEBT OWED TO ME BY DESTINY, STOLEN FROM ME BY A FOOL THESE SIX HUNDRED YEARS GONE BY.
THIS TIME I INTEND TO TAKE WHAT IS MINE. I WILL SLAKE MY ***RIGHTEOUS ANGER*** IN THE BOWELS OF ***WHORISH FATE.***

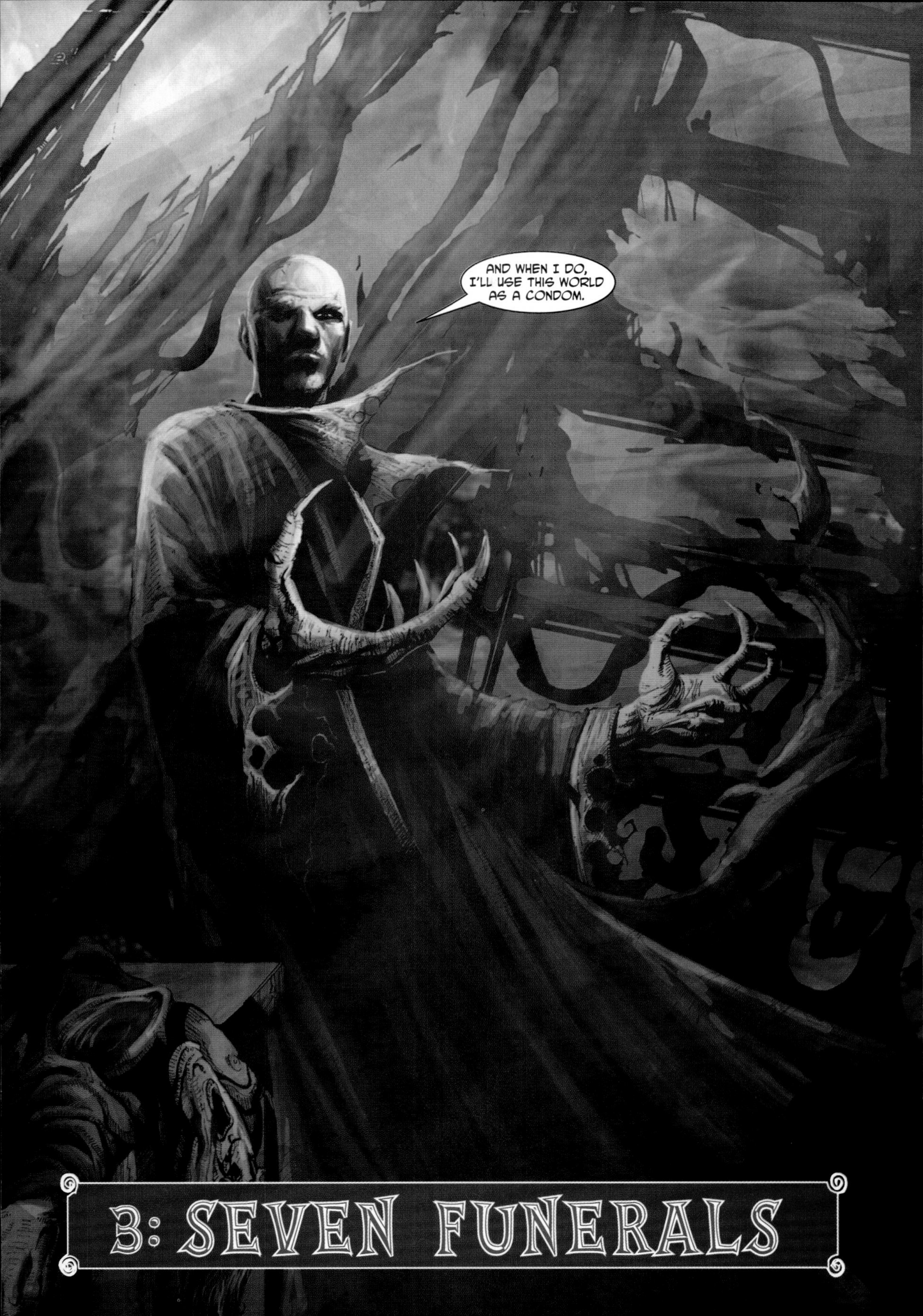
AND WHEN I DO, I'LL USE THIS WORLD AS A CONDOM.

3: SEVEN FUNERALS

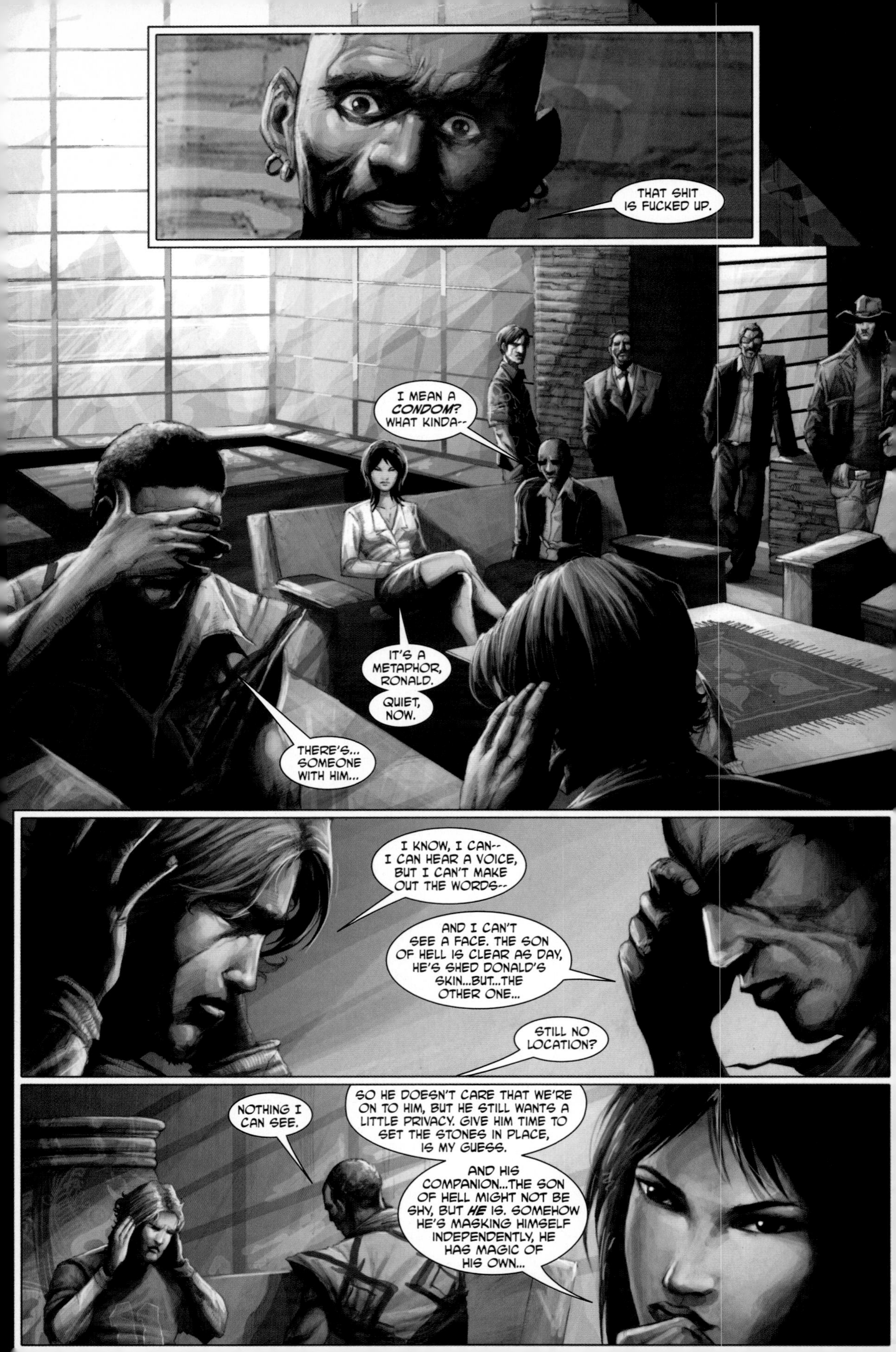
THAT SHIT IS FUCKED UP.
I MEAN A *CONDOM*? WHAT KINDA--
IT'S A METAPHOR, RONALD.
QUIET, NOW.
THERE'S... SOMEONE WITH HIM...
I KNOW, I CAN-- I CAN HEAR A VOICE, BUT I CAN'T MAKE OUT THE WORDS--
AND I CAN'T SEE A FACE. THE SON OF HELL IS CLEAR AS DAY, HE'S SHED DONALD'S SKIN...BUT...THE OTHER ONE...
STILL NO LOCATION?
NOTHING I CAN SEE.
SO HE DOESN'T CARE THAT WE'RE ON TO HIM, BUT HE STILL WANTS A LITTLE PRIVACY. GIVE HIM TIME TO SET THE STONES IN PLACE, IS MY GUESS.
AND HIS COMPANION...THE SON OF HELL MIGHT NOT BE SHY, BUT *HE* IS. SOMEHOW HE'S MASKING HIMSELF INDEPENDENTLY, HE HAS MAGIC OF HIS OWN...

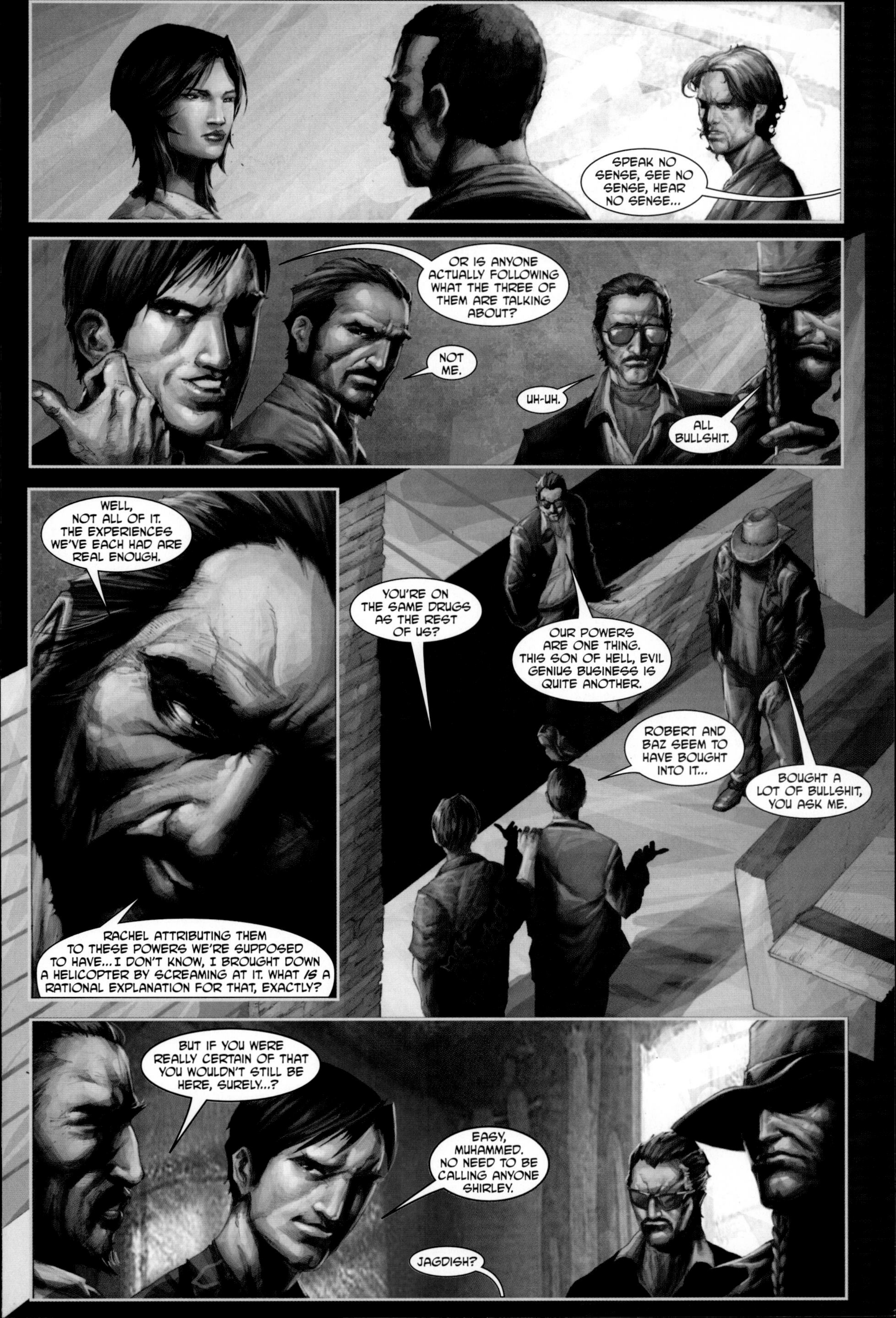
SPEAK NO SENSE, SEE NO SENSE, HEAR NO SENSE...
OR IS ANYONE ACTUALLY FOLLOWING WHAT THE THREE OF THEM ARE TALKING ABOUT?
NOT ME.
UH-UH.
ALL BULLSHIT.
WELL, NOT ALL OF IT. THE EXPERIENCES WE'VE EACH HAD ARE REAL ENOUGH.
RACHEL ATTRIBUTING THEM TO THESE POWERS WE'RE SUPPOSED TO HAVE... I DON'T KNOW, I BROUGHT DOWN A HELICOPTER BY SCREAMING AT IT. WHAT *IS* A RATIONAL EXPLANATION FOR THAT, EXACTLY?
YOU'RE ON THE SAME DRUGS AS THE REST OF US?
OUR POWERS ARE ONE THING. THIS SON OF HELL, EVIL GENIUS BUSINESS IS QUITE ANOTHER.
ROBERT AND BAZ SEEM TO HAVE BOUGHT INTO IT...
BOUGHT A LOT OF BULLSHIT, YOU ASK ME.
BUT IF YOU WERE REALLY CERTAIN OF THAT YOU WOULDN'T STILL BE HERE, SURELY...?
EASY, MUHAMMED. NO NEED TO BE CALLING ANYONE SHIRLEY.
JAGDISH?

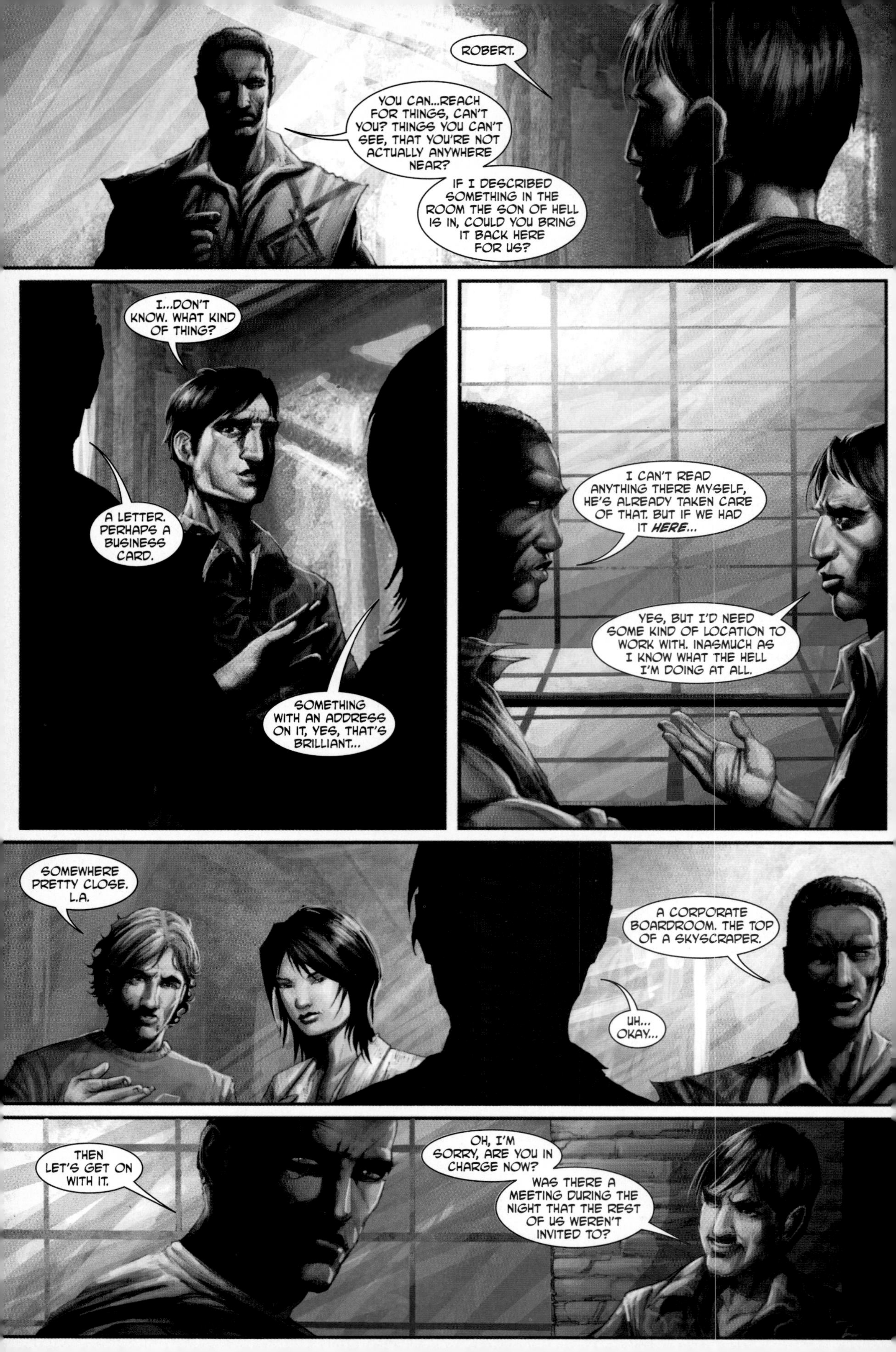
ROBERT.
YOU CAN...REACH FOR THINGS, CAN'T YOU? THINGS YOU CAN'T SEE, THAT YOU'RE NOT ACTUALLY ANYWHERE NEAR?
IF I DESCRIBED SOMETHING IN THE ROOM THE SON OF HELL IS IN, COULD YOU BRING IT BACK HERE FOR US?
I...DON'T KNOW. WHAT KIND OF THING?
A LETTER. PERHAPS A BUSINESS CARD.
SOMETHING WITH AN ADDRESS ON IT, YES, THAT'S BRILLIANT...
I CAN'T READ ANYTHING THERE MYSELF, HE'S ALREADY TAKEN CARE OF THAT. BUT IF WE HAD IT HERE...
YES, BUT I'D NEED SOME KIND OF LOCATION TO WORK WITH. INASMUCH AS I KNOW WHAT THE HELL I'M DOING AT ALL.
SOMEWHERE PRETTY CLOSE. L.A.
A CORPORATE BOARDROOM. THE TOP OF A SKYSCRAPER.
UH... OKAY...
THEN LET'S GET ON WITH IT.
OH, I'M SORRY, ARE YOU IN CHARGE NOW?
WAS THERE A MEETING DURING THE NIGHT THAT THE REST OF US WEREN'T INVITED TO?

I'M NOT IN--

BECAUSE I THOUGHT RACHEL WAS RUNNING THIS LITTLE OUTFIT...

NO, I--

I DIDN'T EVEN KNOW THERE WAS AN OUTFIT. ARE WE SOME KIND OF TEAM NOW, IS THAT THE IDEA?

I GATHERED YOU HERE, AND TOLD YOU WHAT I KNEW OF YOUR HERITAGE, SO THAT YOU COULD FACE THE SON OF HELL. I'LL CONTINUE TO PROVIDE WHATEVER GUIDANCE I CAN. BUT I AM NOT YOUR LEADER.

THAT SAID, YOU ARE GOING TO NEED ONE, SOON...

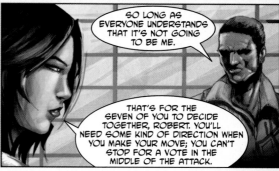

SO LONG AS EVERYONE UNDERSTANDS THAT IT'S NOT GOING TO BE ME.

THAT'S FOR THE SEVEN OF YOU TO DECIDE TOGETHER, ROBERT. YOU'LL NEED SOME KIND OF DIRECTION WHEN YOU MAKE YOUR MOVE; YOU CAN'T STOP FOR A VOTE IN THE MIDDLE OF THE ATTACK.

WHAT ATTACK?

WAIT A MINUTE, WE'RE TAKING ON THE SON OF HELL? WE'RE GOING AFTER HIM?

I THOUGHT IT WAS OBVIOUS. WHY ELSE WOULD YOU BE TRYING TO LOCATE HIM?

I MEAN YOU KNOW YOU HAVE TO STOP HIM, OTHERWISE IT'S THE END OF EVERYTHING. AND WITH THE STAKES AS HIGH AS THEY ARE, THE ONLY WAY TO DO IT WITH ANY CERTAINTY IS TO--

KILL HIM.

EXACTLY, DANIEL. THANK YOU.

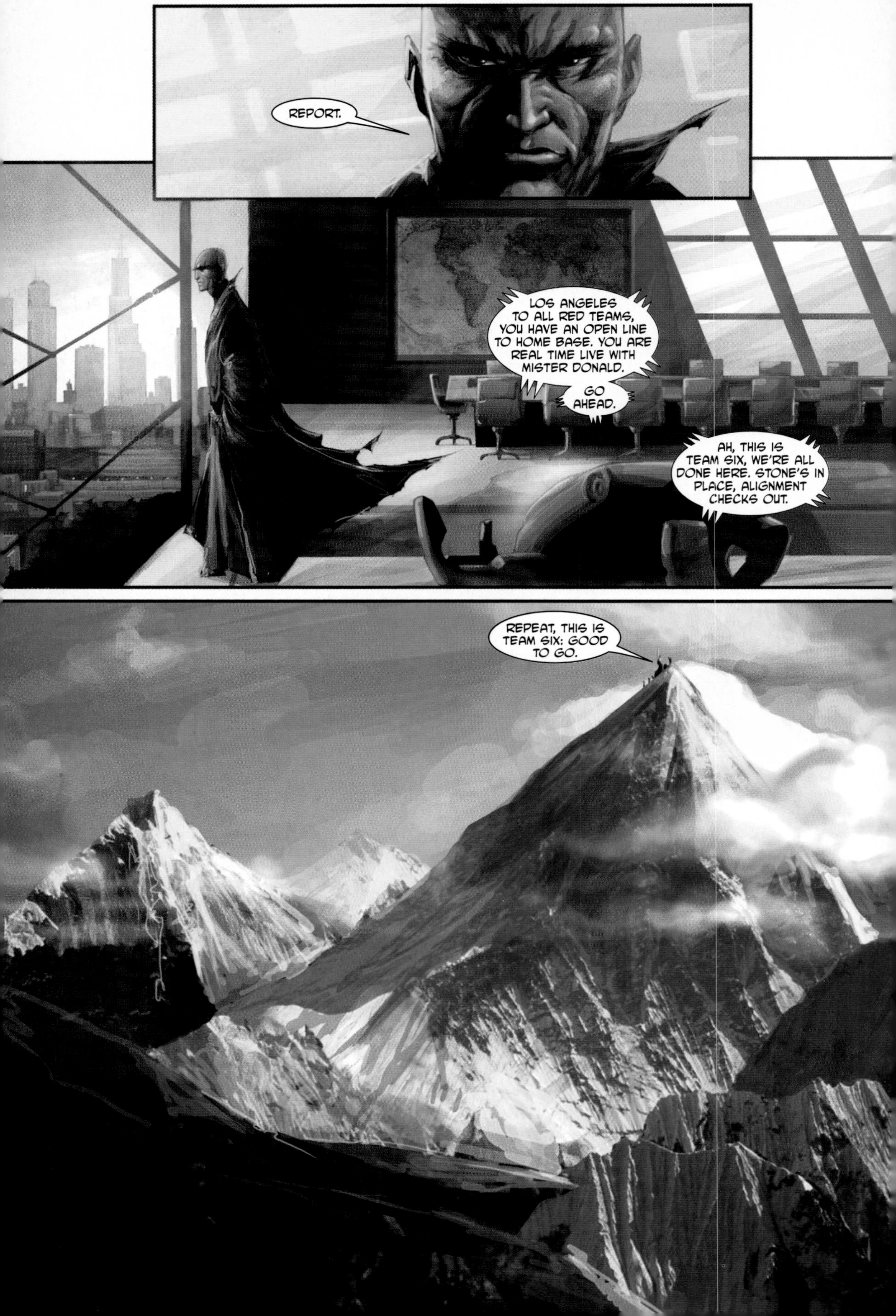
REPORT.
LOS ANGELES TO ALL RED TEAMS, YOU HAVE AN OPEN LINE TO HOME BASE. YOU ARE REAL TIME LIVE WITH MISTER DONALD.
GO AHEAD.
AH, THIS IS TEAM SIX, WE'RE ALL DONE HERE. STONE'S IN PLACE, ALIGNMENT CHECKS OUT.
REPEAT, THIS IS TEAM SIX: GOOD TO GO.

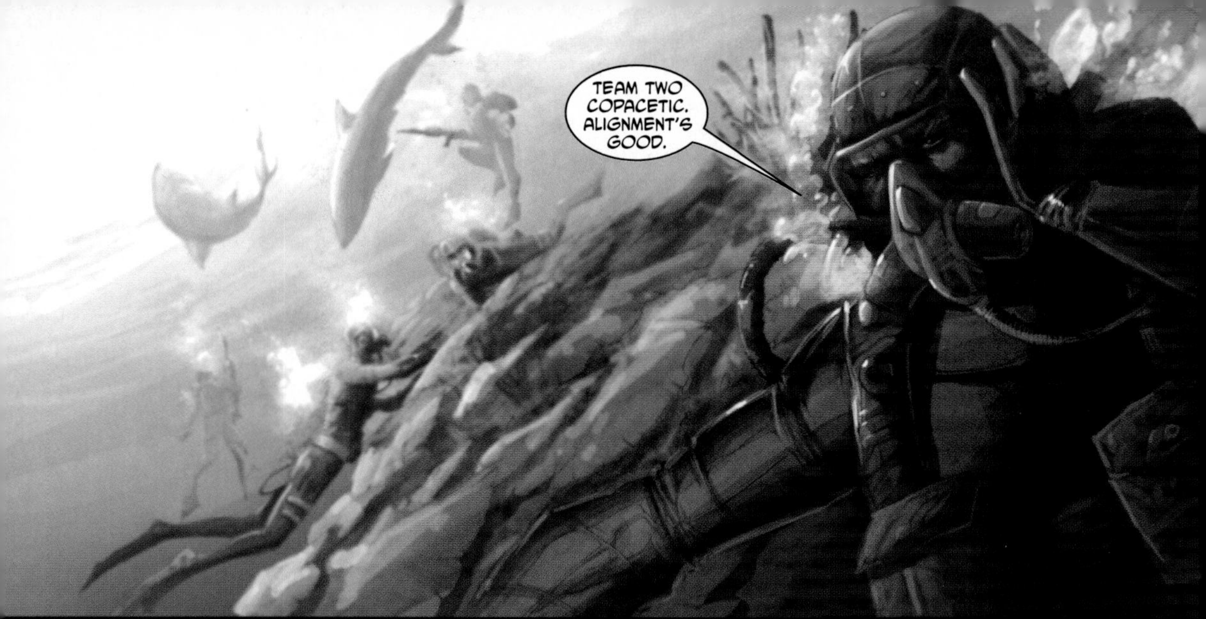
TEAM TWO COPACETIC. ALIGNMENT'S GOOD.

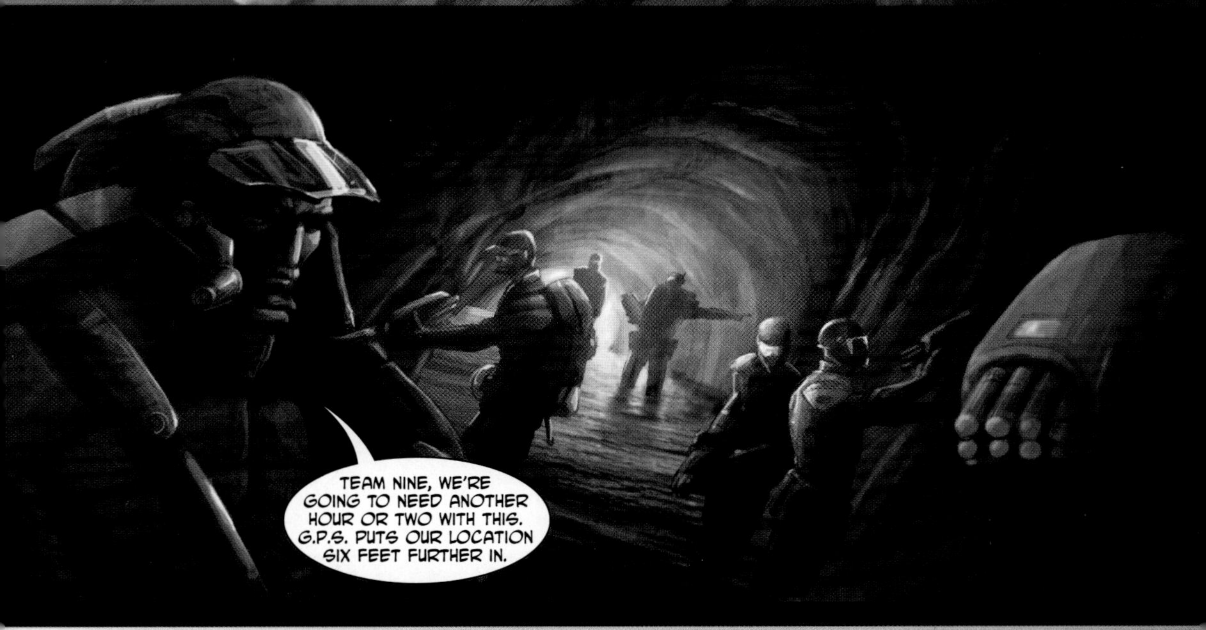
TEAM NINE, WE'RE GOING TO NEED ANOTHER HOUR OR TWO WITH THIS. G.P.S. PUTS OUR LOCATION SIX FEET FURTHER IN.

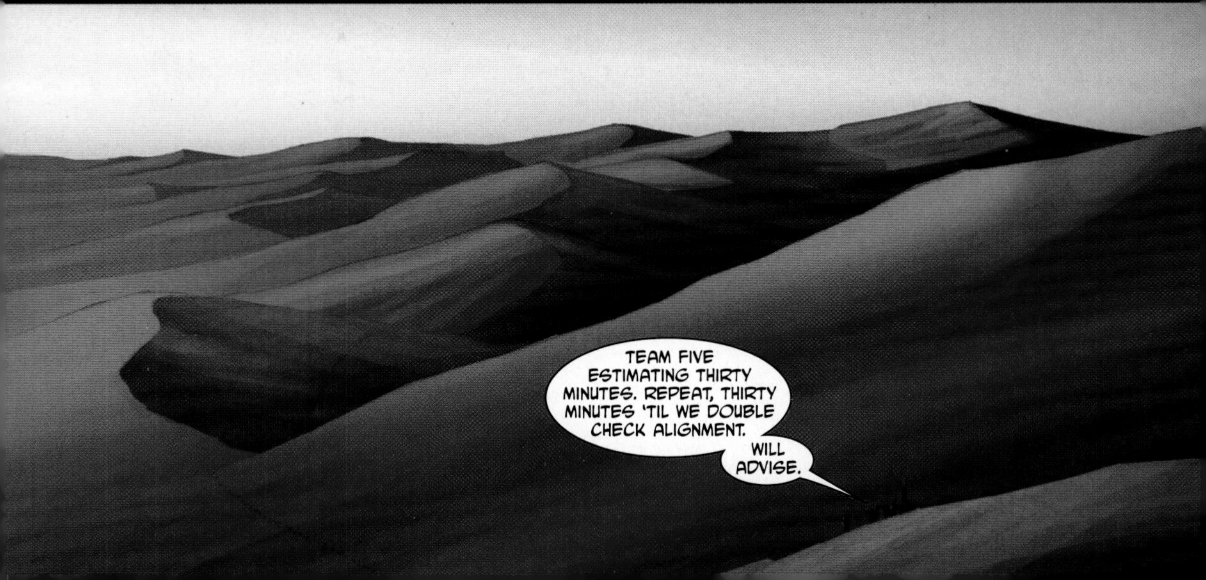
TEAM FIVE ESTIMATING THIRTY MINUTES. REPEAT, THIRTY MINUTES 'TIL WE DOUBLE CHECK ALIGNMENT.
WILL ADVISE.

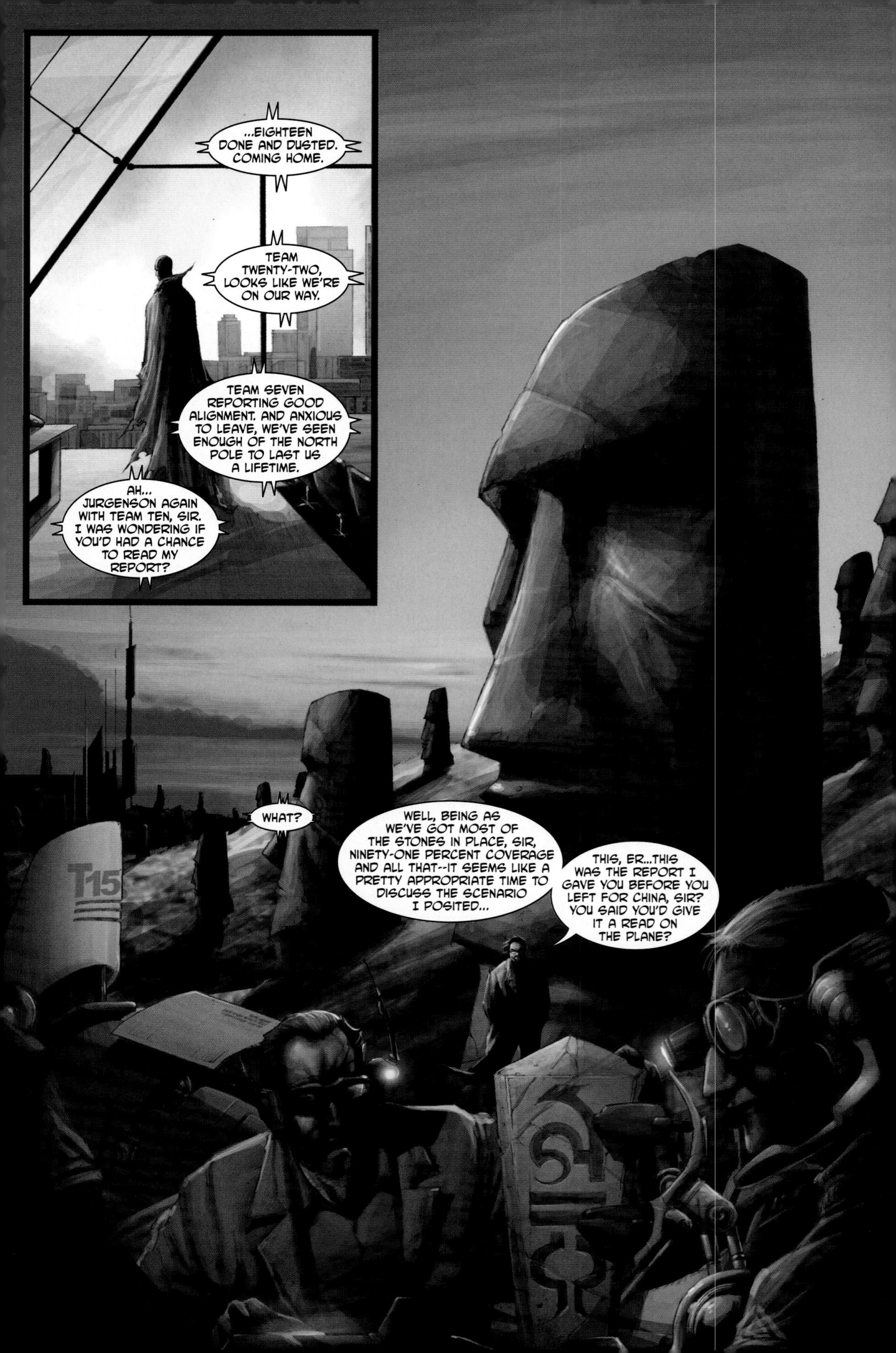
...EIGHTEEN DONE AND DUSTED. COMING HOME.
TEAM TWENTY-TWO, LOOKS LIKE WE'RE ON OUR WAY.
TEAM SEVEN REPORTING GOOD ALIGNMENT. AND ANXIOUS TO LEAVE, WE'VE SEEN ENOUGH OF THE NORTH POLE TO LAST US A LIFETIME.
AH... JURGENSON AGAIN WITH TEAM TEN, SIR. I WAS WONDERING IF YOU'D HAD A CHANCE TO READ MY REPORT?
WHAT?
WELL, BEING AS WE'VE GOT MOST OF THE STONES IN PLACE, SIR, NINETY-ONE PERCENT COVERAGE AND ALL THAT--IT SEEMS LIKE A PRETTY APPROPRIATE TIME TO DISCUSS THE SCENARIO I POSITED...
THIS, ER...THIS WAS THE REPORT I GAVE YOU BEFORE YOU LEFT FOR CHINA, SIR? YOU SAID YOU'D GIVE IT A READ ON THE PLANE?
T15

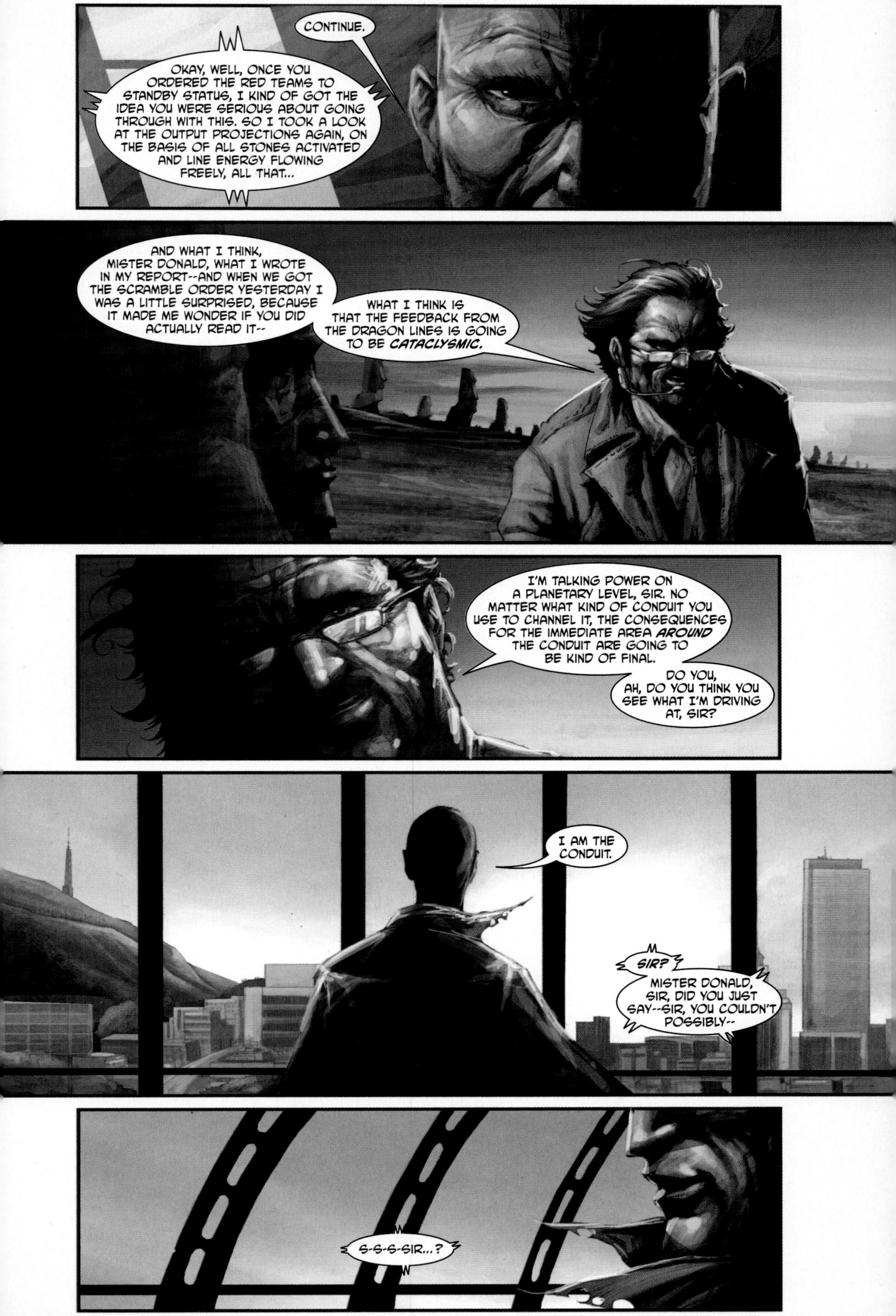
CONTINUE.
OKAY, WELL, ONCE YOU ORDERED THE RED TEAMS TO STANDBY STATUS, I KIND OF GOT THE IDEA YOU WERE SERIOUS ABOUT GOING THROUGH WITH THIS. SO I TOOK A LOOK AT THE OUTPUT PROJECTIONS AGAIN, ON THE BASIS OF ALL STONES ACTIVATED AND LINE ENERGY FLOWING FREELY, ALL THAT...
AND WHAT I THINK, MISTER DONALD, WHAT I WROTE IN MY REPORT--AND WHEN WE GOT THE SCRAMBLE ORDER YESTERDAY I WAS A LITTLE SURPRISED, BECAUSE IT MADE ME WONDER IF YOU DID ACTUALLY READ IT--
WHAT I THINK IS THAT THE FEEDBACK FROM THE DRAGON LINES IS GOING TO BE *CATACLYSMIC.*
I'M TALKING POWER ON A PLANETARY LEVEL, SIR. NO MATTER WHAT KIND OF CONDUIT YOU USE TO CHANNEL IT, THE CONSEQUENCES FOR THE IMMEDIATE AREA *AROUND* THE CONDUIT ARE GOING TO BE KIND OF FINAL.
DO YOU, AH, DO YOU THINK YOU SEE WHAT I'M DRIVING AT, SIR?
I AM THE CONDUIT.
SIR?
MISTER DONALD, SIR, DID YOU JUST SAY--SIR, YOU COULDN'T POSSIBLY--
S-S-S-SIR...?

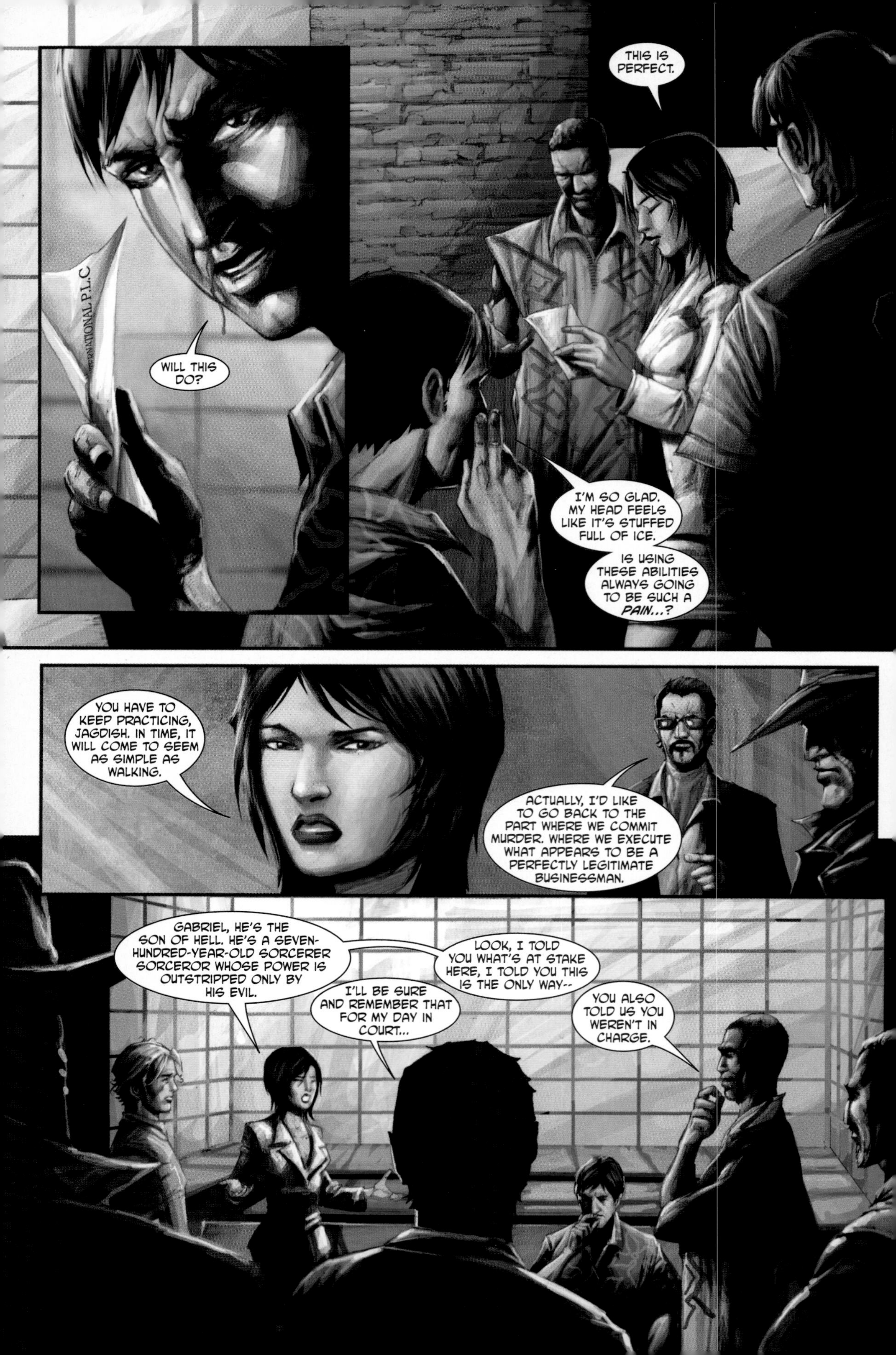
INTERNATIONAL P.L.C
WILL THIS DO?
THIS IS PERFECT.
I'M SO GLAD. MY HEAD FEELS LIKE IT'S STUFFED FULL OF ICE.
IS USING THESE ABILITIES ALWAYS GOING TO BE SUCH A *PAIN*...?
YOU HAVE TO KEEP PRACTICING, JAGDISH. IN TIME, IT WILL COME TO SEEM AS SIMPLE AS WALKING.
ACTUALLY, I'D LIKE TO GO BACK TO THE PART WHERE WE COMMIT MURDER. WHERE WE EXECUTE WHAT APPEARS TO BE A PERFECTLY LEGITIMATE BUSINESSMAN.
GABRIEL, HE'S THE SON OF HELL. HE'S A SEVEN-HUNDRED-YEAR-OLD SORCERER SORCEROR WHOSE POWER IS OUTSTRIPPED ONLY BY HIS EVIL.
LOOK, I TOLD YOU WHAT'S AT STAKE HERE, I TOLD YOU THIS IS THE ONLY WAY--
I'LL BE SURE AND REMEMBER THAT FOR MY DAY IN COURT...
YOU ALSO TOLD US YOU WEREN'T IN CHARGE.

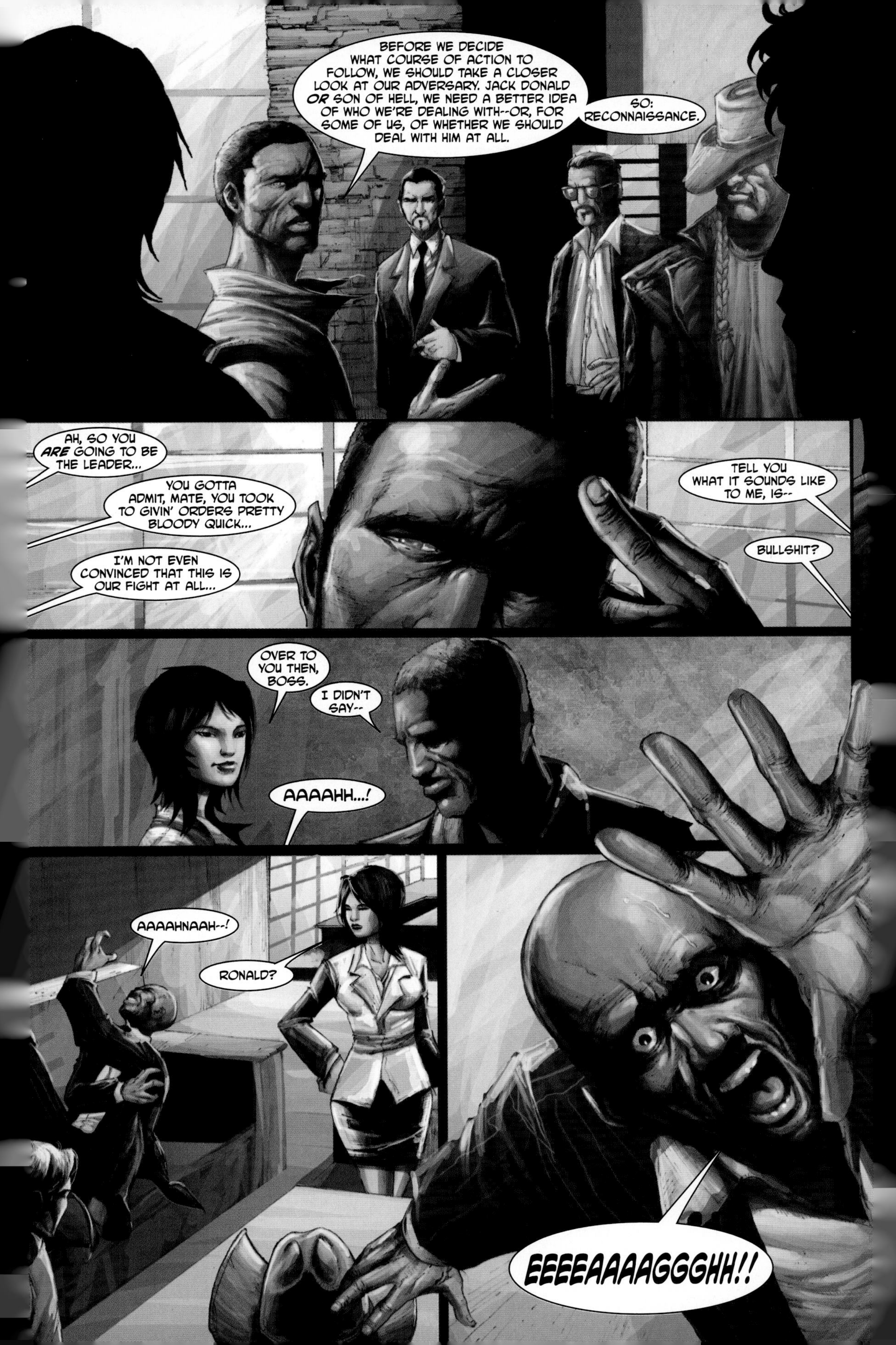
BEFORE WE DECIDE WHAT COURSE OF ACTION TO FOLLOW, WE SHOULD TAKE A CLOSER LOOK AT OUR ADVERSARY. JACK DONALD *OR* SON OF HELL, WE NEED A BETTER IDEA OF WHO WE'RE DEALING WITH--OR, FOR SOME OF US, OF WHETHER WE SHOULD DEAL WITH HIM AT ALL.
SO: RECONNAISSANCE.
AH, SO YOU *ARE* GOING TO BE THE LEADER...
YOU GOTTA ADMIT, MATE, YOU TOOK TO GIVIN' ORDERS PRETTY BLOODY QUICK...
I'M NOT EVEN CONVINCED THAT THIS IS OUR FIGHT AT ALL...
TELL YOU WHAT IT SOUNDS LIKE TO ME, IS--
BULLSHIT?
OVER TO YOU THEN, BOSS.
I DIDN'T SAY--
AAAAHH...!
AAAAHNAAH--!
RONALD?
EEEEAAAAGGGHH!!

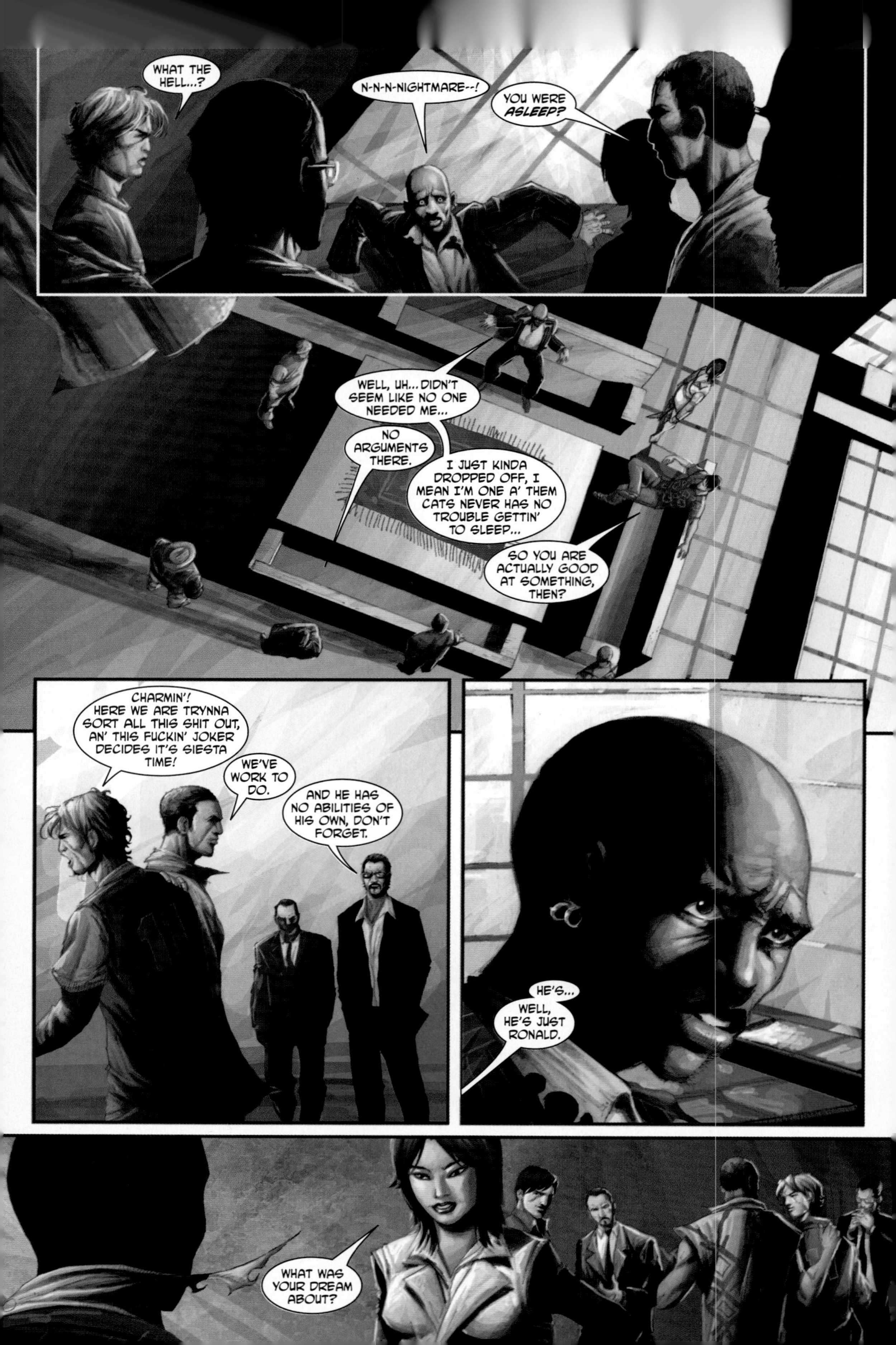

WHAT THE HELL...?
N-N-N-NIGHTMARE--!
YOU WERE ASLEEP?
WELL, UH... DIDN'T SEEM LIKE NO ONE NEEDED ME...
NO ARGUMENTS THERE.
I JUST KINDA DROPPED OFF, I MEAN I'M ONE A' THEM CATS NEVER HAS NO TROUBLE GETTIN' TO SLEEP...
SO YOU ARE ACTUALLY GOOD AT SOMETHING, THEN?
CHARMIN'! HERE WE ARE TRYNNA SORT ALL THIS SHIT OUT, AN' THIS FUCKIN' JOKER DECIDES IT'S SIESTA TIME!
WE'VE WORK TO DO.
AND HE HAS NO ABILITIES OF HIS OWN, DON'T FORGET.
HE'S...
WELL, HE'S JUST RONALD.
WHAT WAS YOUR DREAM ABOUT?

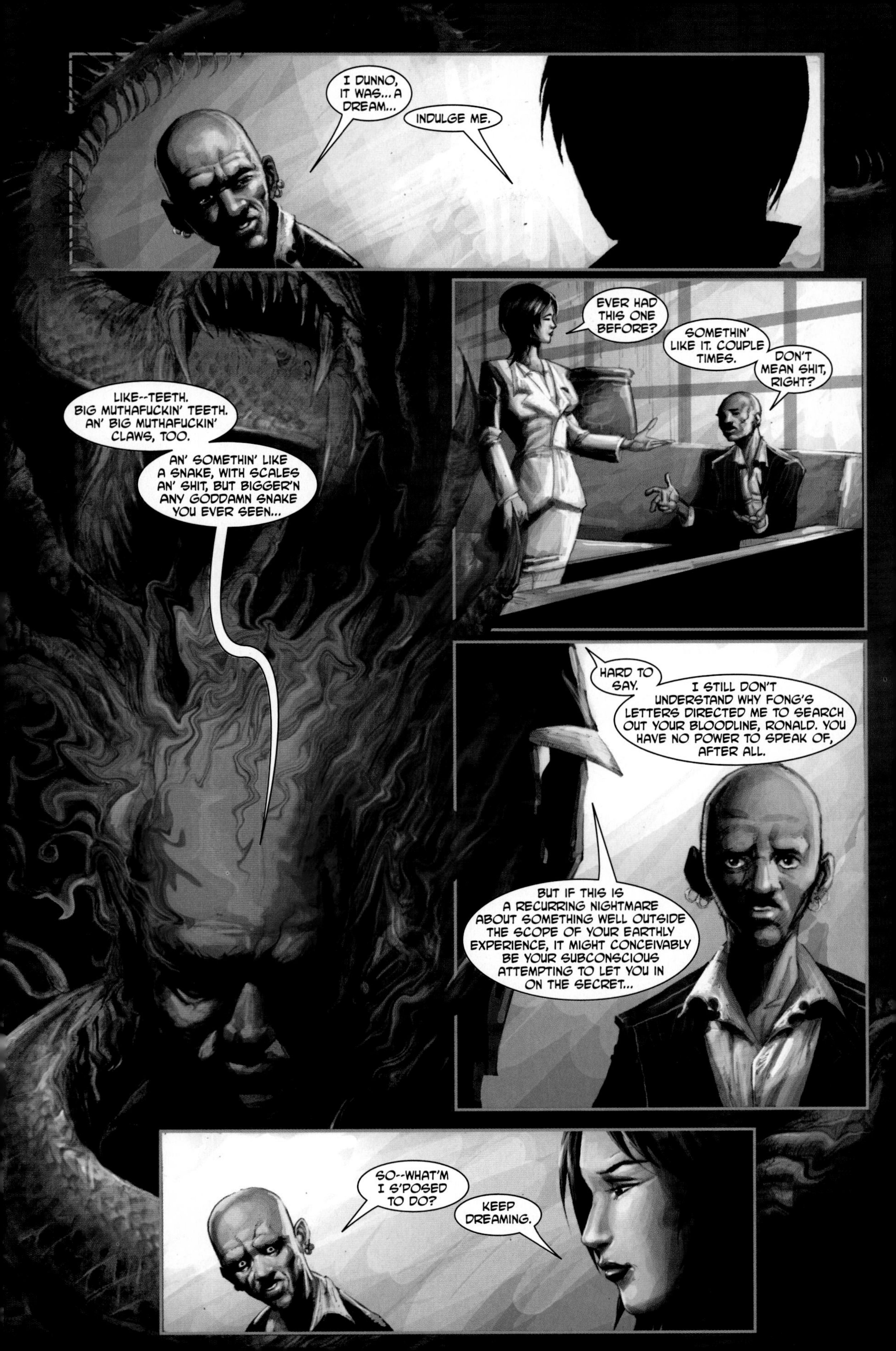
I DUNNO, IT WAS... A DREAM...
INDULGE ME.
EVER HAD THIS ONE BEFORE?
SOMETHIN' LIKE IT. COUPLE TIMES.
DON'T MEAN SHIT, RIGHT?
LIKE--TEETH. BIG MUTHAFUCKIN' TEETH. AN' BIG MUTHAFUCKIN' CLAWS, TOO.
AN' SOMETHIN' LIKE A SNAKE, WITH SCALES AN' SHIT, BUT BIGGER'N ANY GODDAMN SNAKE YOU EVER SEEN...
HARD TO SAY.
I STILL DON'T UNDERSTAND WHY FONG'S LETTERS DIRECTED ME TO SEARCH OUT YOUR BLOODLINE, RONALD. YOU HAVE NO POWER TO SPEAK OF, AFTER ALL.
BUT IF THIS IS A RECURRING NIGHTMARE ABOUT SOMETHING WELL OUTSIDE THE SCOPE OF YOUR EARTHLY EXPERIENCE, IT MIGHT CONCEIVABLY BE YOUR SUBCONSCIOUS ATTEMPTING TO LET YOU IN ON THE SECRET...
SO--WHAT'M I S'POSED TO DO?
KEEP DREAMING.

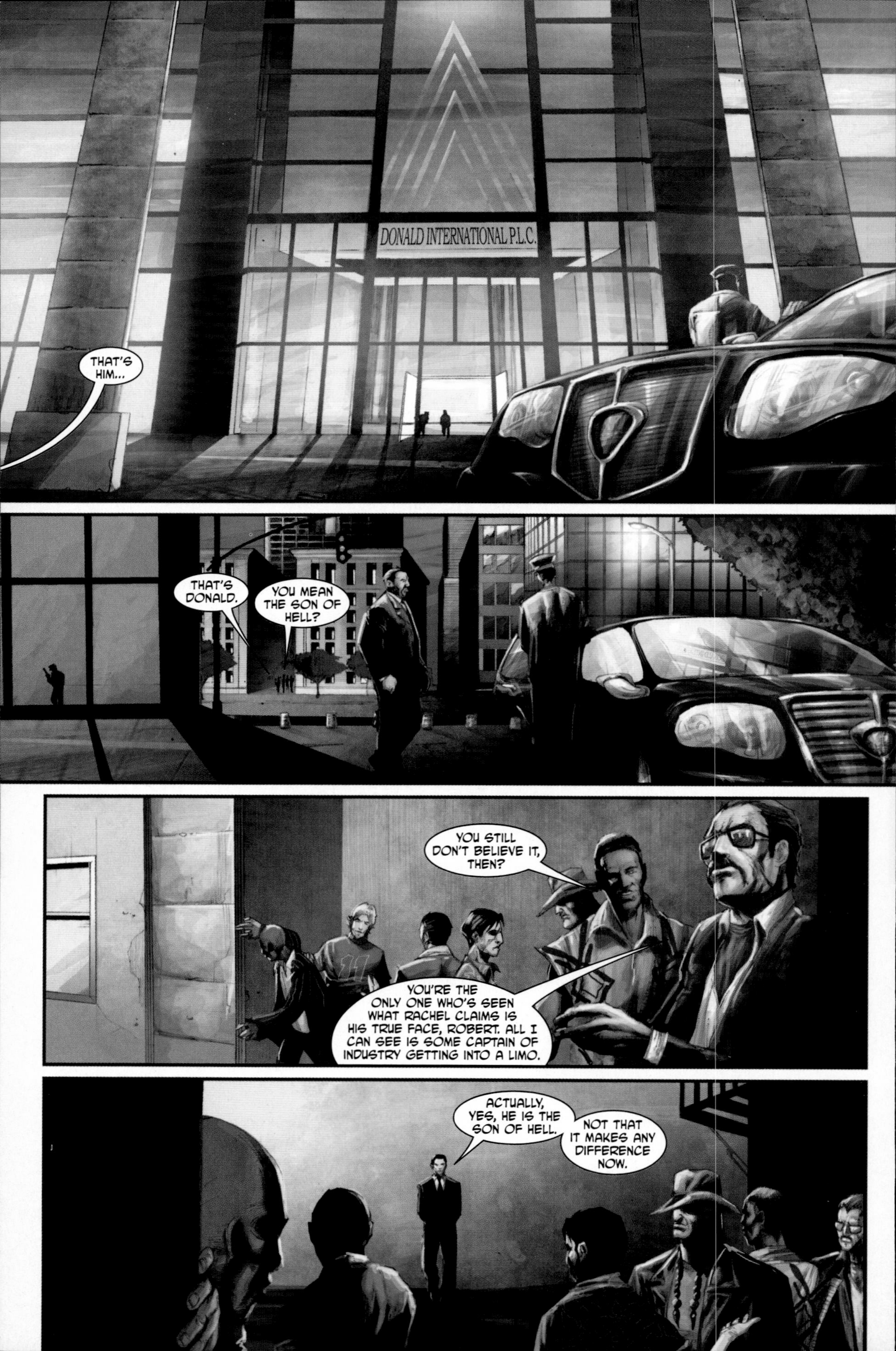
DONALD INTERNATIONAL P.L.C.
THAT'S HIM...
THAT'S DONALD.
YOU MEAN THE SON OF HELL?
YOU STILL DON'T BELIEVE IT, THEN?
YOU'RE THE ONLY ONE WHO'S SEEN WHAT RACHEL CLAIMS IS HIS TRUE FACE, ROBERT. ALL I CAN SEE IS SOME CAPTAIN OF INDUSTRY GETTING INTO A LIMO.
ACTUALLY, YES, HE IS THE SON OF HELL.
NOT THAT IT MAKES ANY DIFFERENCE NOW.

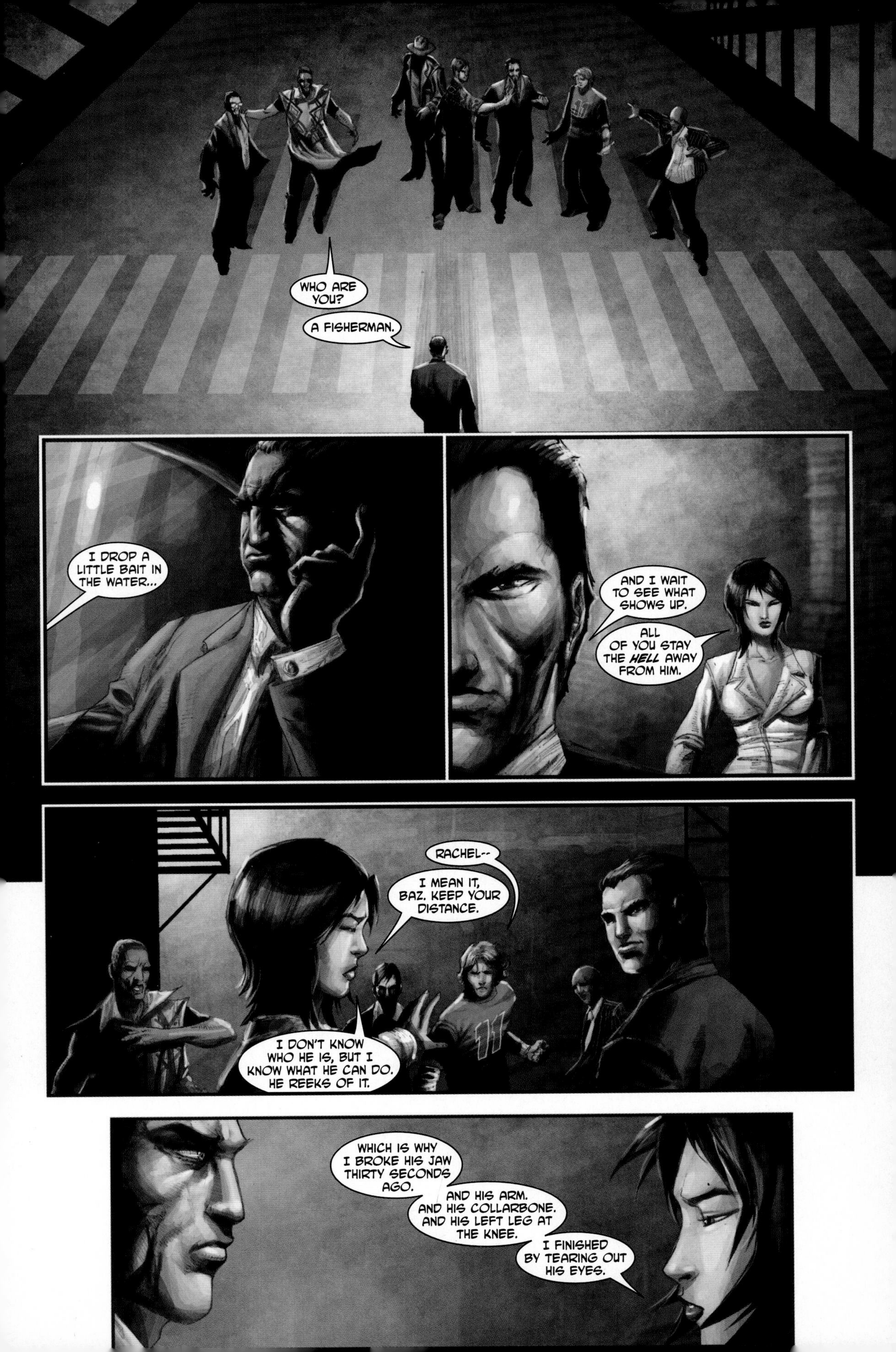
WHO ARE YOU?
A FISHERMAN.
I DROP A LITTLE BAIT IN THE WATER...
AND I WAIT TO SEE WHAT SHOWS UP.
ALL OF YOU STAY THE *HELL* AWAY FROM HIM.
RACHEL--
I MEAN IT, BAZ. KEEP YOUR DISTANCE.
I DON'T KNOW WHO HE IS, BUT I KNOW WHAT HE CAN DO. HE REEKS OF IT.
WHICH IS WHY I BROKE HIS JAW THIRTY SECONDS AGO.
AND HIS ARM. AND HIS COLLARBONE. AND HIS LEFT LEG AT THE KNEE.
I FINISHED BY TEARING OUT HIS EYES.

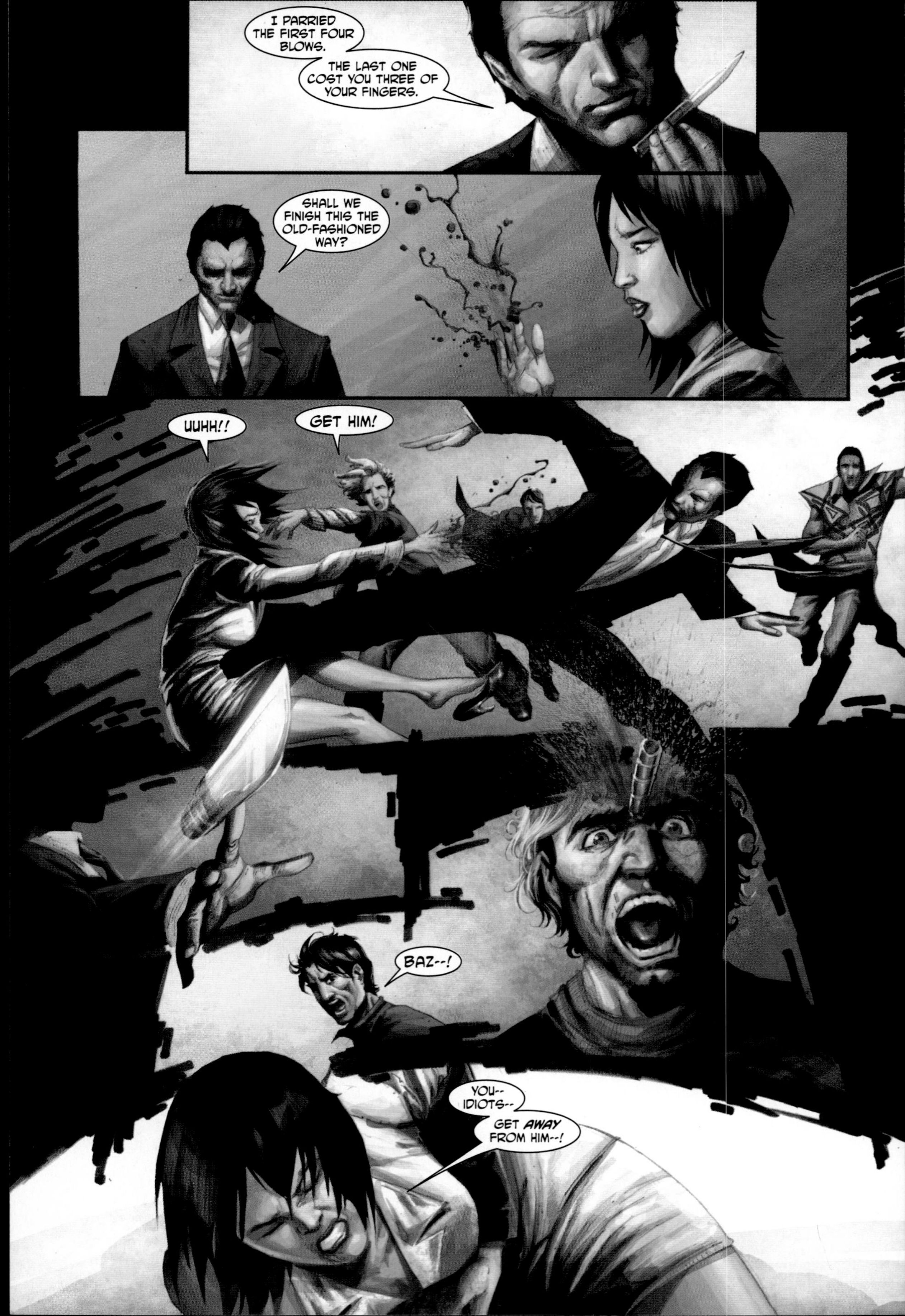
I PARRIED THE FIRST FOUR BLOWS.
THE LAST ONE COST YOU THREE OF YOUR FINGERS.
SHALL WE FINISH THIS THE OLD-FASHIONED WAY?
UUHH!!
GET HIM!
BAZ--!
YOU-- IDIOTS--
GET *AWAY* FROM HIM--!

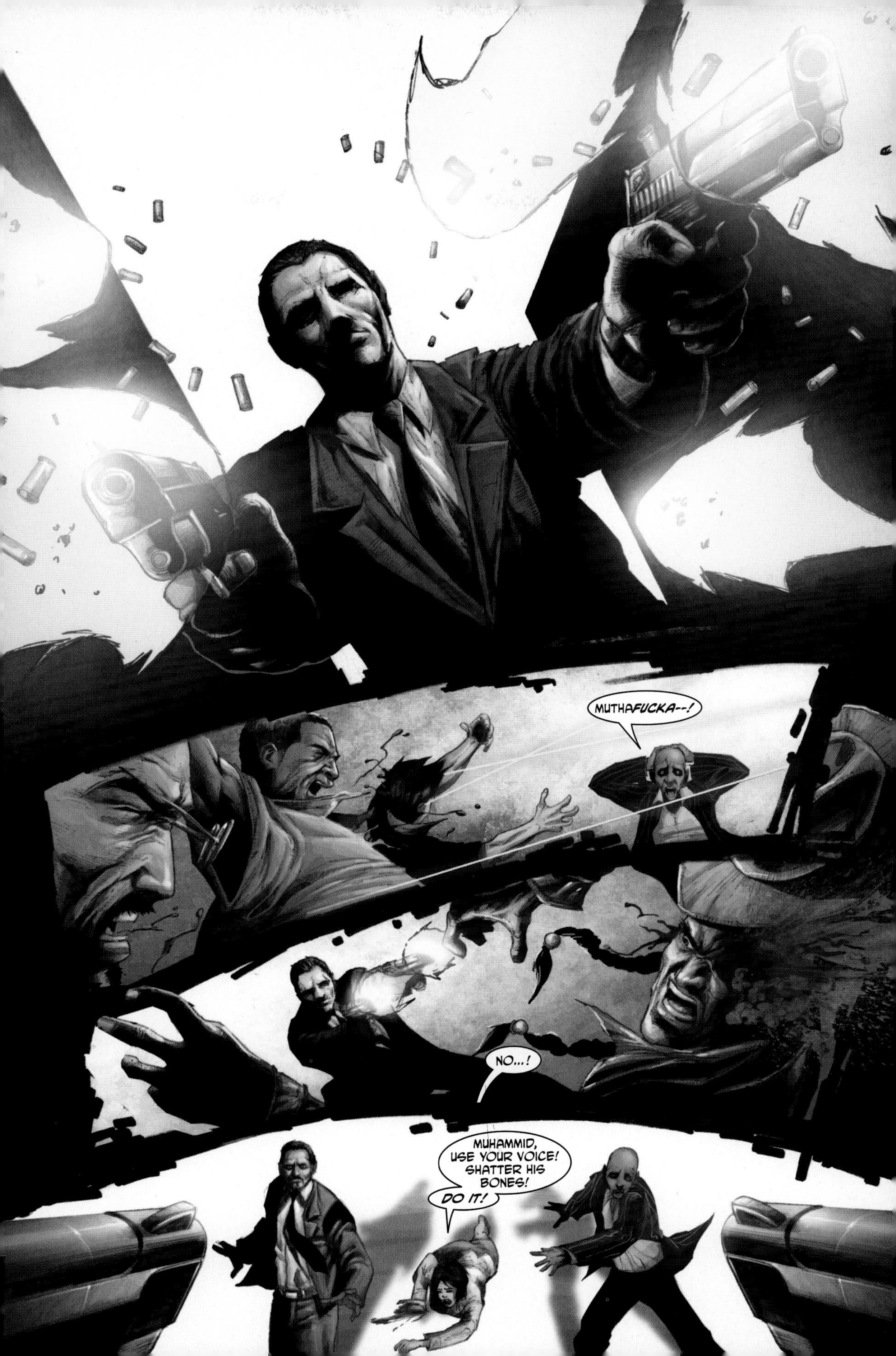
MUTHAFUCKA--!
NO...!
MUHAMMID, USE YOUR VOICE! SHATTER HIS BONES!
DO IT!

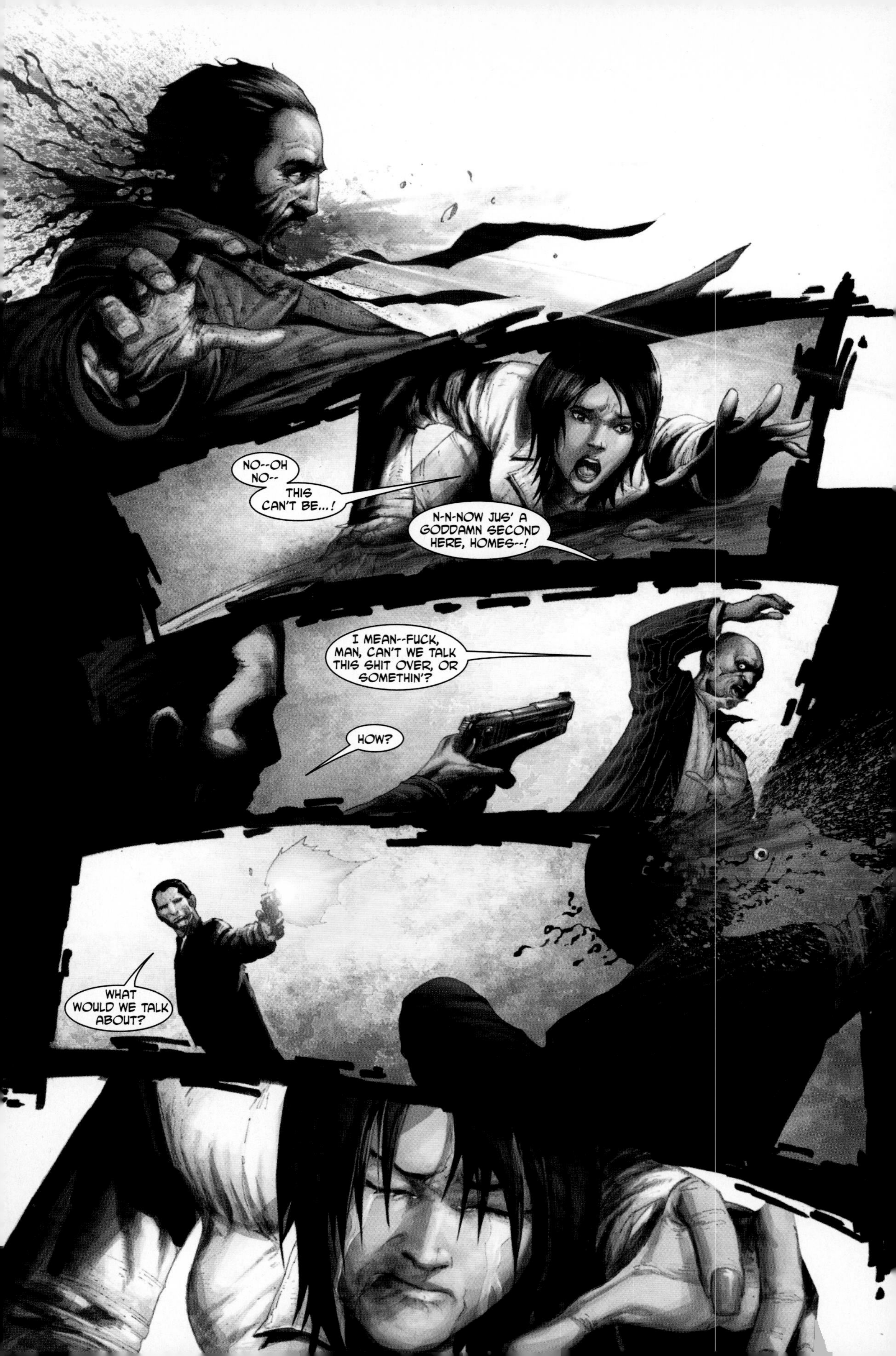
NO--OH NO-- THIS CAN'T BE...!
N-N-NOW JUS' A GODDAMN SECOND HERE, HOMES--!
I MEAN--FUCK, MAN, CAN'T WE TALK THIS SHIT OVER, OR SOMETHIN'?
HOW?
WHAT WOULD WE TALK ABOUT?

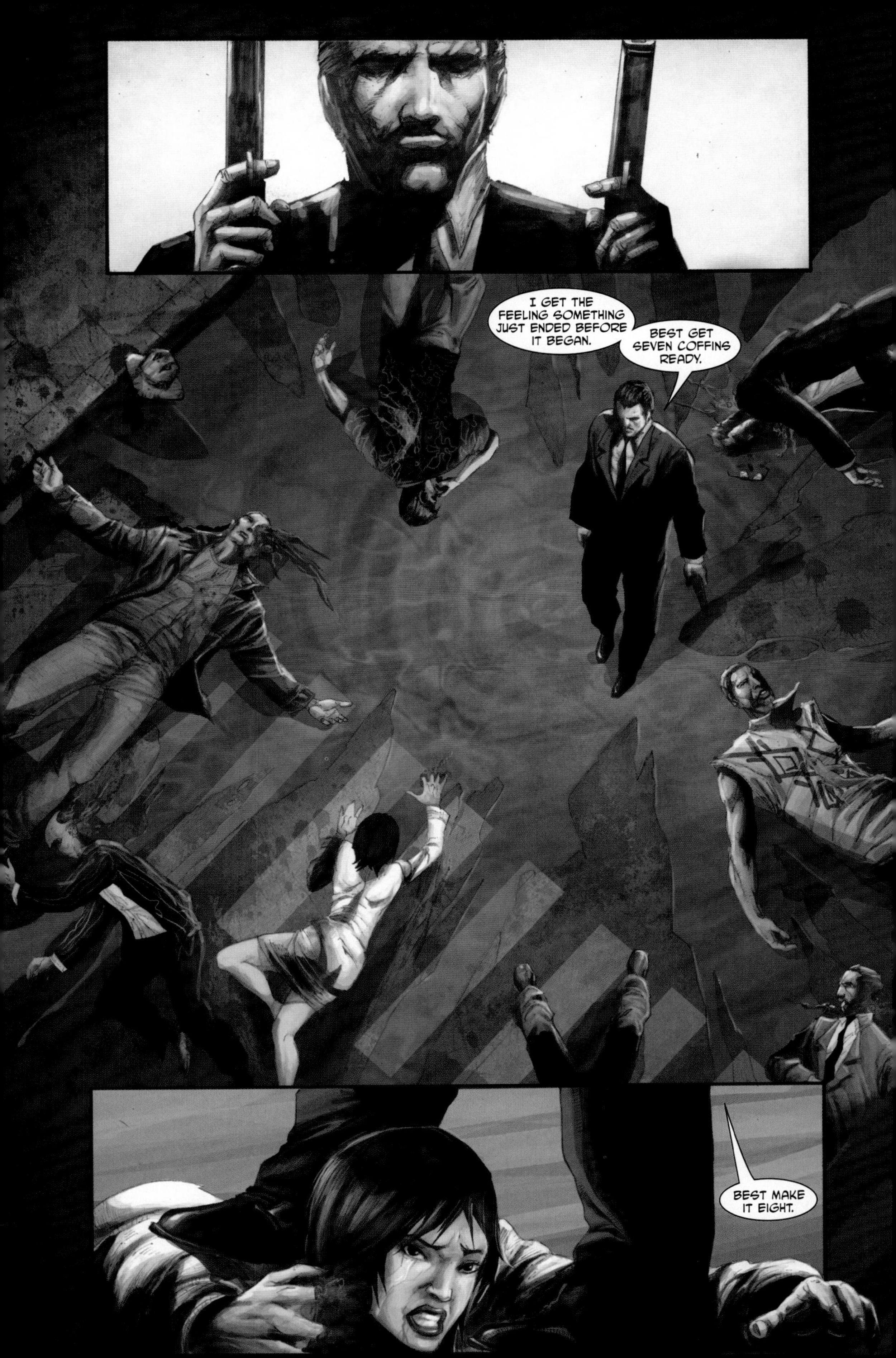
I GET THE FEELING SOMETHING JUST ENDED BEFORE IT BEGAN.
BEST GET SEVEN COFFINS READY.
BEST MAKE IT EIGHT.

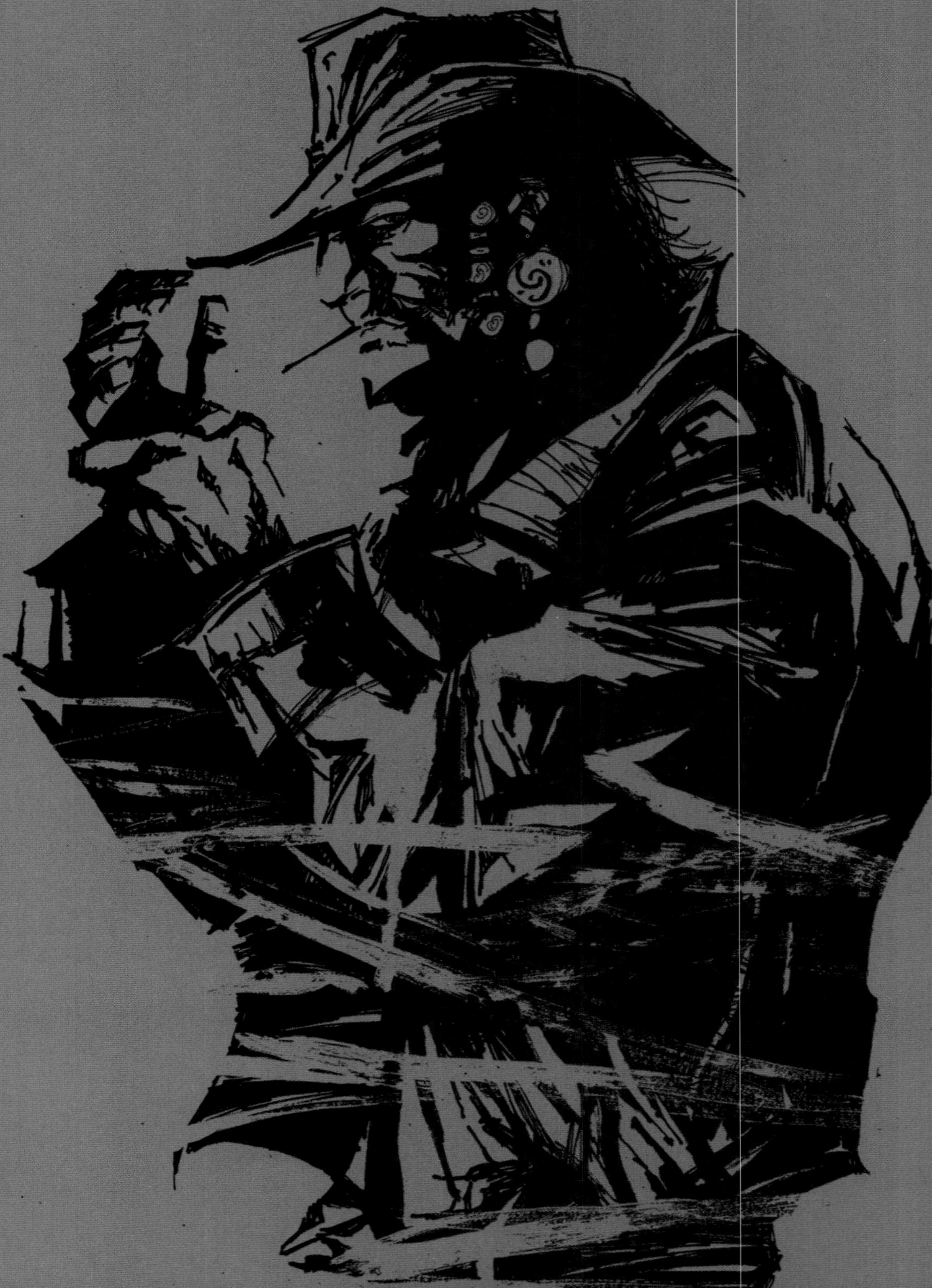

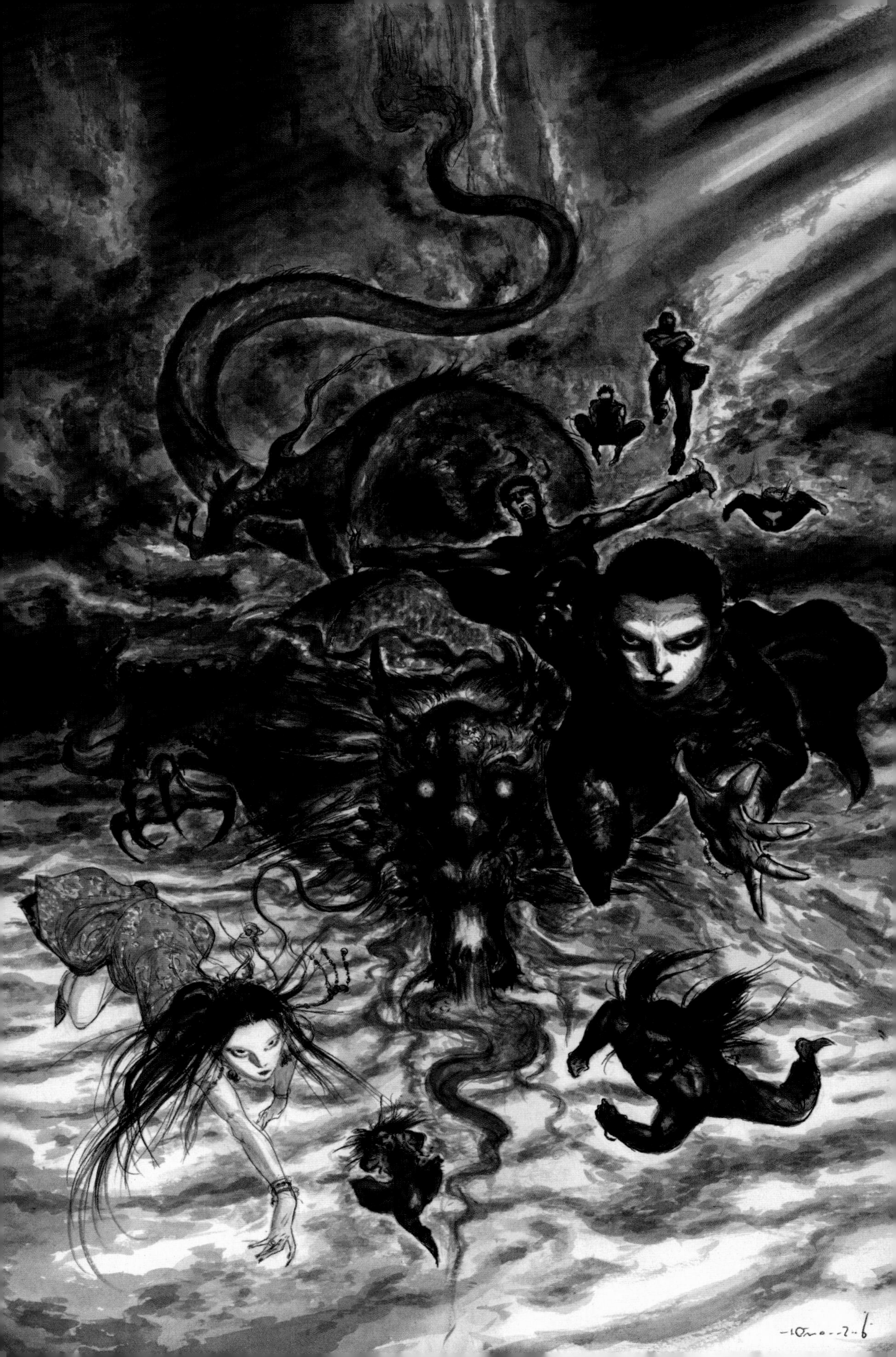

4: THE LONG ROAD HOME

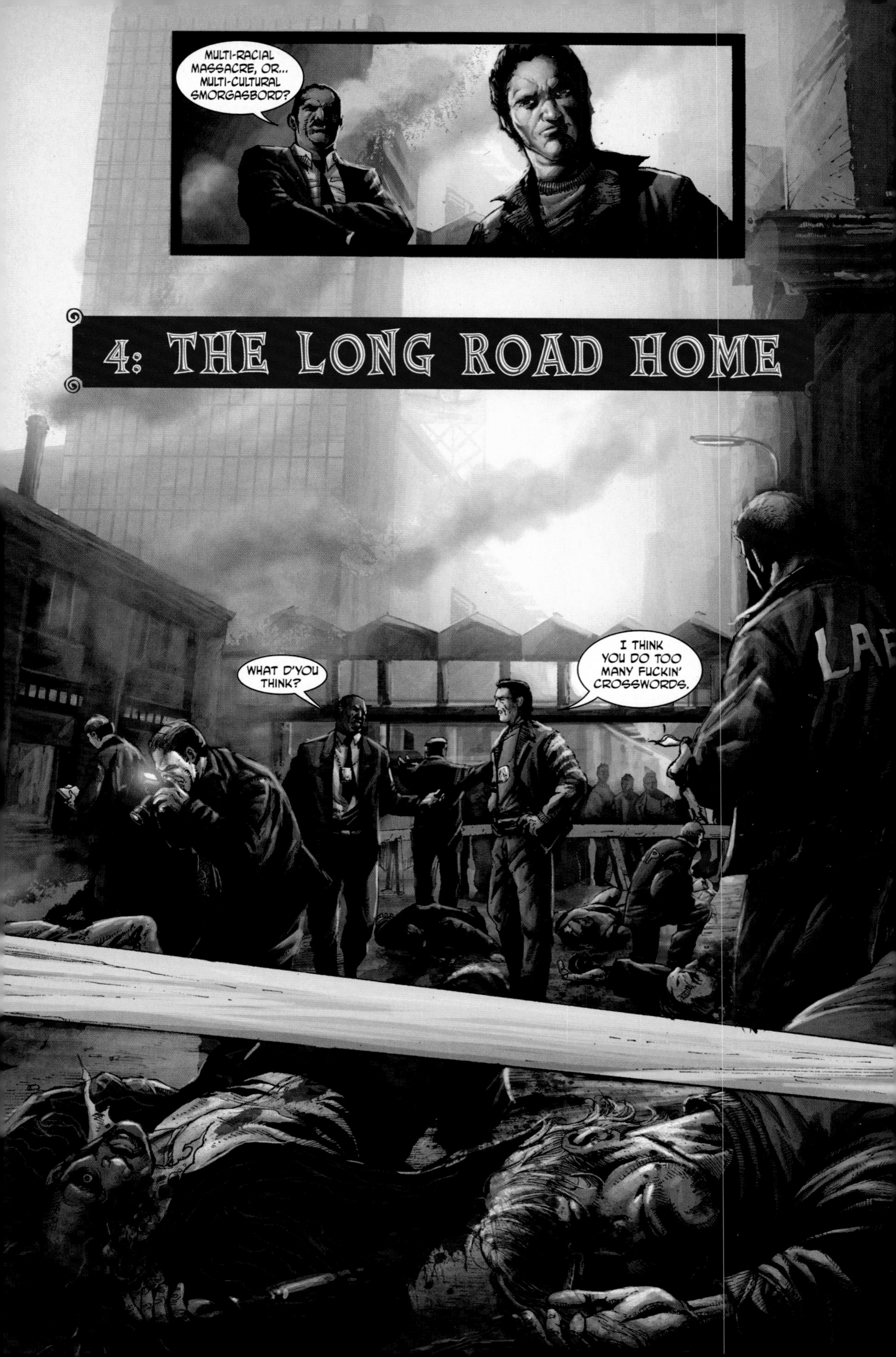
MULTI-RACIAL MASSACRE, OR... MULTI-CULTURAL SMORGASBORD?
WHAT D'YOU THINK?
I THINK YOU DO TOO MANY FUCKIN' CROSSWORDS.

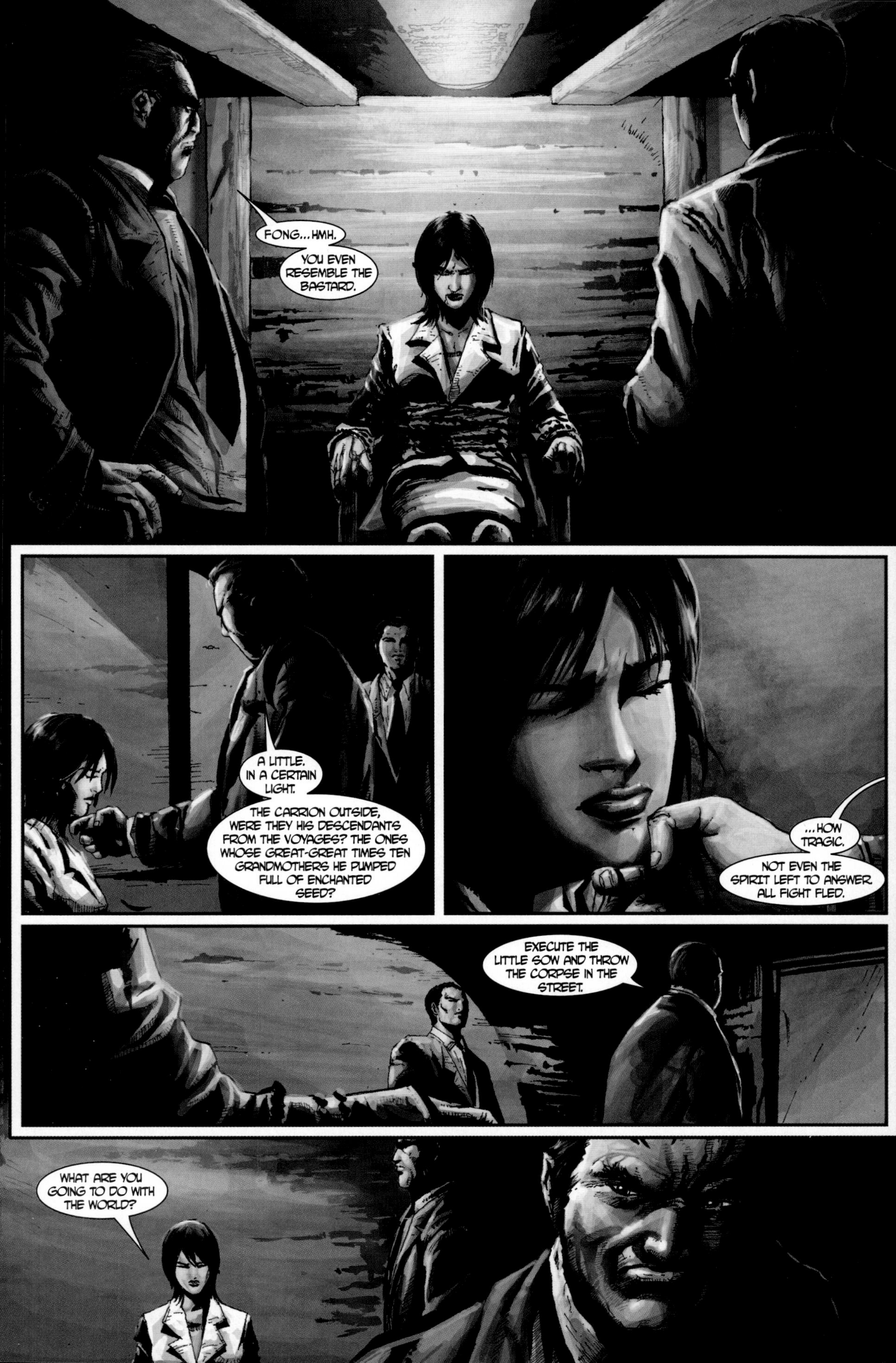
FONG...HMH.
YOU EVEN RESEMBLE THE BASTARD.
A LITTLE. IN A CERTAIN LIGHT.
THE CARRION OUTSIDE, WERE THEY HIS DESCENDANTS FROM THE VOYAGES? THE ONES WHOSE GREAT-GREAT TIMES TEN GRANDMOTHERS HE PUMPED FULL OF ENCHANTED SEED?
...HOW TRAGIC.
NOT EVEN THE SPIRIT LEFT TO ANSWER. ALL FIGHT FLED.
EXECUTE THE LITTLE SOW AND THROW THE CORPSE IN THE STREET.
WHAT ARE YOU GOING TO DO WITH THE WORLD?

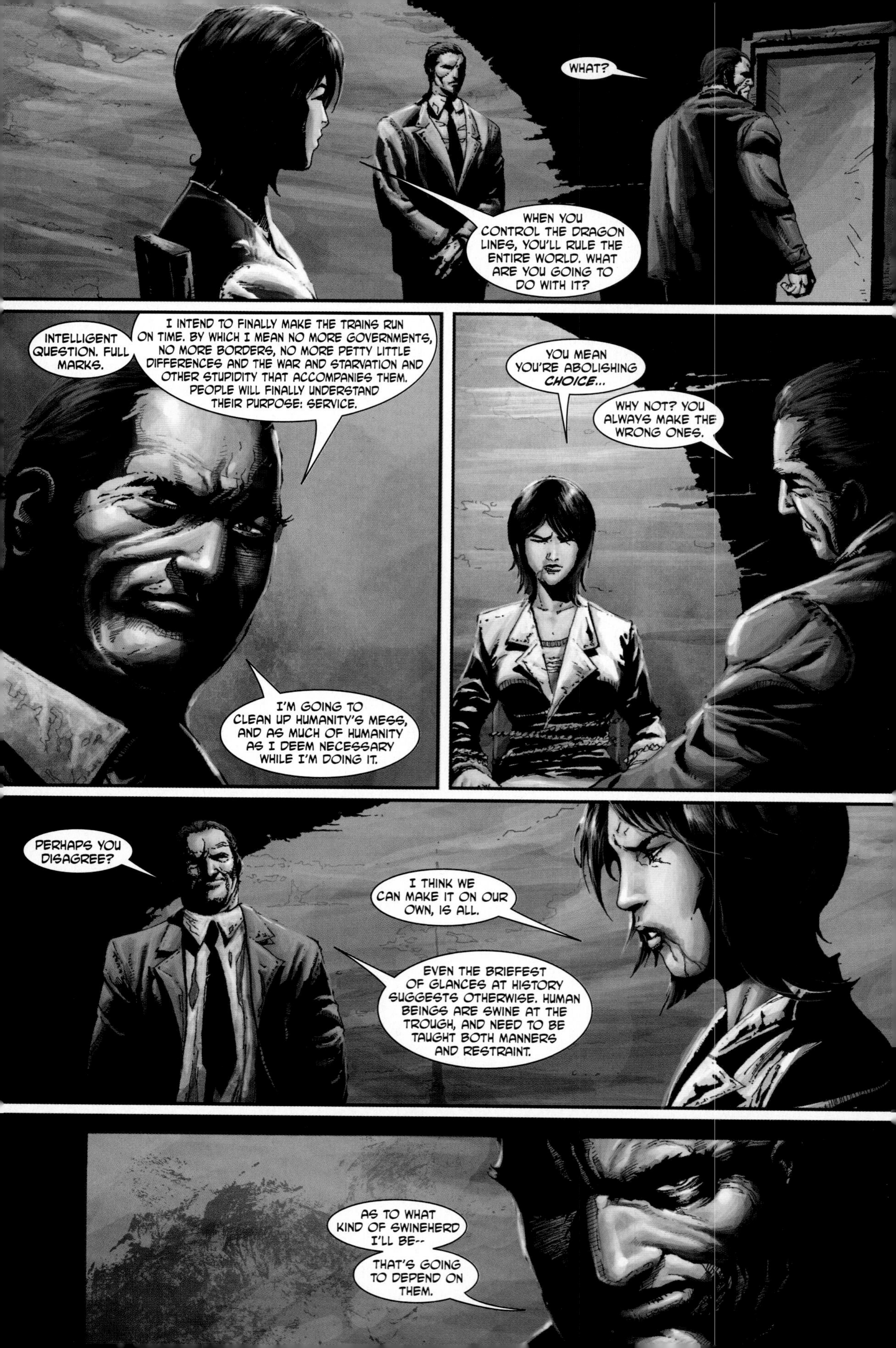
WHAT?
WHEN YOU CONTROL THE DRAGON LINES, YOU'LL RULE THE ENTIRE WORLD. WHAT ARE YOU GOING TO DO WITH IT?
INTELLIGENT QUESTION. FULL MARKS.
I INTEND TO FINALLY MAKE THE TRAINS RUN ON TIME. BY WHICH I MEAN NO MORE GOVERNMENTS, NO MORE BORDERS, NO MORE PETTY LITTLE DIFFERENCES AND THE WAR AND STARVATION AND OTHER STUPIDITY THAT ACCOMPANIES THEM. PEOPLE WILL FINALLY UNDERSTAND THEIR PURPOSE: SERVICE.
I'M GOING TO CLEAN UP HUMANITY'S MESS, AND AS MUCH OF HUMANITY AS I DEEM NECESSARY WHILE I'M DOING IT.
YOU MEAN YOU'RE ABOLISHING *CHOICE*...
WHY NOT? YOU ALWAYS MAKE THE WRONG ONES.
PERHAPS YOU DISAGREE?
I THINK WE CAN MAKE IT ON OUR OWN, IS ALL.
EVEN THE BRIEFEST OF GLANCES AT HISTORY SUGGESTS OTHERWISE. HUMAN BEINGS ARE SWINE AT THE TROUGH, AND NEED TO BE TAUGHT BOTH MANNERS AND RESTRAINT.
AS TO WHAT KIND OF SWINEHERD I'LL BE--
THAT'S GOING TO DEPEND ON THEM.

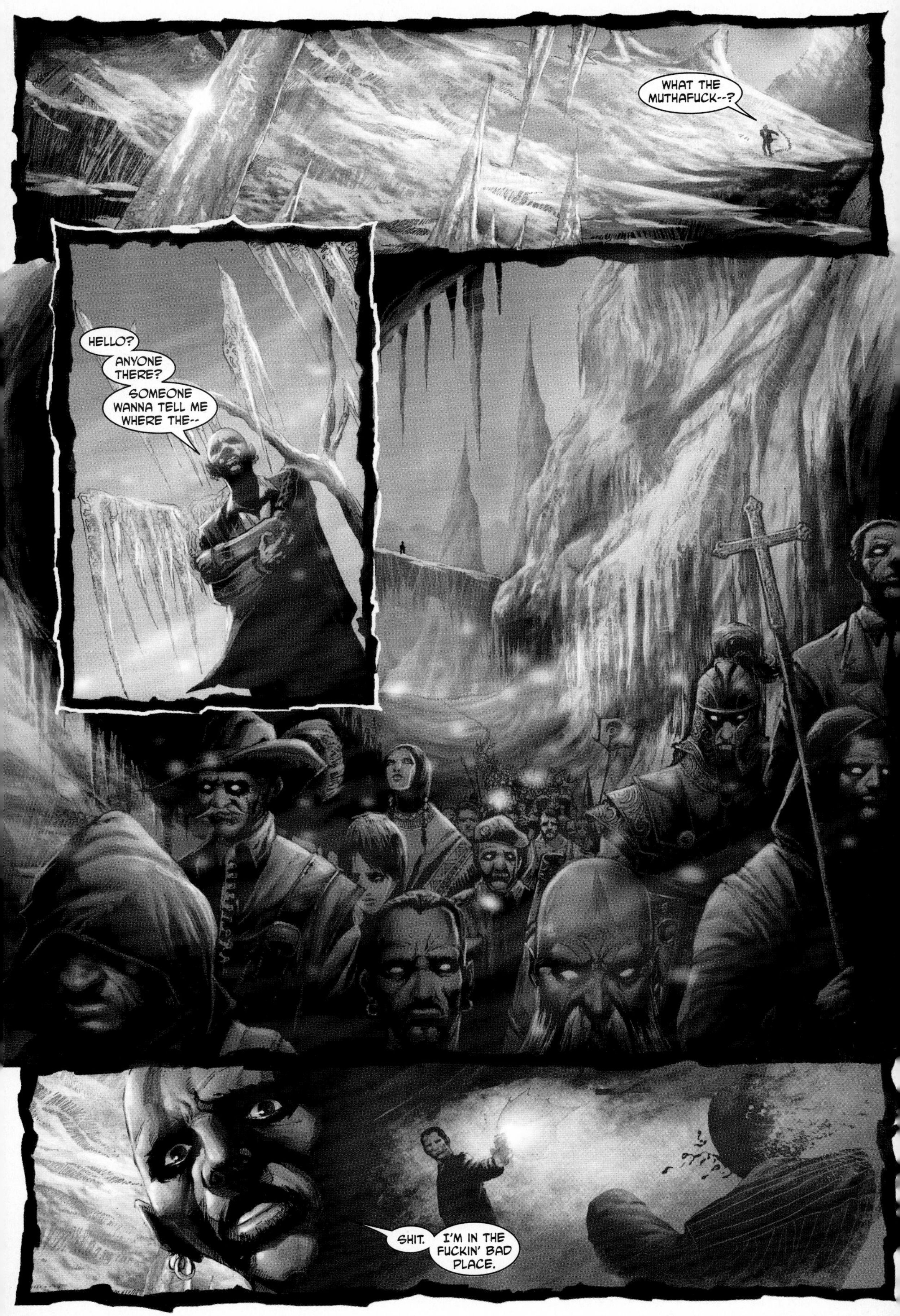
WHAT THE MUTHAFUCK--?
HELLO?
ANYONE THERE?
SOMEONE WANNA TELL ME WHERE THE--
SHIT.
I'M IN THE FUCKIN' BAD PLACE.

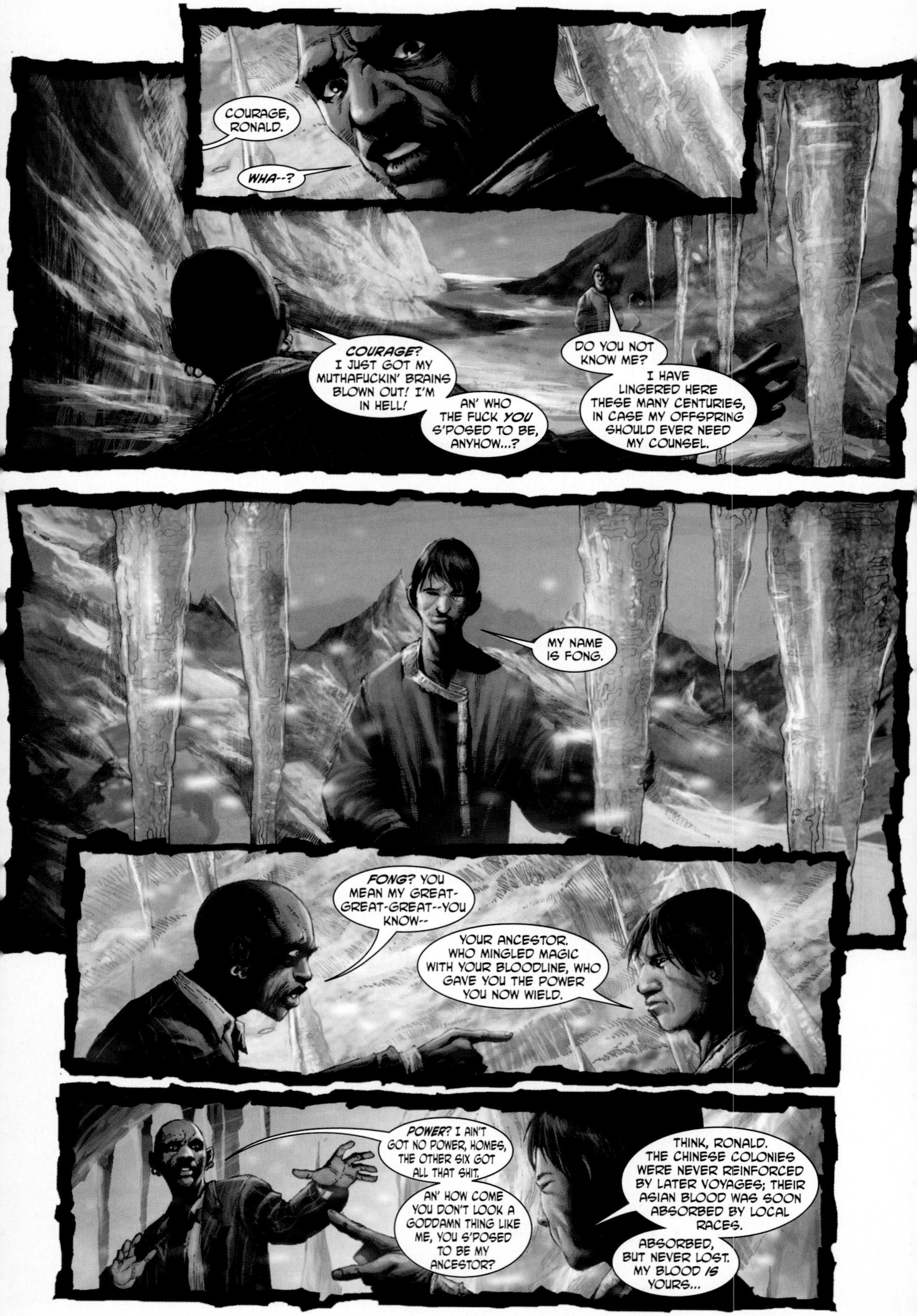
COURAGE, RONALD.
WHA--?
COURAGE? I JUST GOT MY MUTHAFUCKIN' BRAINS BLOWN OUT! I'M IN HELL!
AN' WHO THE FUCK YOU S'POSED TO BE, ANYHOW...?
DO YOU NOT KNOW ME?
I HAVE LINGERED HERE THESE MANY CENTURIES, IN CASE MY OFFSPRING SHOULD EVER NEED MY COUNSEL.
MY NAME IS FONG.
FONG? YOU MEAN MY GREAT-GREAT-GREAT--YOU KNOW--
YOUR ANCESTOR. WHO MINGLED MAGIC WITH YOUR BLOODLINE, WHO GAVE YOU THE POWER YOU NOW WIELD.
POWER? I AIN'T GOT NO POWER, HOMES, THE OTHER SIX GOT ALL THAT SHIT.
AN' HOW COME YOU DON'T LOOK A GODDAMN THING LIKE ME, YOU S'POSED TO BE MY ANCESTOR?
THINK, RONALD. THE CHINESE COLONIES WERE NEVER REINFORCED BY LATER VOYAGES; THEIR ASIAN BLOOD WAS SOON ABSORBED BY LOCAL RACES.
ABSORBED, BUT NEVER LOST. MY BLOOD IS YOURS...

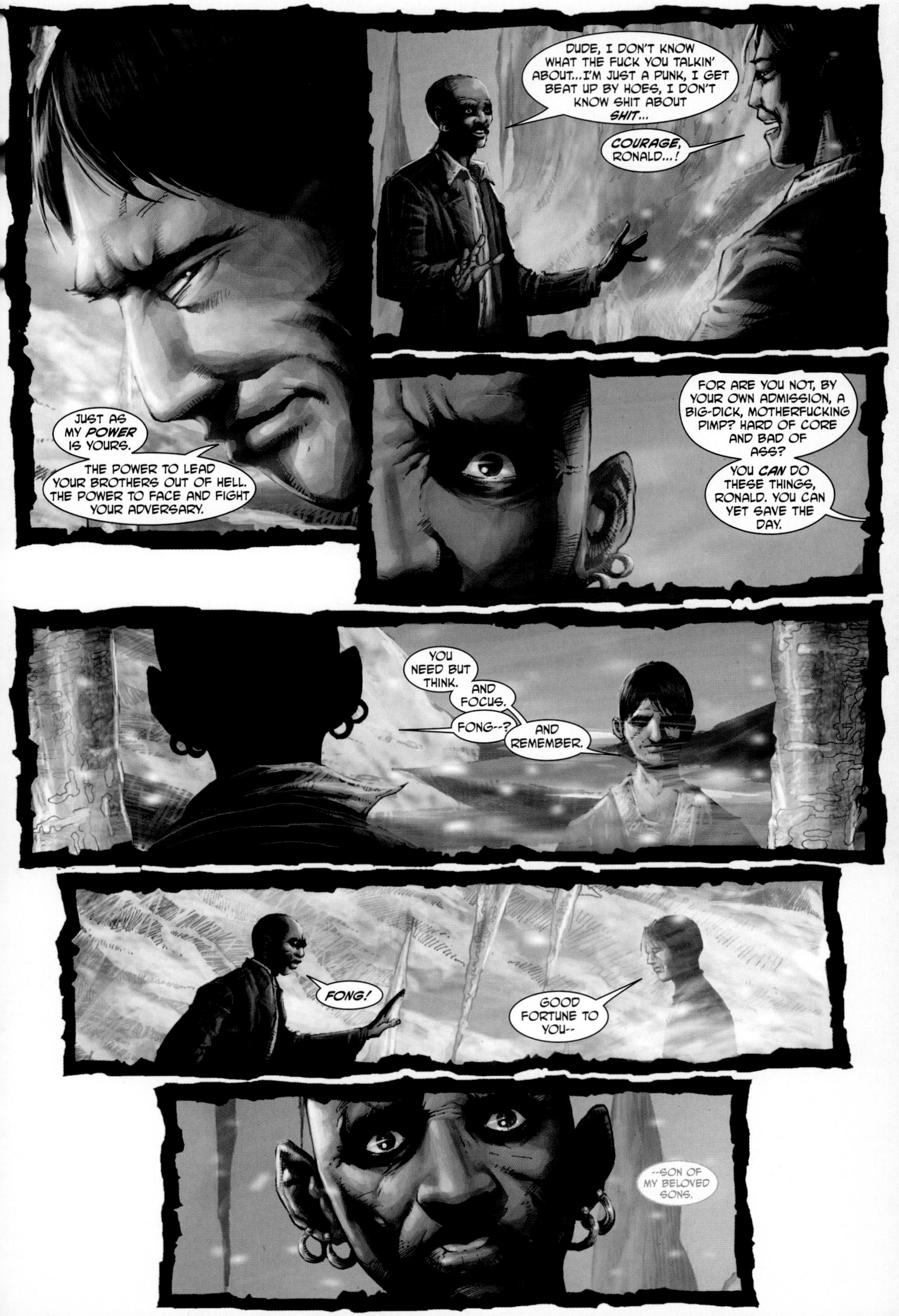
DUDE, I DON'T KNOW WHAT THE FUCK YOU TALKIN' ABOUT...I'M JUST A PUNK, I GET BEAT UP BY HOES, I DON'T KNOW SHIT ABOUT SHIT...
COURAGE, RONALD...!
JUST AS MY POWER IS YOURS.
THE POWER TO LEAD YOUR BROTHERS OUT OF HELL. THE POWER TO FACE AND FIGHT YOUR ADVERSARY.
FOR ARE YOU NOT, BY YOUR OWN ADMISSION, A BIG-DICK, MOTHERFUCKING PIMP? HARD OF CORE AND BAD OF ASS?
YOU CAN DO THESE THINGS, RONALD. YOU CAN YET SAVE THE DAY.
YOU NEED BUT THINK.
AND FOCUS.
FONG--?
AND REMEMBER.
FONG!
GOOD FORTUNE TO YOU--
--SON OF MY BELOVED SONS.

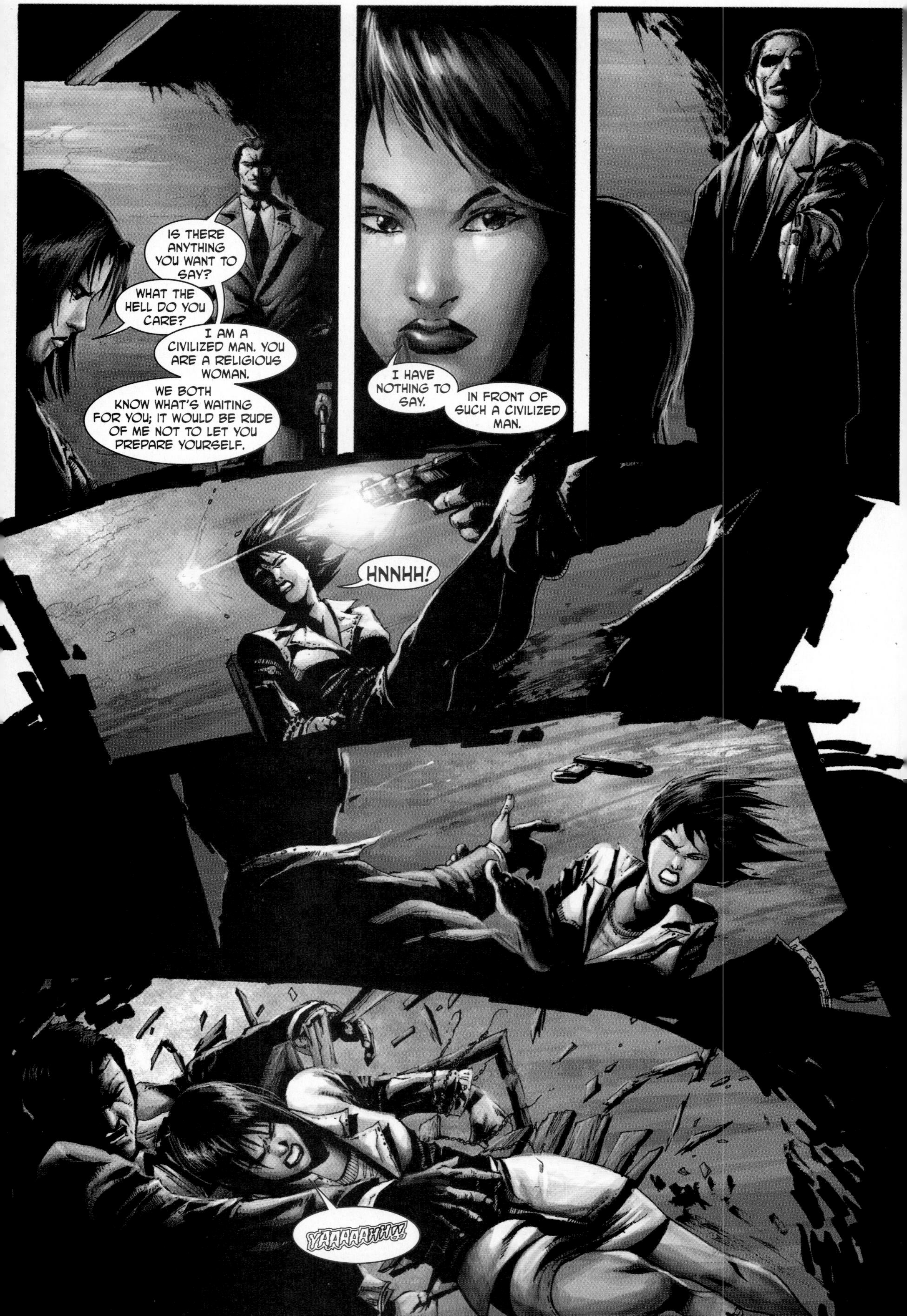
IS THERE ANYTHING YOU WANT TO SAY?
WHAT THE HELL DO YOU CARE?
I AM A CIVILIZED MAN. YOU ARE A RELIGIOUS WOMAN.
WE BOTH KNOW WHAT'S WAITING FOR YOU; IT WOULD BE RUDE OF ME NOT TO LET YOU PREPARE YOURSELF.
I HAVE NOTHING TO SAY.
IN FRONT OF SUCH A CIVILIZED MAN.
HNNHH!
YAAAAAHH!!

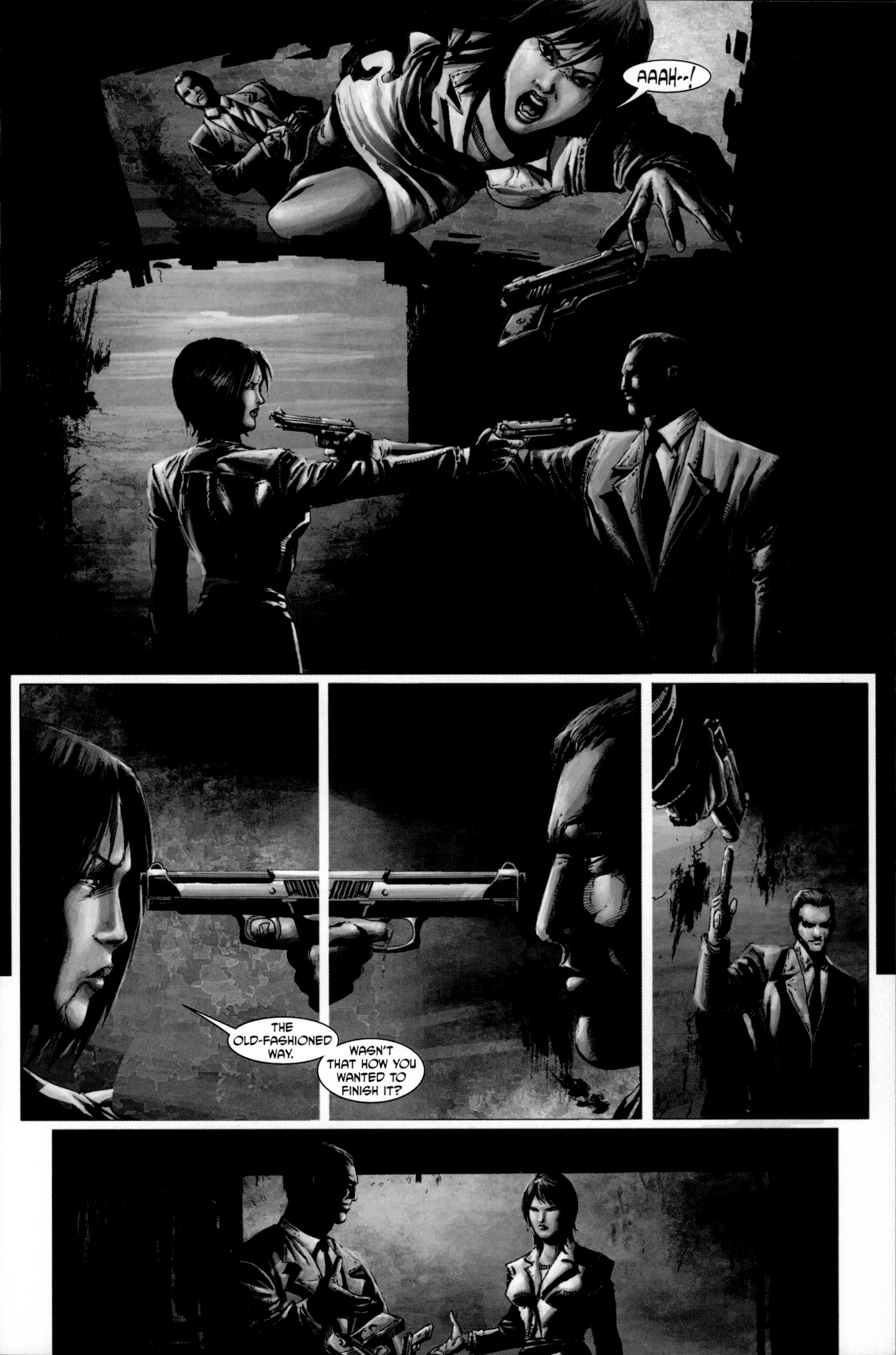
AAAH--!
THE OLD-FASHIONED WAY.
WASN'T THAT HOW YOU WANTED TO FINISH IT?

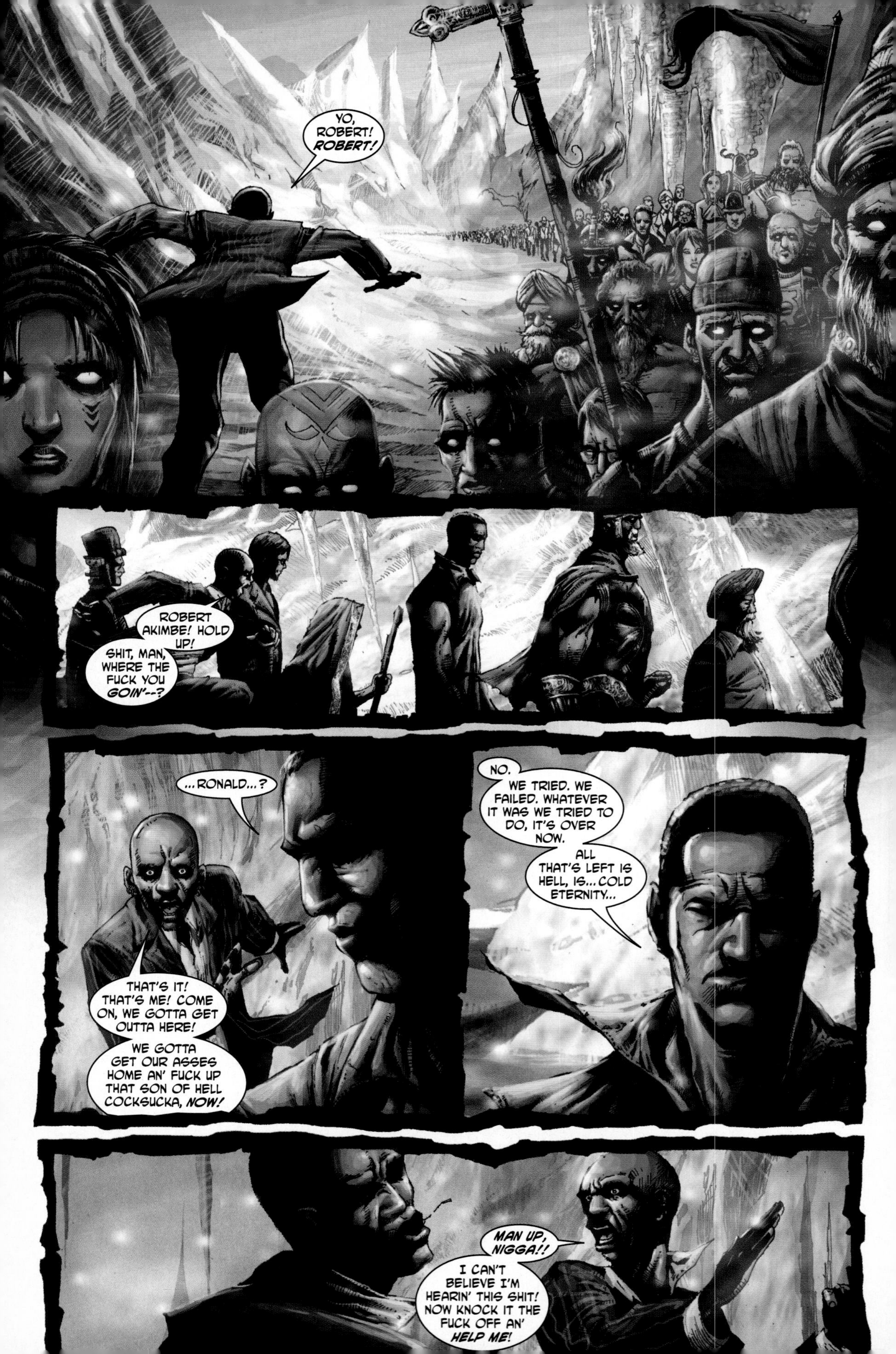
YO, ROBERT! ROBERT!
ROBERT AKIMBE! HOLD UP!
SHIT, MAN, WHERE THE FUCK YOU GOIN'--?
...RONALD...?
THAT'S IT! THAT'S ME! COME ON, WE GOTTA GET OUTTA HERE!
WE GOTTA GET OUR ASSES HOME AN' FUCK UP THAT SON OF HELL COCKSUCKA, NOW!
NO.
WE TRIED. WE FAILED. WHATEVER IT WAS WE TRIED TO DO, IT'S OVER NOW.
ALL THAT'S LEFT IS HELL, IS...COLD ETERNITY...
MAN UP, NIGGA!!
I CAN'T BELIEVE I'M HEARIN' THIS SHIT! NOW KNOCK IT THE FUCK OFF AN' HELP ME!

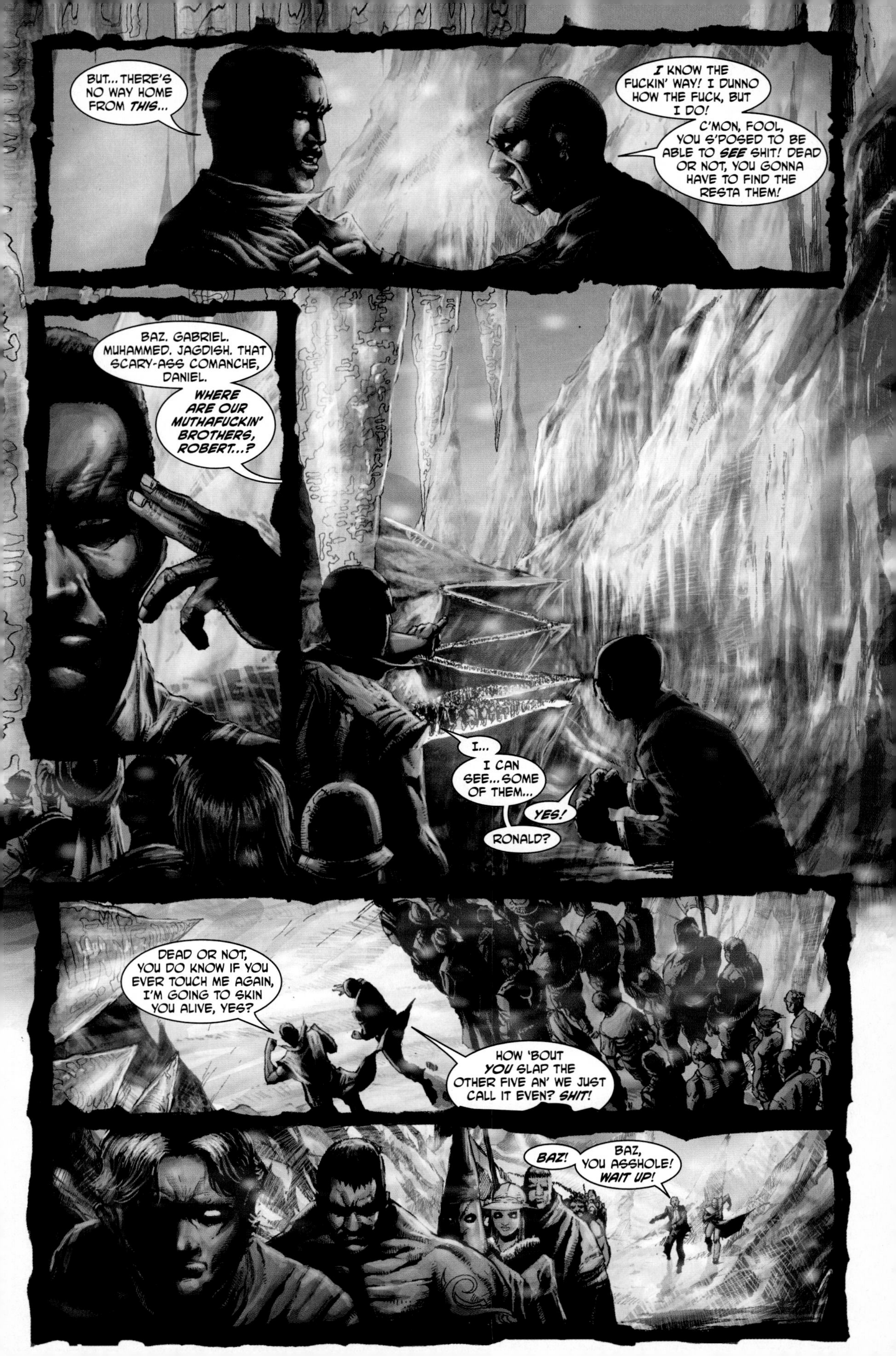
BUT... THERE'S NO WAY HOME FROM *THIS*...
I KNOW THE FUCKIN' WAY! I DUNNO HOW THE FUCK, BUT I DO!
C'MON, FOOL, YOU S'POSED TO BE ABLE TO *SEE* SHIT! DEAD OR NOT, YOU GONNA HAVE TO FIND THE RESTA THEM!
BAZ. GABRIEL. MUHAMMED. JAGDISH. THAT SCARY-ASS COMANCHE, DANIEL.
WHERE ARE OUR MUTHAFUCKIN' BROTHERS, ROBERT...?
I... I CAN SEE... SOME OF THEM...
YES!
RONALD?
DEAD OR NOT, YOU DO KNOW IF YOU EVER TOUCH ME AGAIN, I'M GOING TO SKIN YOU ALIVE, YES?
HOW 'BOUT *YOU* SLAP THE OTHER FIVE AN' WE JUST CALL IT EVEN? *SHIT!*
BAZ!
BAZ, YOU ASSHOLE! *WAIT UP!*

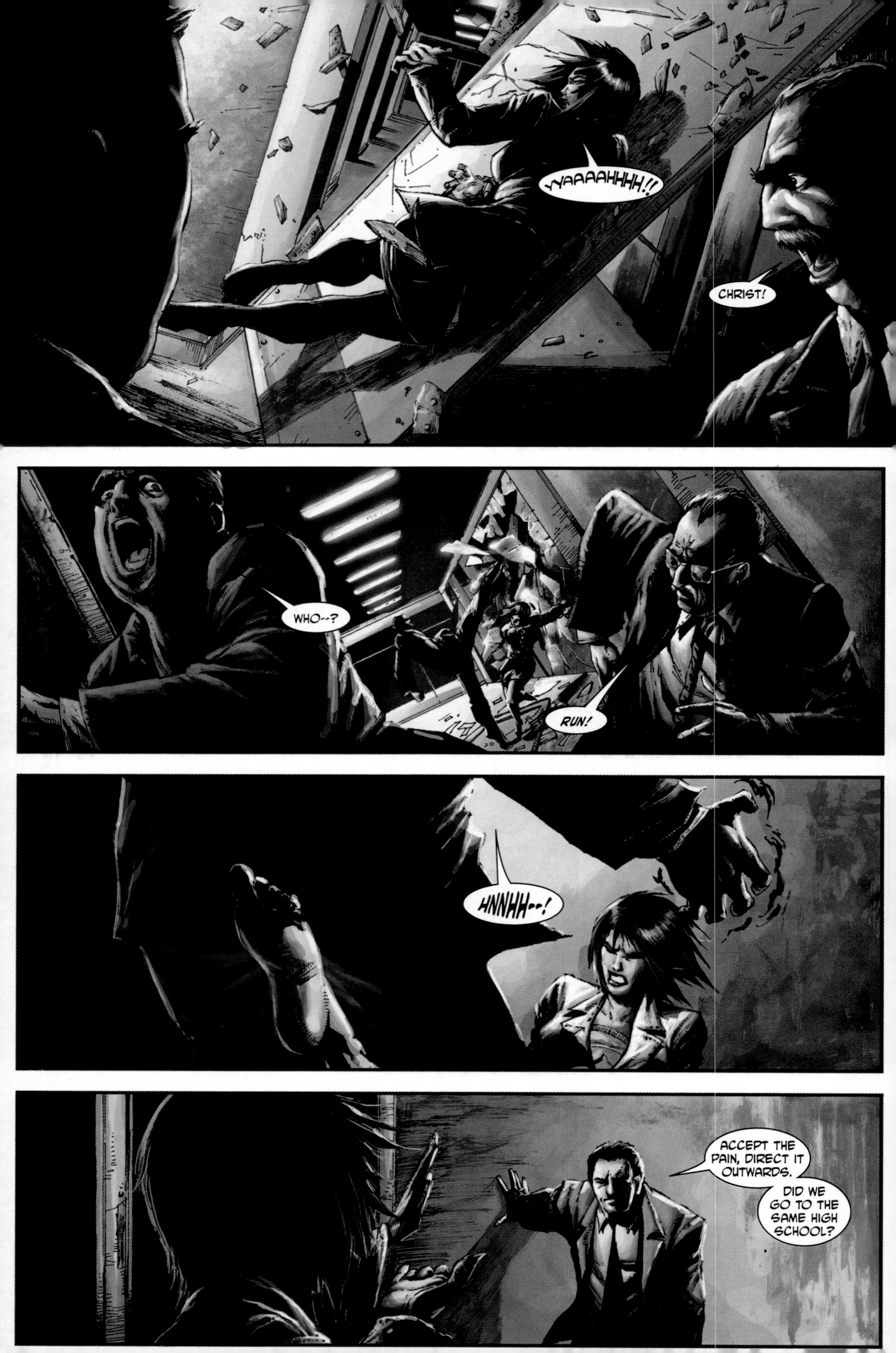
YYAAAAHHHH!!
CHRIST!
WHO--?
RUN!
HNNHH--!
ACCEPT THE PAIN, DIRECT IT OUTWARDS.
DID WE GO TO THE SAME HIGH SCHOOL?

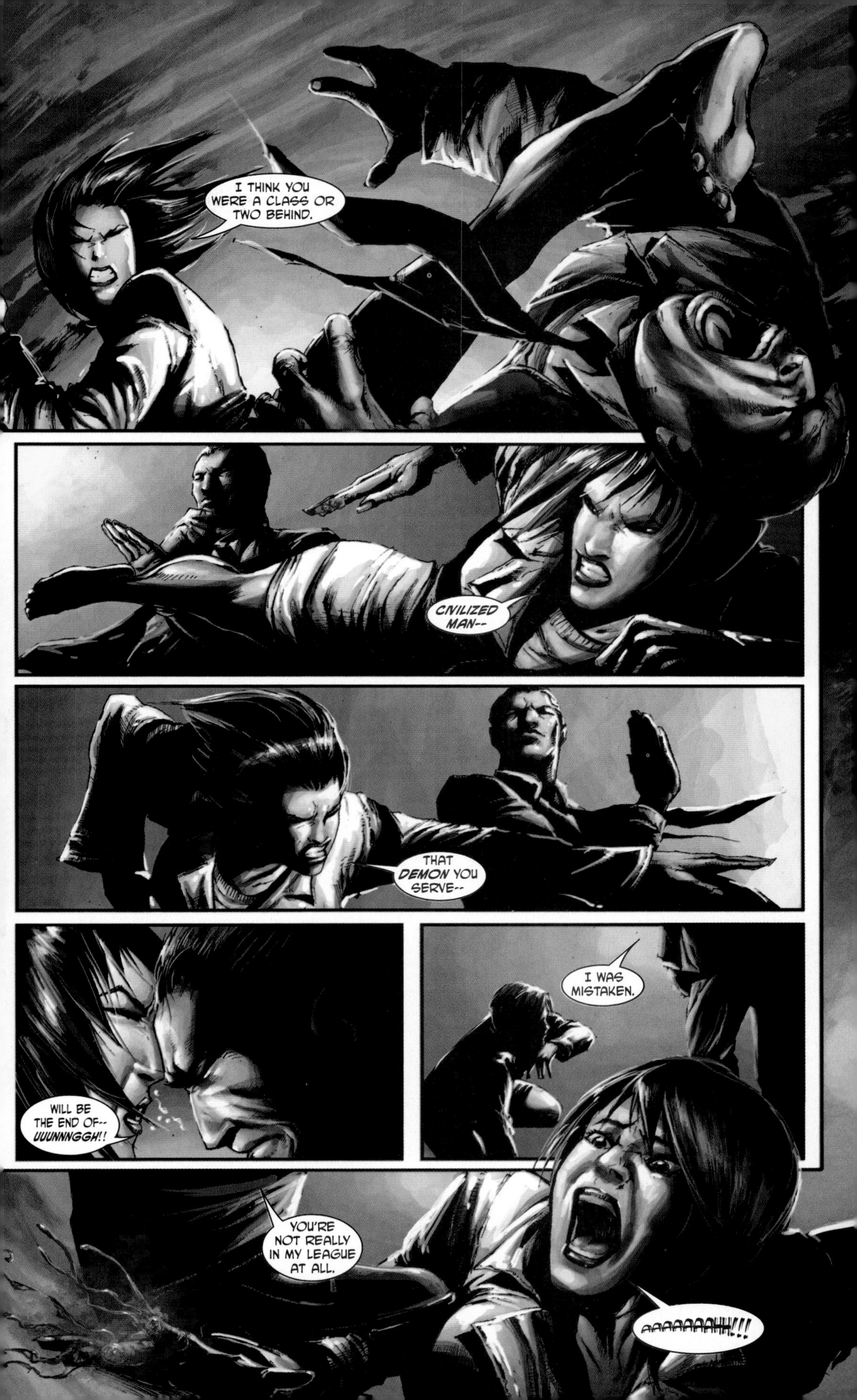
I THINK YOU WERE A CLASS OR TWO BEHIND.
CIVILIZED MAN--
THAT DEMON YOU SERVE--
WILL BE THE END OF-- UUUNNNGGH!!
I WAS MISTAKEN.
YOU'RE NOT REALLY IN MY LEAGUE AT ALL.
AAAAAAAAHH!!!

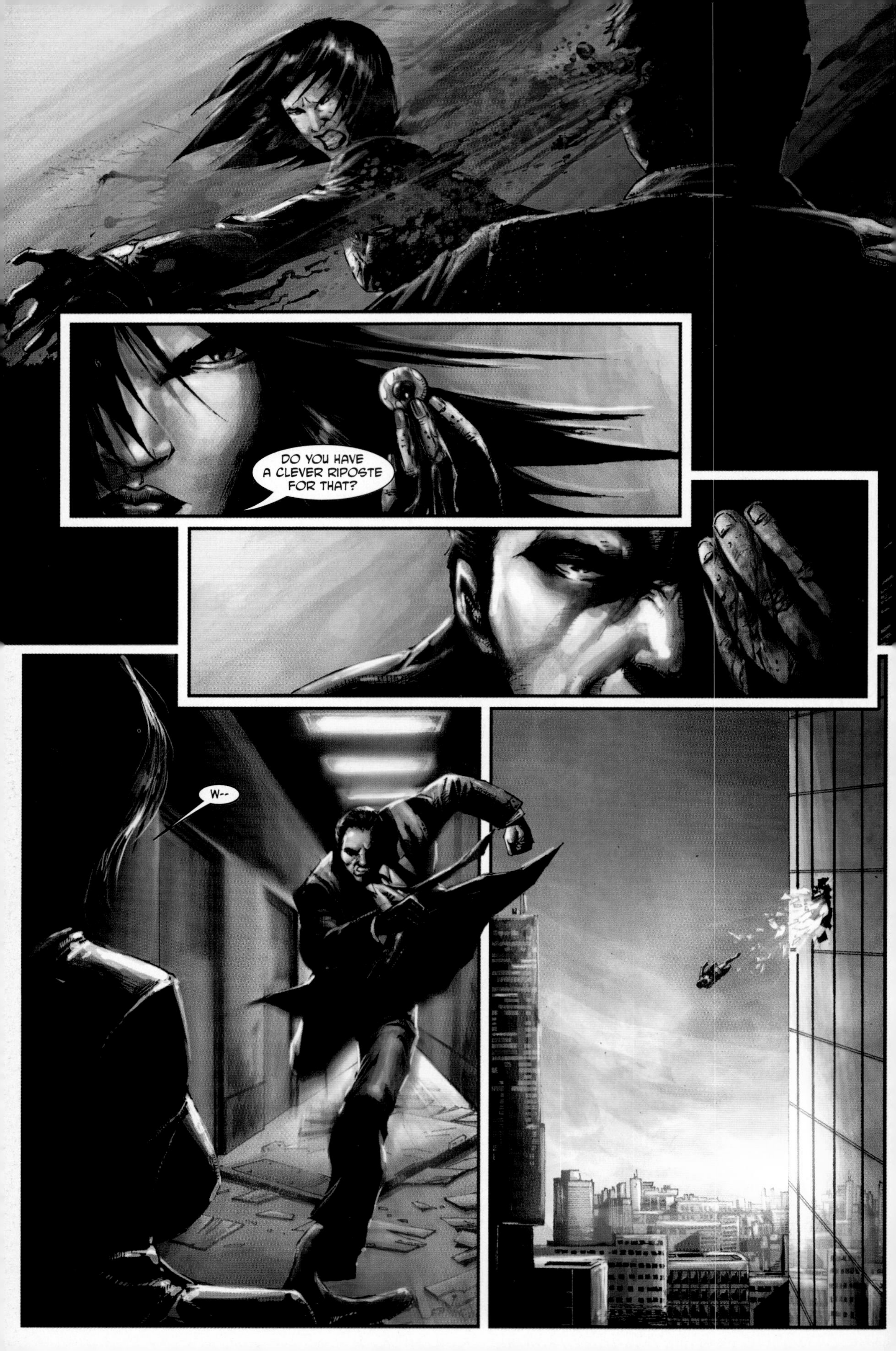
DO YOU HAVE A CLEVER RIPOSTE FOR THAT?
W--

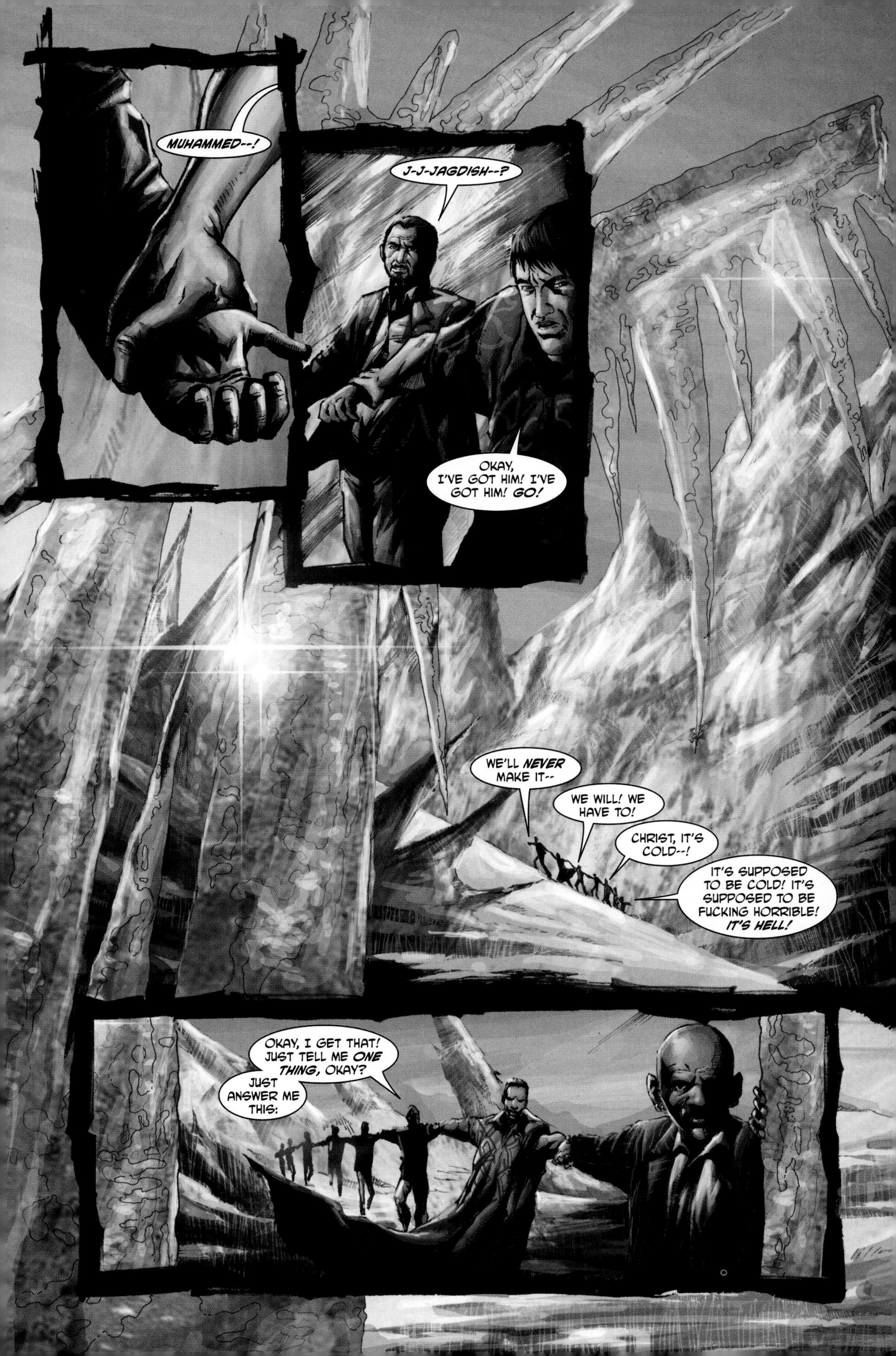
MUHAMMED--!
J-J-JAGDISH--?
OKAY, I'VE GOT HIM! I'VE GOT HIM! *GO!*
WE'LL *NEVER* MAKE IT--
WE WILL! WE HAVE TO!
CHRIST, IT'S COLD--!
IT'S SUPPOSED TO BE COLD! IT'S SUPPOSED TO BE FUCKING HORRIBLE! *IT'S HELL!*
OKAY, I GET THAT! JUST TELL ME *ONE THING,* OKAY?
JUST ANSWER ME THIS:

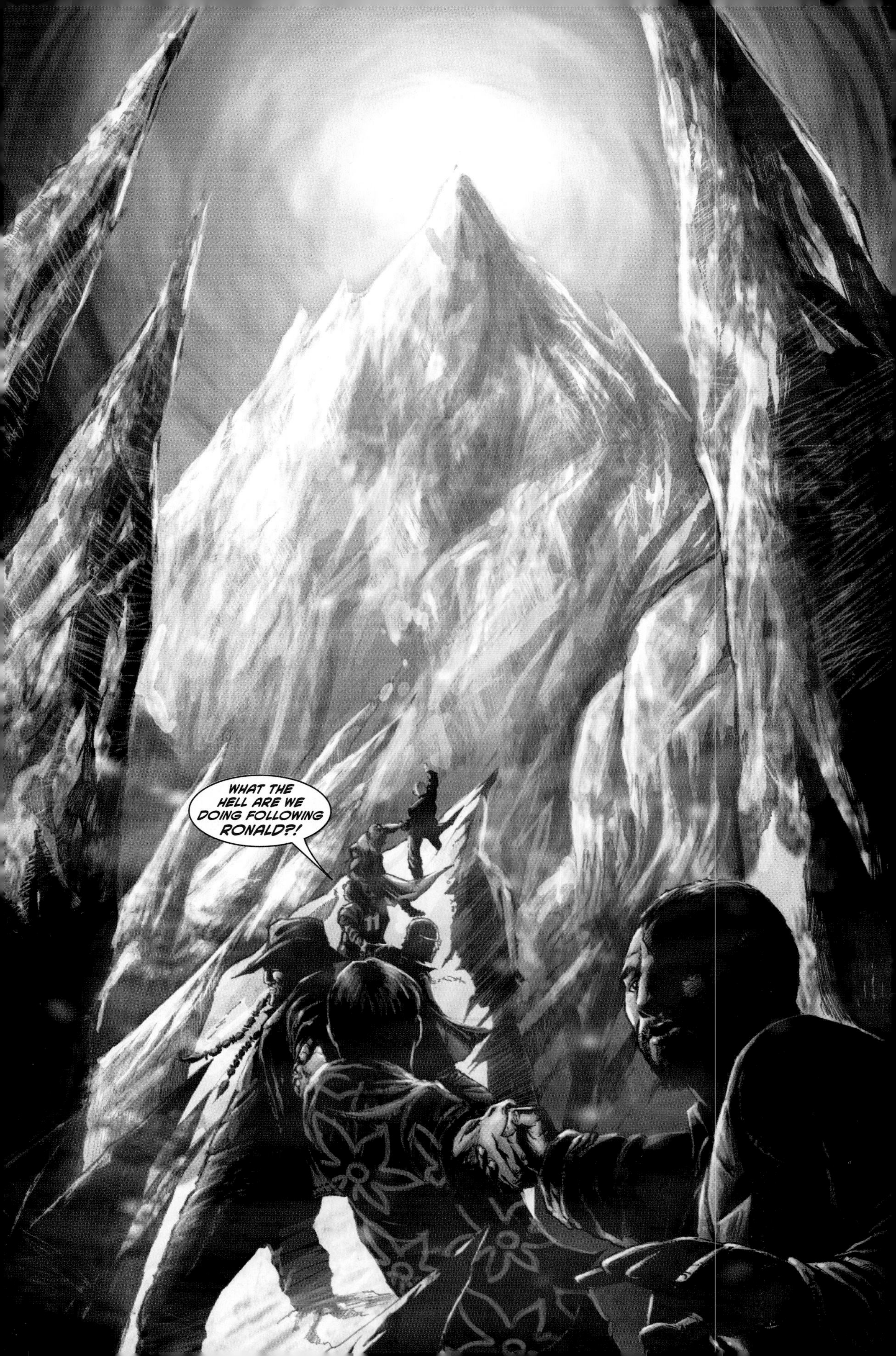
WHAT THE HELL ARE WE DOING FOLLOWING RONALD?!

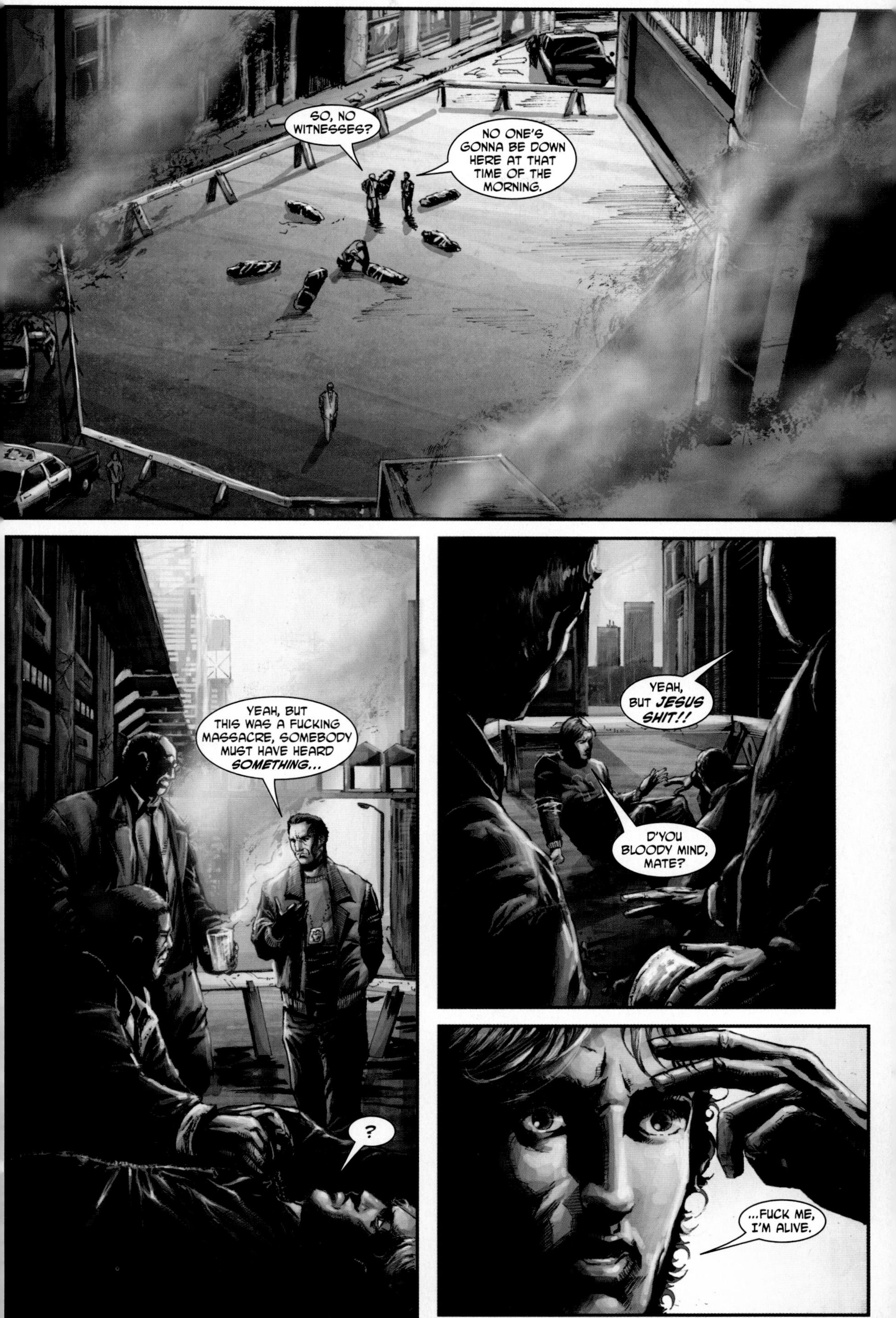
SO, NO WITNESSES?
NO ONE'S GONNA BE DOWN HERE AT THAT TIME OF THE MORNING.
YEAH, BUT THIS WAS A FUCKING MASSACRE, SOMEBODY MUST HAVE HEARD SOMETHING...
?
YEAH, BUT JESUS SHIT!!
D'YOU BLOODY MIND, MATE?
...FUCK ME, I'M ALIVE.

SO ARE WE. APPARENTLY.

MMFFF!!

MMFFF!! FFGGG! MMMNNGGHH!!

RONALD!

OUT YOU COME, MATE!

HHHHHHH, GODDAMN MUTHA*FUCKA*!

THOUGHT I WAS GONNA FUCKIN' SUFFOCATE IN THERE!

SO WHAT? AIN'T YOU THE BLOKE THAT KNOWS THE WAY OUTTA HELL?

YES, HOW EXACTLY DID YOU ACCOMPLISH THAT, RONALD...?

NOT NOW, JAGDISH. WE HAVE TO FIND RACHEL, AND THE SON OF HELL ALONG WITH HER.

MOTHER OF GOD, *LOOK*--!

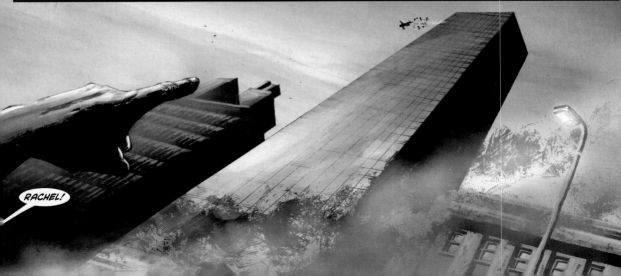

RACHEL!

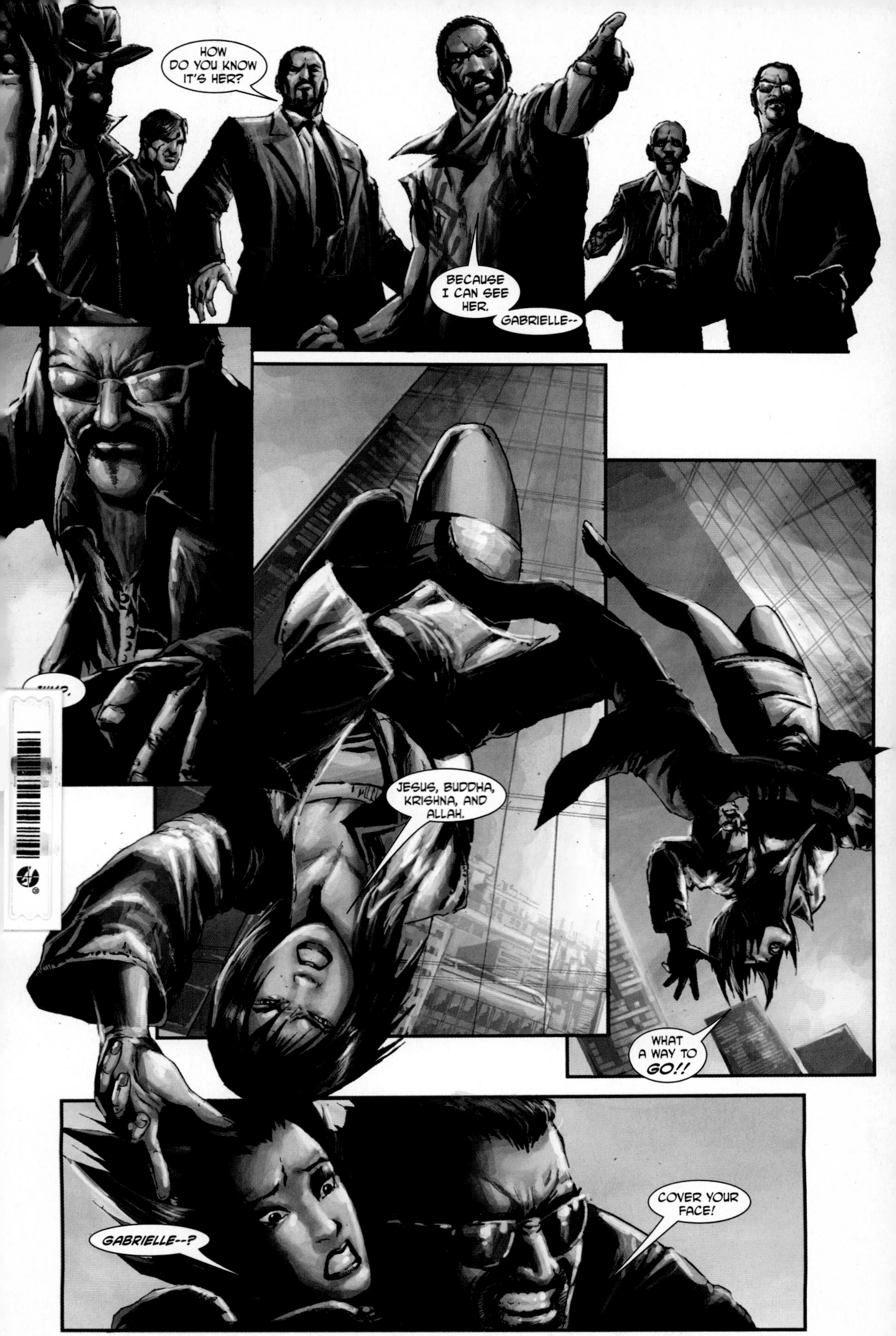

HOW DO YOU KNOW IT'S HER?
BECAUSE I CAN SEE HER.
GABRIELLE--
JESUS, BUDDHA, KRISHNA, AND ALLAH.
WHAT A WAY TO GO!!
GABRIELLE--?
COVER YOUR FACE!

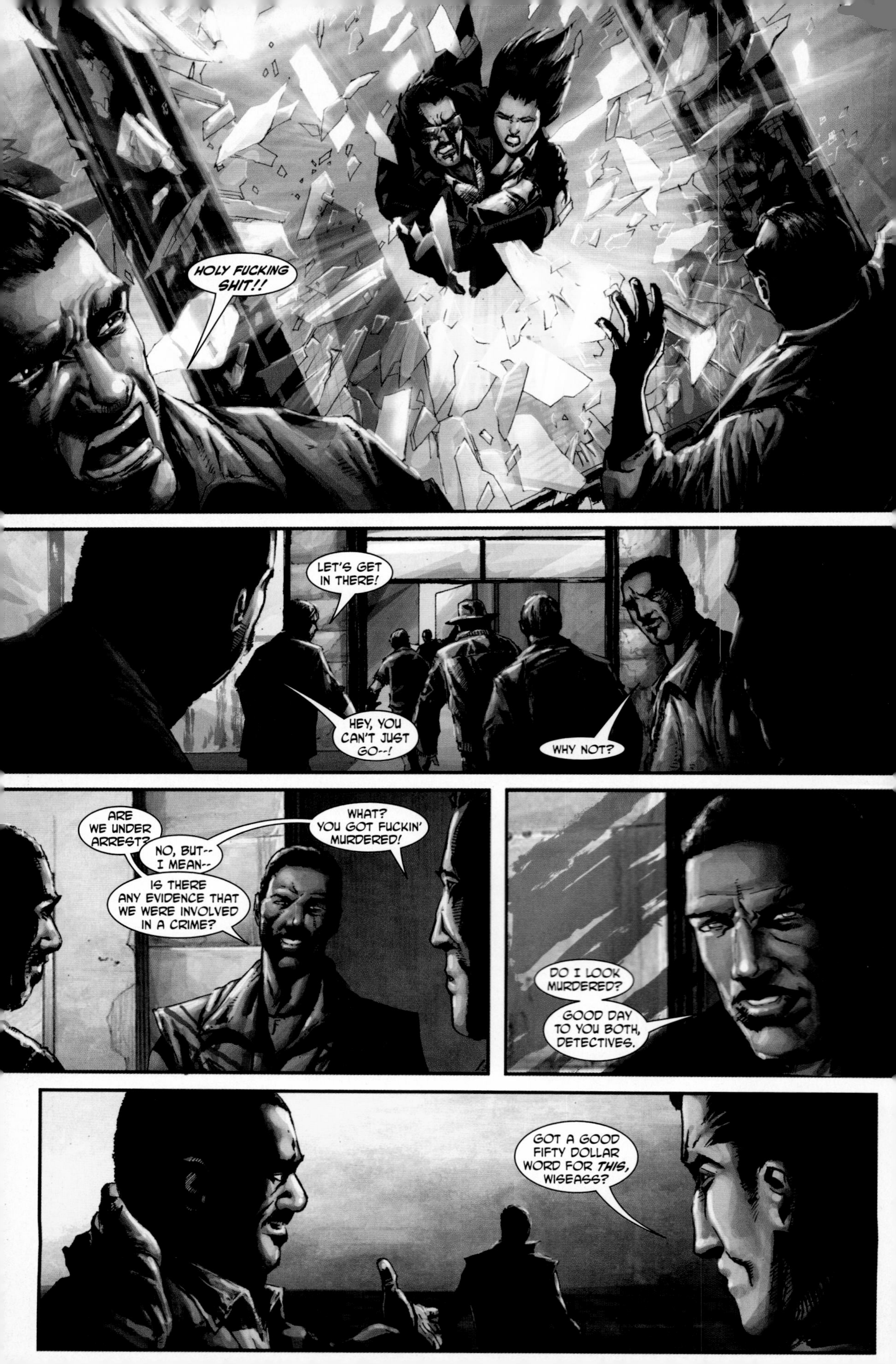
HOLY FUCKING SHIT!!
LET'S GET IN THERE!
HEY, YOU CAN'T JUST GO--!
WHY NOT?
ARE WE UNDER ARREST?
NO, BUT-- I MEAN--
IS THERE ANY EVIDENCE THAT WE WERE INVOLVED IN A CRIME?
WHAT? YOU GOT FUCKIN' MURDERED!
DO I LOOK MURDERED?
GOOD DAY TO YOU BOTH, DETECTIVES.
GOT A GOOD FIFTY DOLLAR WORD FOR *THIS*, WISEASS?

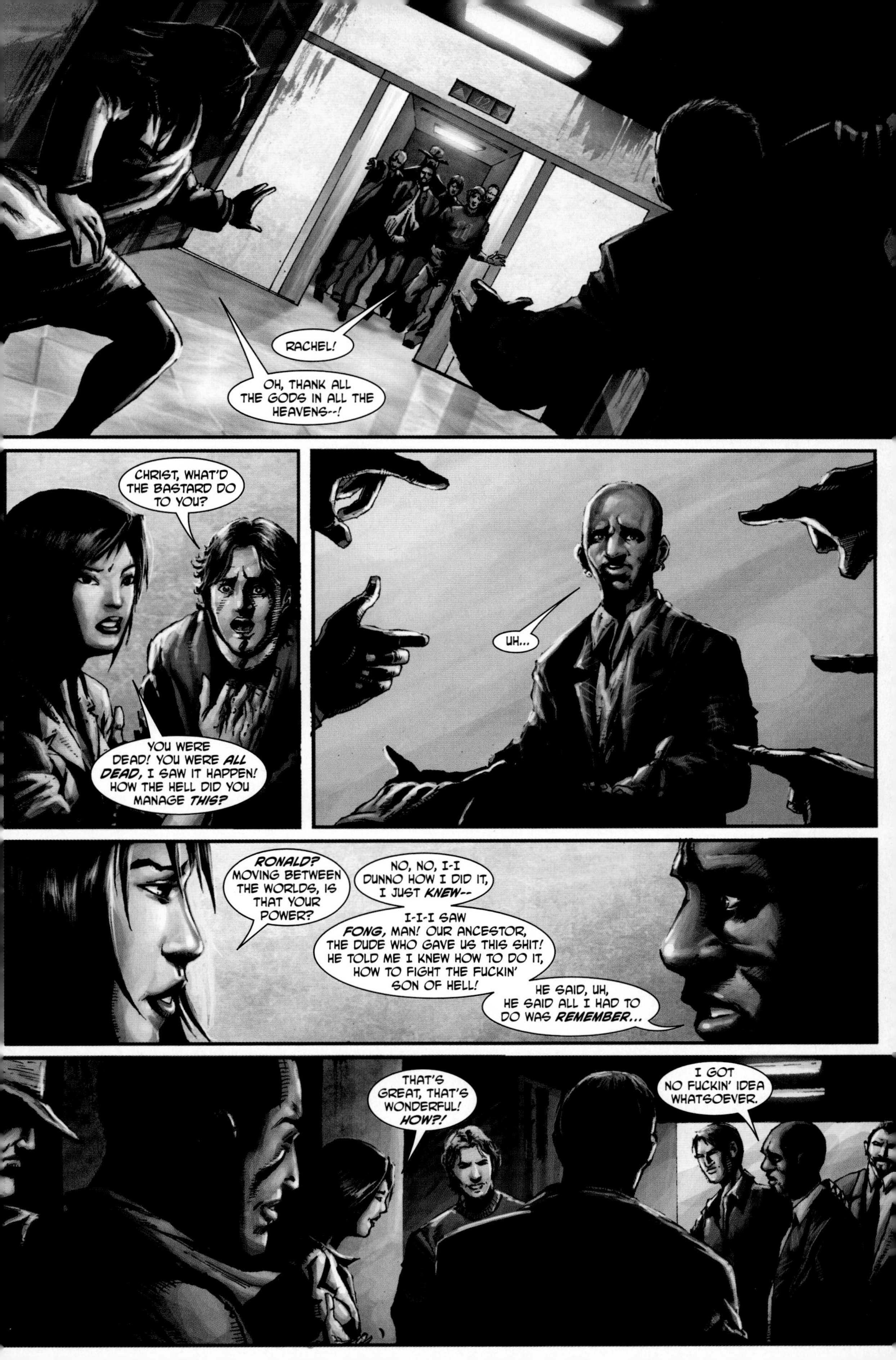
RACHEL!
OH, THANK ALL THE GODS IN ALL THE HEAVENS--!
CHRIST, WHAT'D THE BASTARD DO TO YOU?
YOU WERE DEAD! YOU WERE ALL DEAD, I SAW IT HAPPEN! HOW THE HELL DID YOU MANAGE THIS?
UH...
RONALD? MOVING BETWEEN THE WORLDS, IS THAT YOUR POWER?
NO, NO, I-I DUNNO HOW I DID IT, I JUST KNEW--
I-I-I SAW FONG, MAN! OUR ANCESTOR, THE DUDE WHO GAVE US THIS SHIT! HE TOLD ME I KNEW HOW TO DO IT, HOW TO FIGHT THE FUCKIN' SON OF HELL!
HE SAID, UH, HE SAID ALL I HAD TO DO WAS REMEMBER...
THAT'S GREAT, THAT'S WONDERFUL! HOW?!
I GOT NO FUCKIN' IDEA WHATSOEVER.

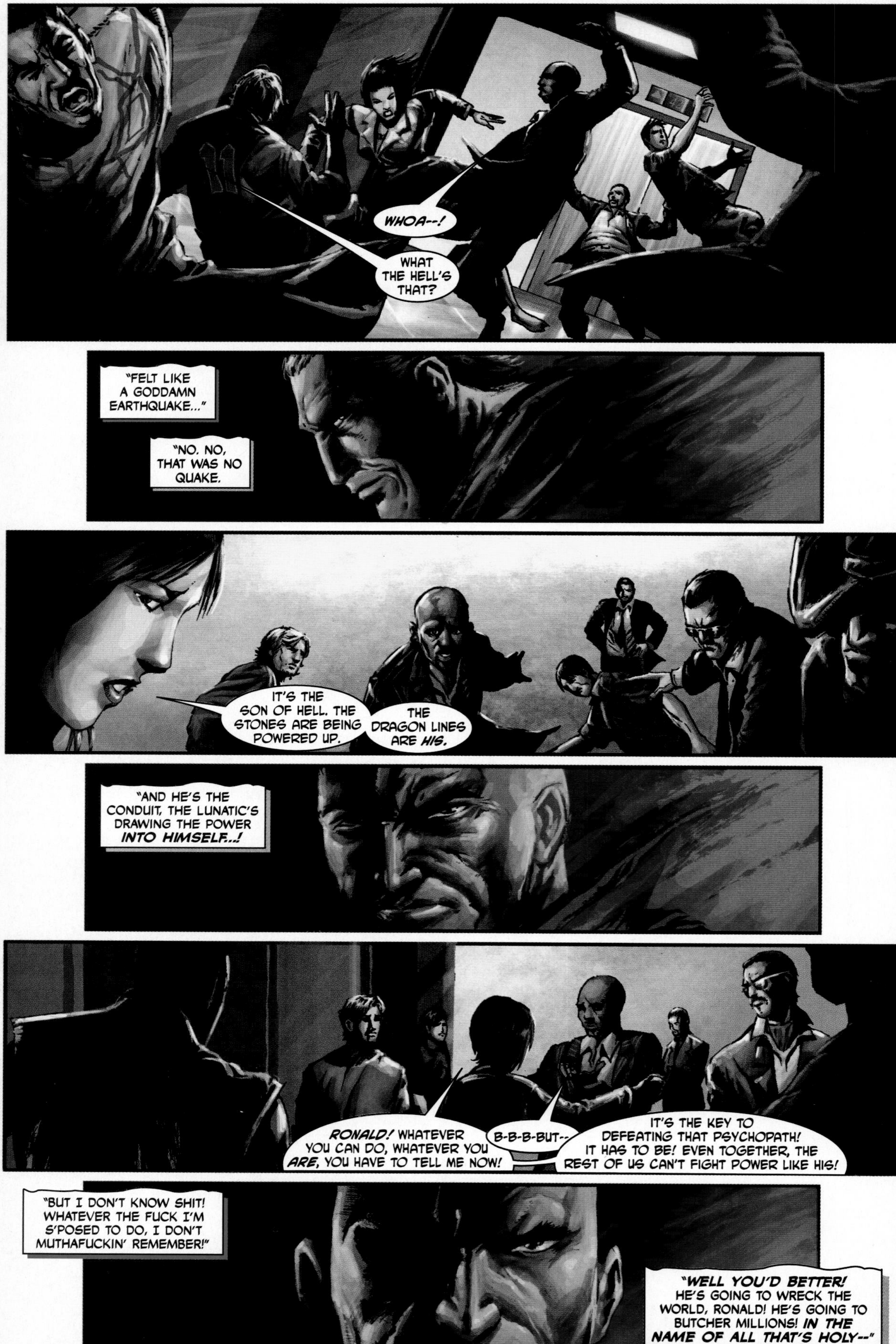
WHOA--!
WHAT THE HELL'S THAT?
"FELT LIKE A GODDAMN EARTHQUAKE..."
"NO. NO, THAT WAS NO QUAKE.
IT'S THE SON OF HELL. THE STONES ARE BEING POWERED UP.
THE DRAGON LINES ARE *HIS*.
"AND HE'S THE CONDUIT, THE LUNATIC'S DRAWING THE POWER ***INTO HIMSELF...!***
RONALD! WHATEVER YOU CAN DO, WHATEVER YOU *ARE*, YOU HAVE TO TELL ME NOW!
B-B-B-BUT--
IT'S THE KEY TO DEFEATING THAT PSYCHOPATH! IT HAS TO BE! EVEN TOGETHER, THE REST OF US CAN'T FIGHT POWER LIKE HIS!
"BUT I DON'T KNOW SHIT! WHATEVER THE FUCK I'M S'POSED TO DO, I DON'T MUTHAFUCKIN' REMEMBER!"
"***WELL YOU'D BETTER!*** HE'S GOING TO WRECK THE WORLD, RONALD! HE'S GOING TO BUTCHER MILLIONS! ***IN THE NAME OF ALL THAT'S HOLY--"***

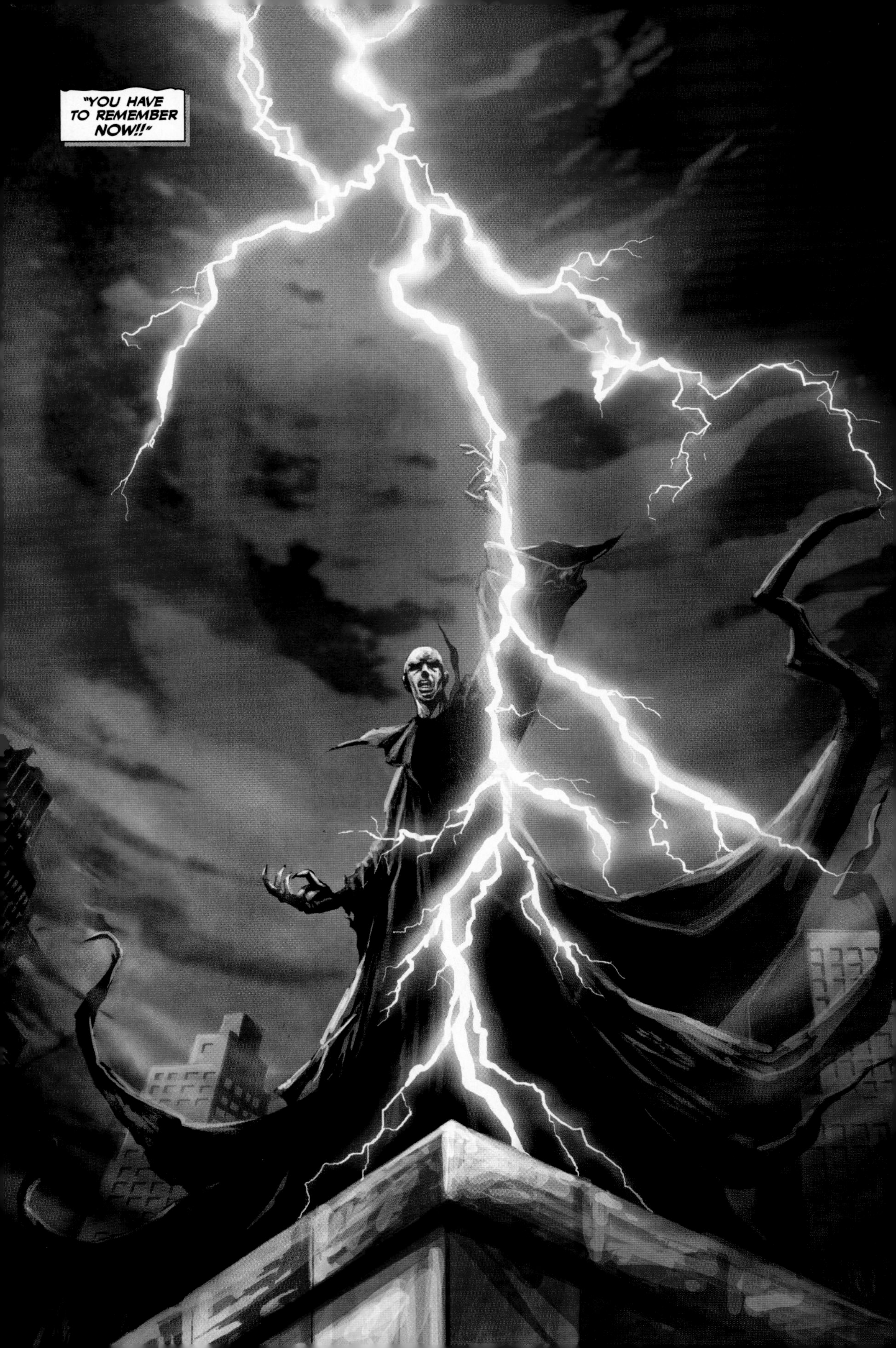
"YOU HAVE TO REMEMBER NOW!!"

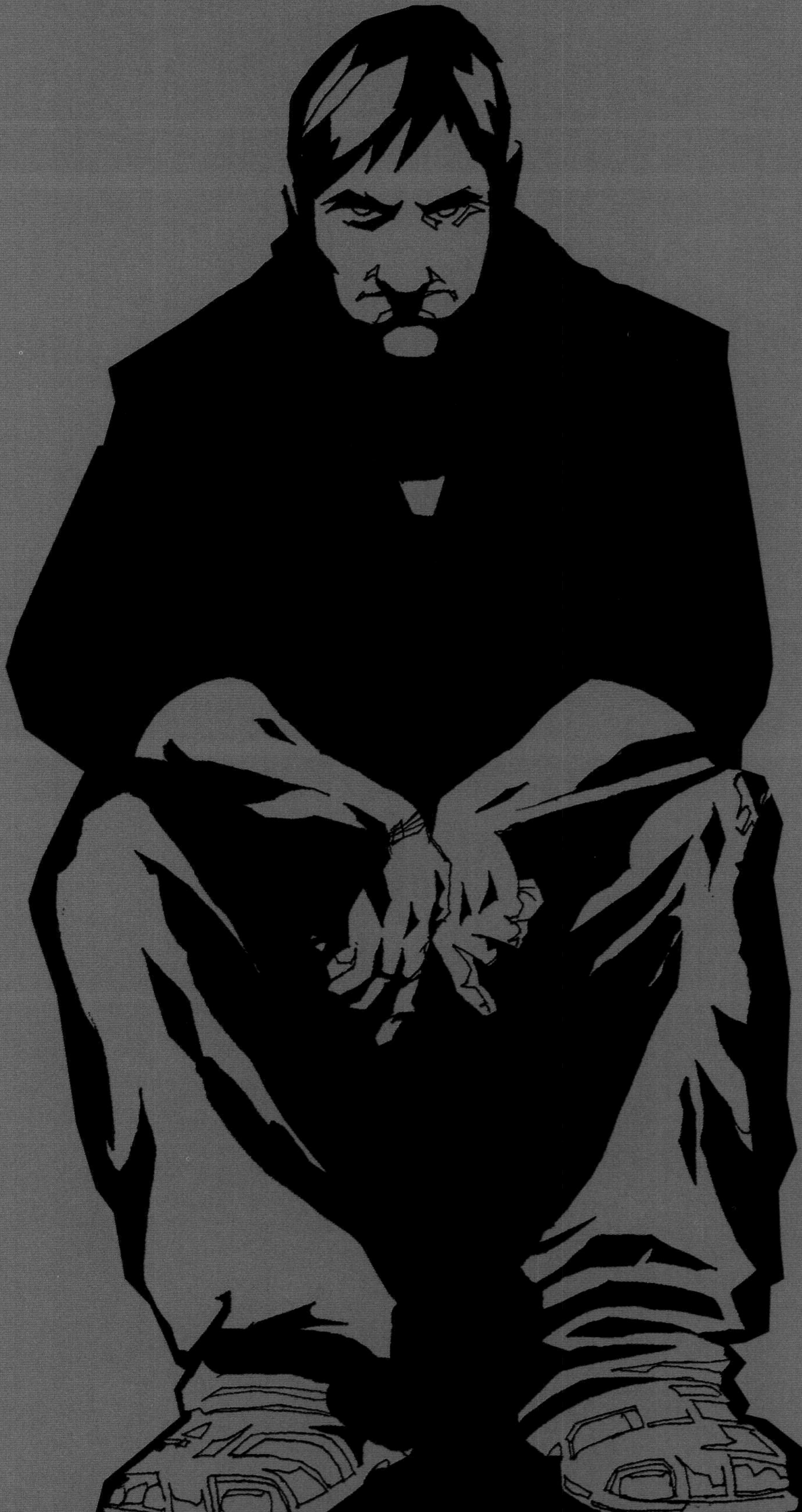

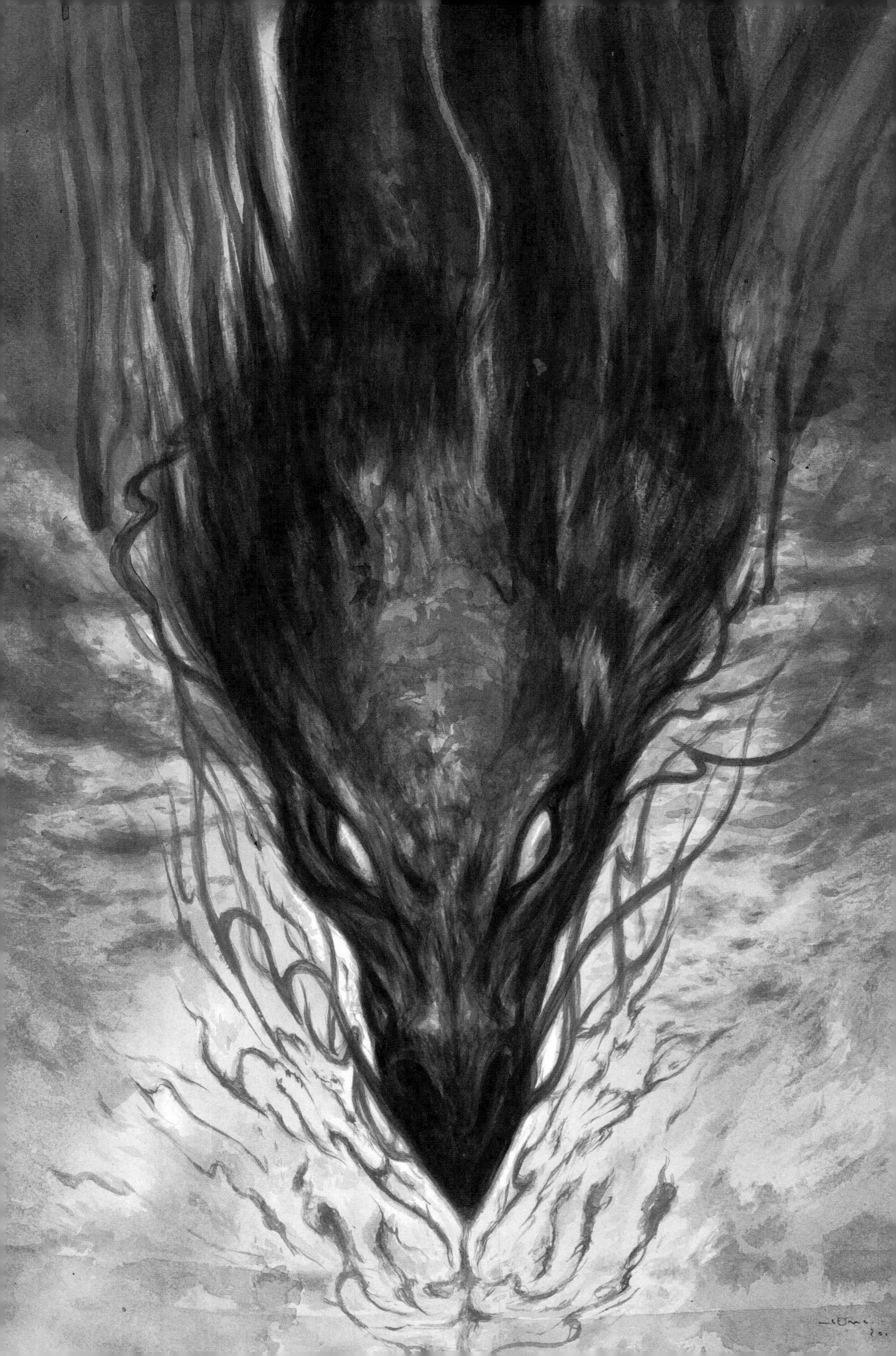

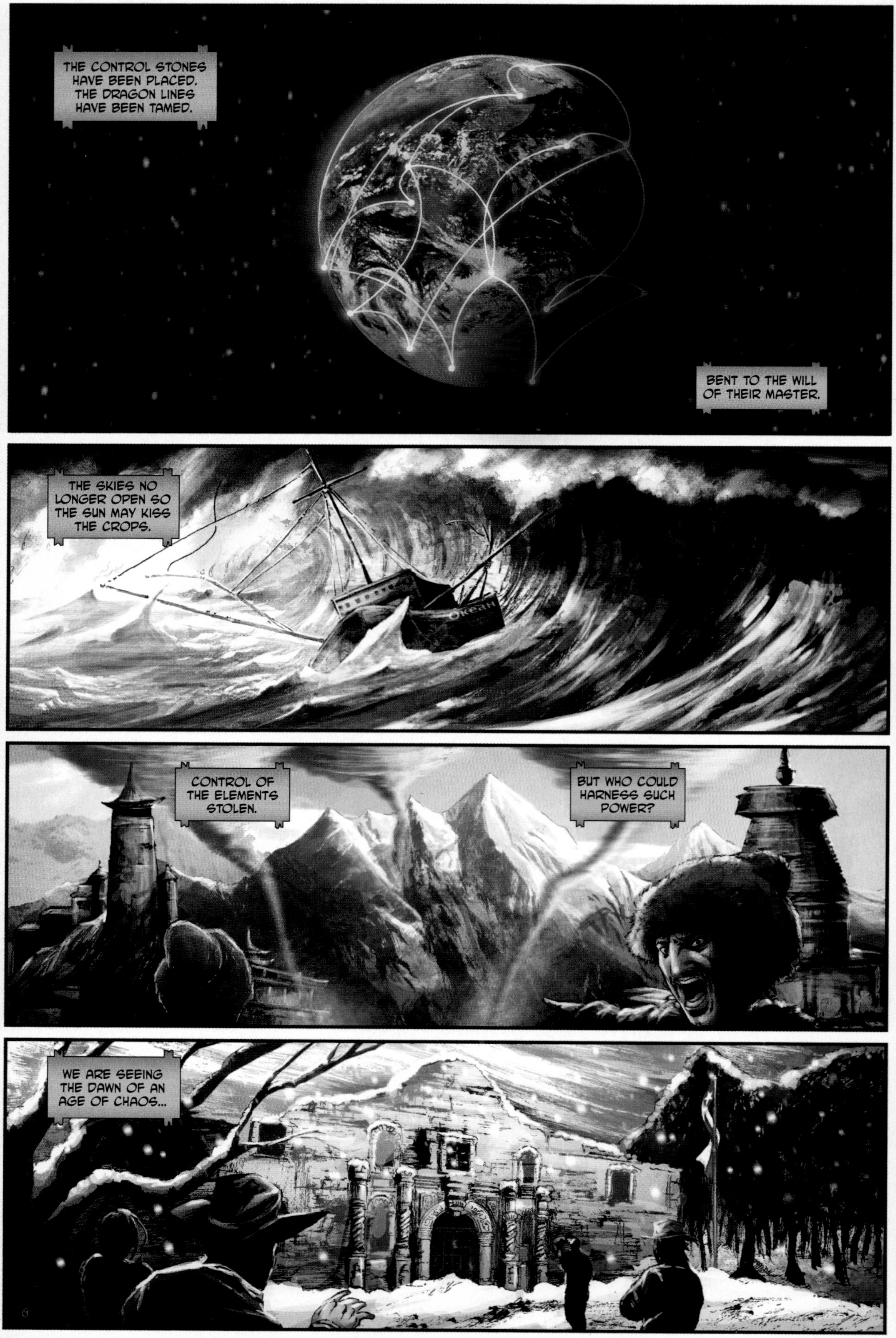
THE CONTROL STONES HAVE BEEN PLACED. THE DRAGON LINES HAVE BEEN TAMED.
BENT TO THE WILL OF THEIR MASTER.
THE SKIES NO LONGER OPEN SO THE SUN MAY KISS THE CROPS.
Океан
CONTROL OF THE ELEMENTS STOLEN.
BUT WHO COULD HARNESS SUCH POWER?
WE ARE SEEING THE DAWN OF AN AGE OF CHAOS...

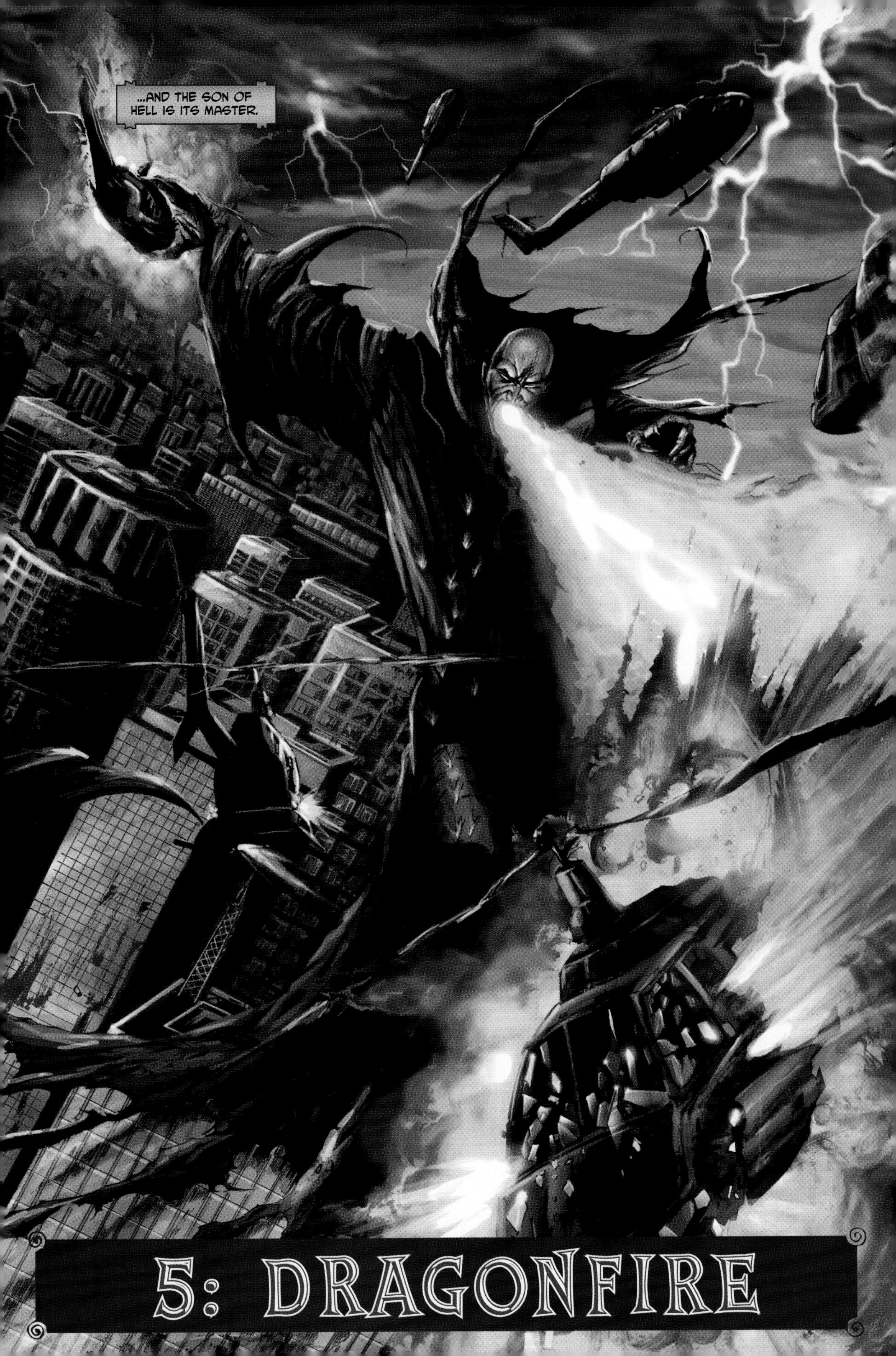

...AND THE SON OF HELL IS ITS MASTER.
5: DRAGONFIRE

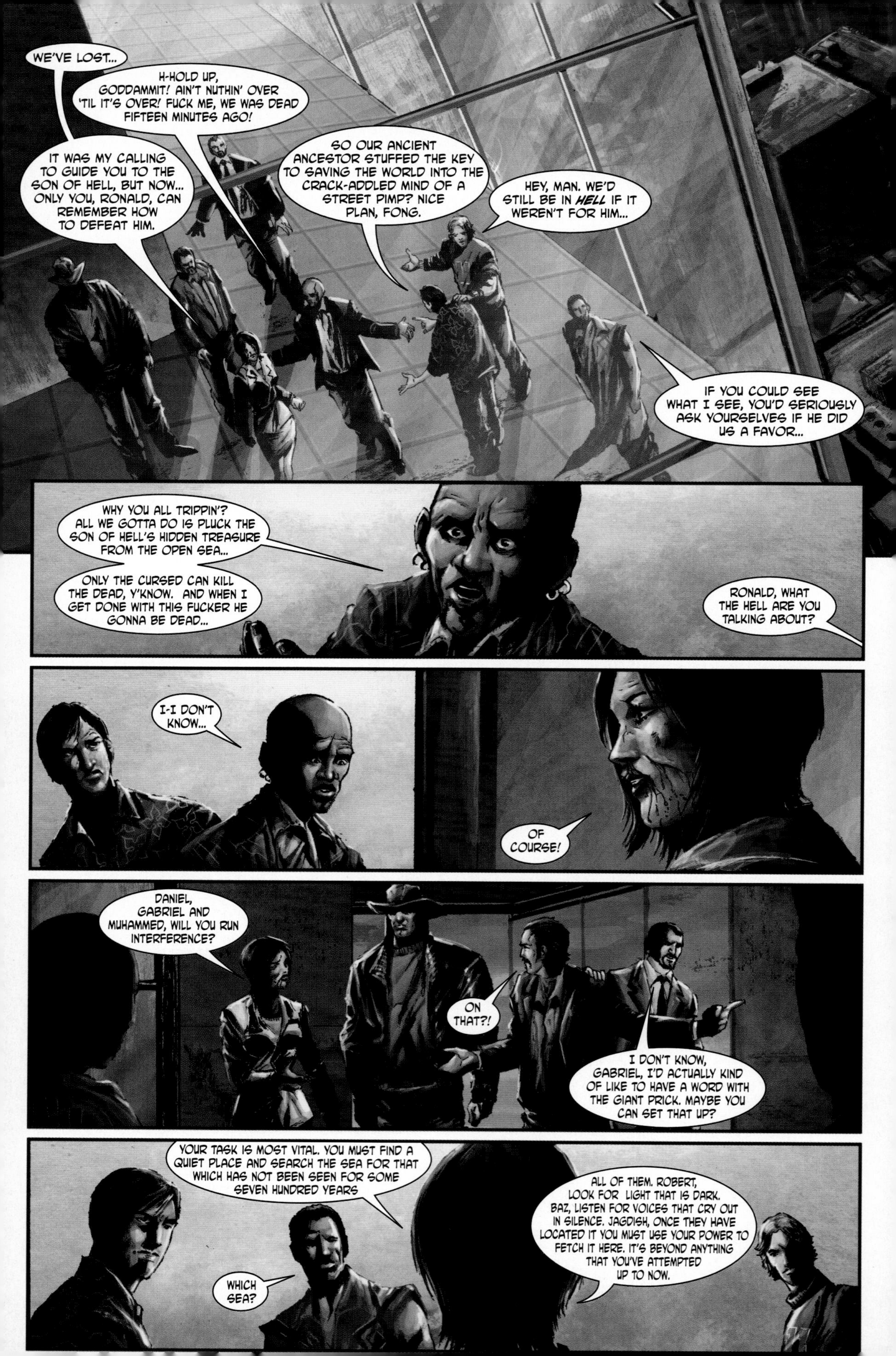
WE'VE LOST...
H-HOLD UP, GODDAMMIT! AIN'T NUTHIN' OVER 'TIL IT'S OVER! FUCK ME, WE WAS DEAD FIFTEEN MINUTES AGO!
IT WAS MY CALLING TO GUIDE YOU TO THE SON OF HELL, BUT NOW... ONLY YOU, RONALD, CAN REMEMBER HOW TO DEFEAT HIM.
SO OUR ANCIENT ANCESTOR STUFFED THE KEY TO SAVING THE WORLD INTO THE CRACK-ADDLED MIND OF A STREET PIMP? NICE PLAN, FONG.
HEY, MAN. WE'D STILL BE IN *HELL* IF IT WEREN'T FOR HIM...
IF YOU COULD SEE WHAT I SEE, YOU'D SERIOUSLY ASK YOURSELVES IF HE DID US A FAVOR...
WHY YOU ALL TRIPPIN'? ALL WE GOTTA DO IS PLUCK THE SON OF HELL'S HIDDEN TREASURE FROM THE OPEN SEA...
ONLY THE CURSED CAN KILL THE DEAD, Y'KNOW. AND WHEN I GET DONE WITH THIS FUCKER HE GONNA BE DEAD...
RONALD, WHAT THE HELL ARE YOU TALKING ABOUT?
I-I DON'T KNOW...
OF COURSE!
DANIEL, GABRIEL AND MUHAMMED, WILL YOU RUN INTERFERENCE?
ON THAT?!
I DON'T KNOW, GABRIEL, I'D ACTUALLY KIND OF LIKE TO HAVE A WORD WITH THE GIANT PRICK. MAYBE YOU CAN SET THAT UP?
YOUR TASK IS MOST VITAL. YOU MUST FIND A QUIET PLACE AND SEARCH THE SEA FOR THAT WHICH HAS NOT BEEN SEEN FOR SOME SEVEN HUNDRED YEARS
WHICH SEA?
ALL OF THEM. ROBERT, LOOK FOR LIGHT THAT IS DARK. BAZ, LISTEN FOR VOICES THAT CRY OUT IN SILENCE. JAGDISH, ONCE THEY HAVE LOCATED IT YOU MUST USE YOUR POWER TO FETCH IT HERE. IT'S BEYOND ANYTHING THAT YOU'VE ATTEMPTED UP TO NOW.

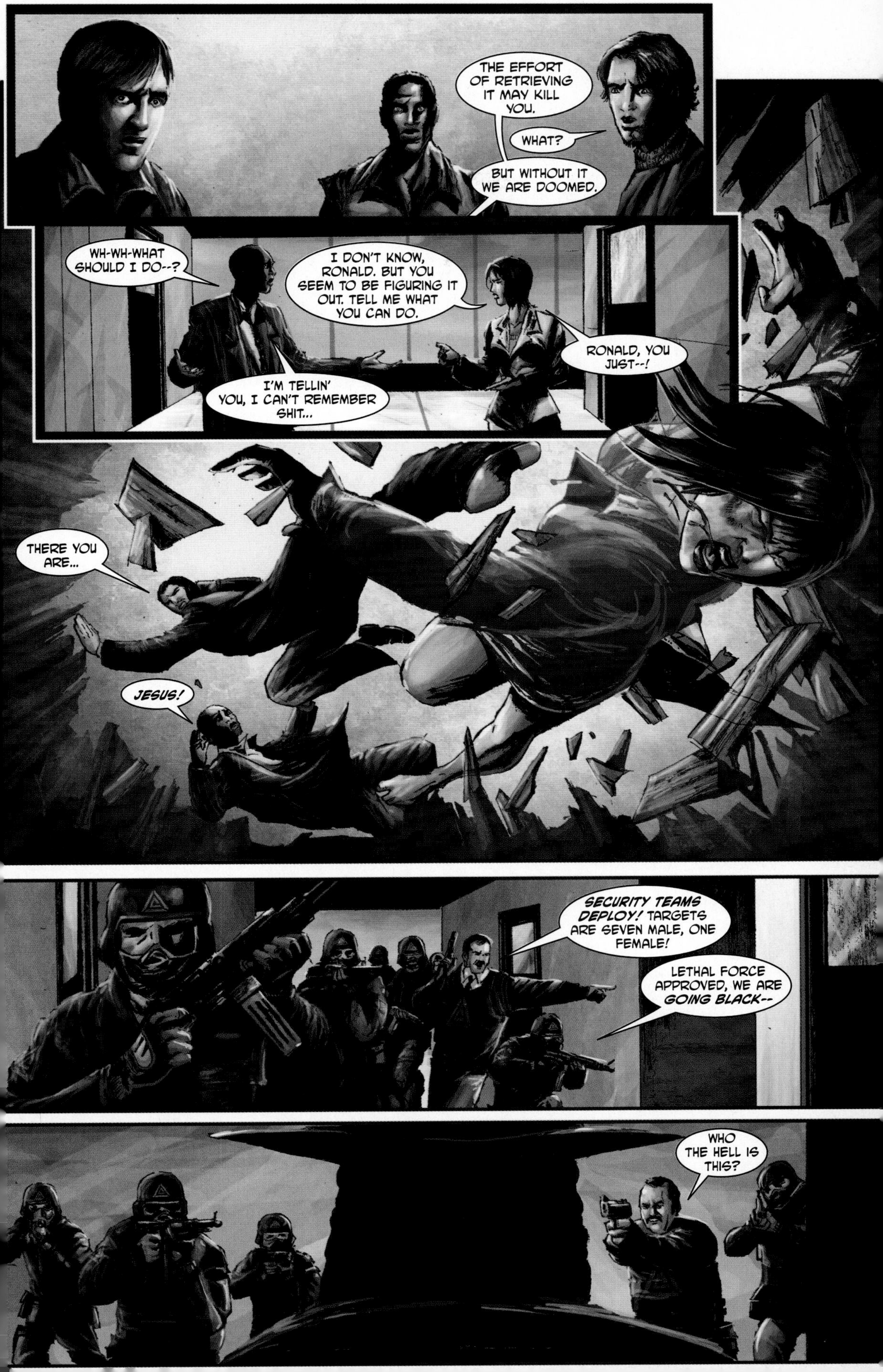
THE EFFORT OF RETRIEVING IT MAY KILL YOU.
WHAT?
BUT WITHOUT IT WE ARE DOOMED.
WH-WH-WHAT SHOULD I DO--?
I DON'T KNOW, RONALD. BUT YOU SEEM TO BE FIGURING IT OUT. TELL ME WHAT YOU CAN DO.
I'M TELLIN' YOU, I CAN'T REMEMBER SHIT...
RONALD, YOU JUST--!
THERE YOU ARE...
JESUS!
SECURITY TEAMS DEPLOY! TARGETS ARE SEVEN MALE, ONE FEMALE!
LETHAL FORCE APPROVED, WE ARE GOING BLACK--
WHO THE HELL IS THIS?

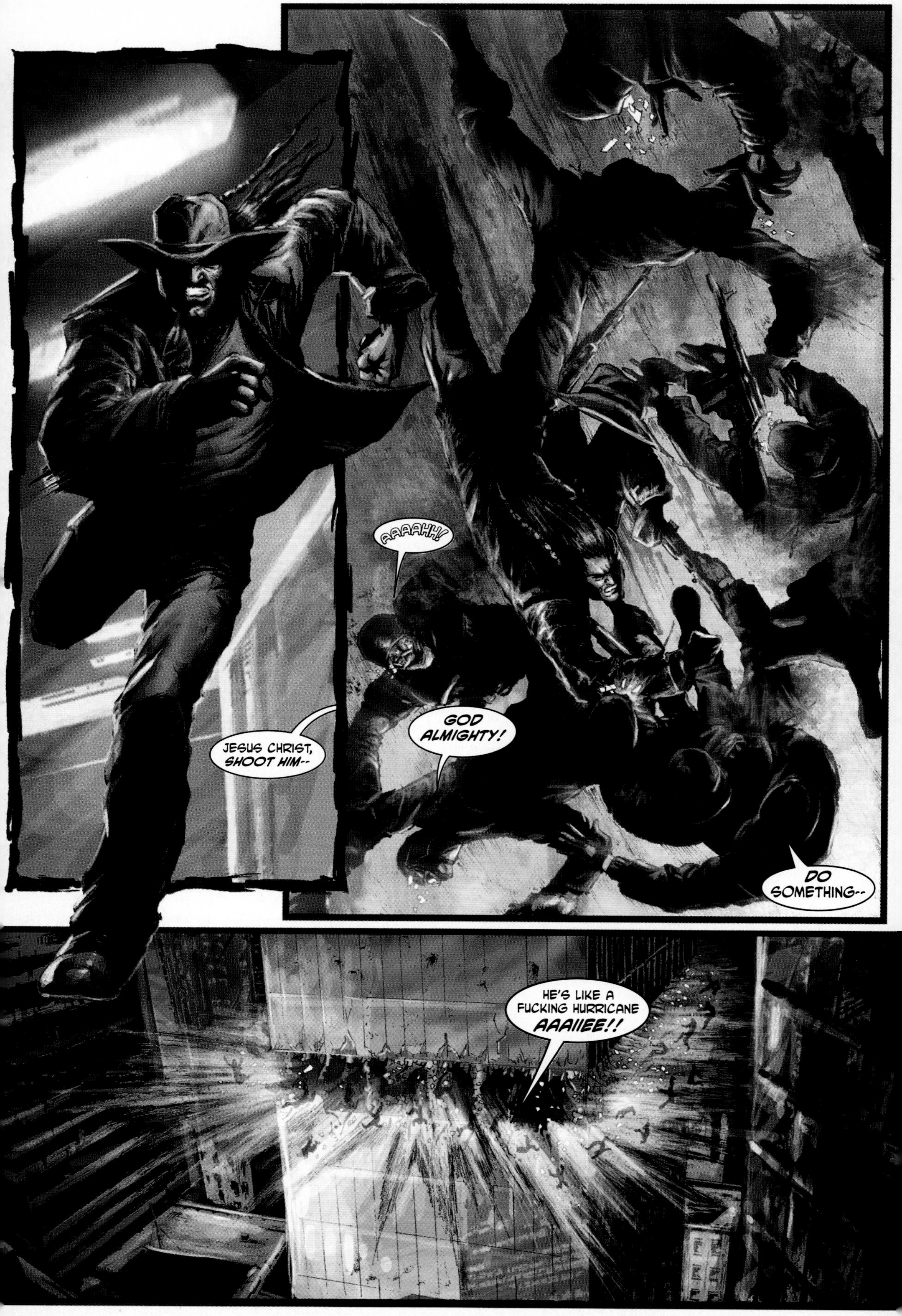
AAAAHH!
JESUS CHRIST, SHOOT HIM--
GOD ALMIGHTY!
DO SOMETHING--
HE'S LIKE A FUCKING HURRICANE AAAIIEE!!

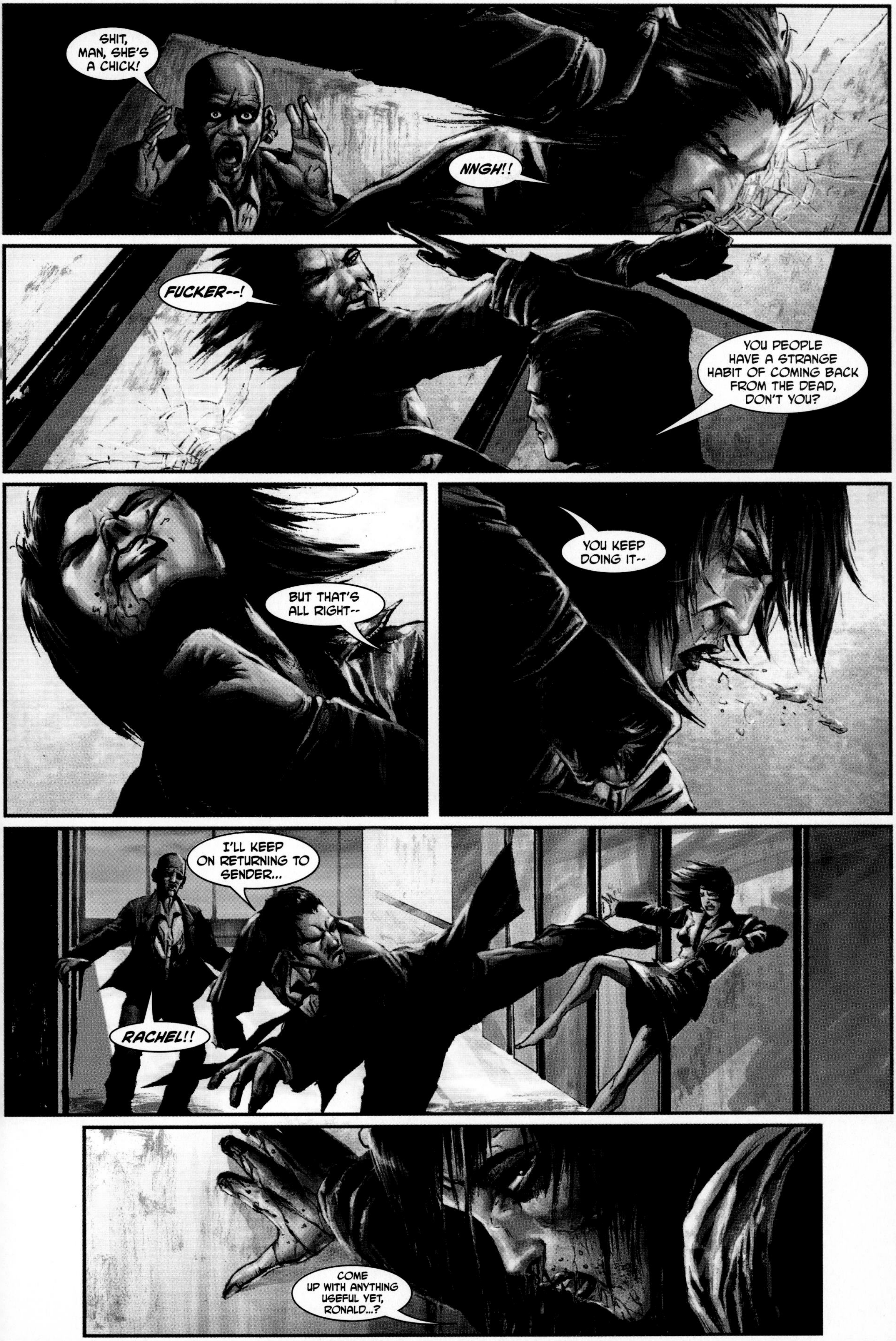
SHIT, MAN, SHE'S A CHICK!
NNGH!!
FUCKER--!
YOU PEOPLE HAVE A STRANGE HABIT OF COMING BACK FROM THE DEAD, DON'T YOU?
BUT THAT'S ALL RIGHT--
YOU KEEP DOING IT--
I'LL KEEP ON RETURNING TO SENDER...
RACHEL!!
COME UP WITH ANYTHING USEFUL YET, RONALD...?

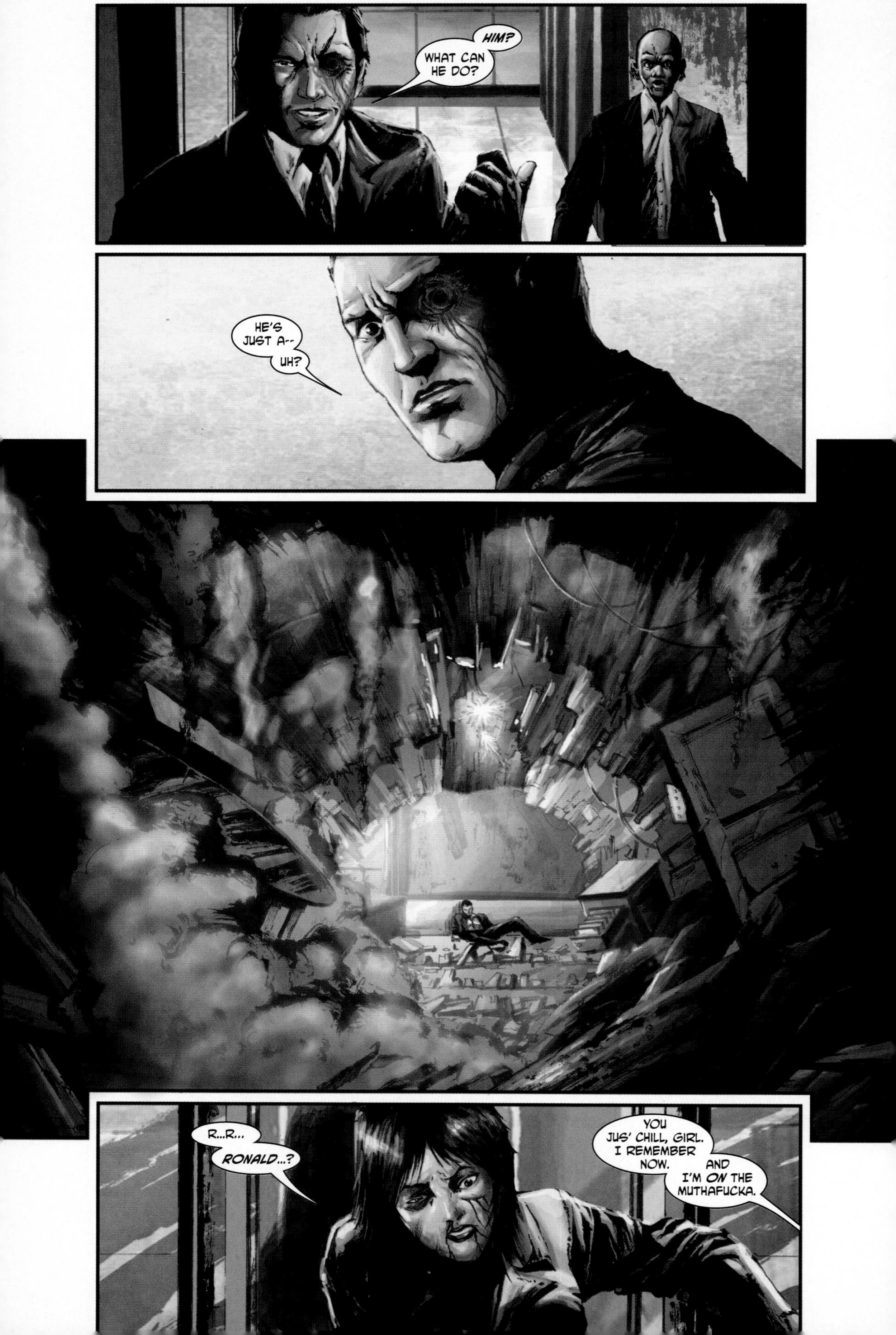
HIM?
WHAT CAN HE DO?
HE'S JUST A--
UH?
R...R...
RONALD...?
YOU JUS' CHILL, GIRL. I REMEMBER NOW.
AND I'M ON THE MUTHAFUCKA.

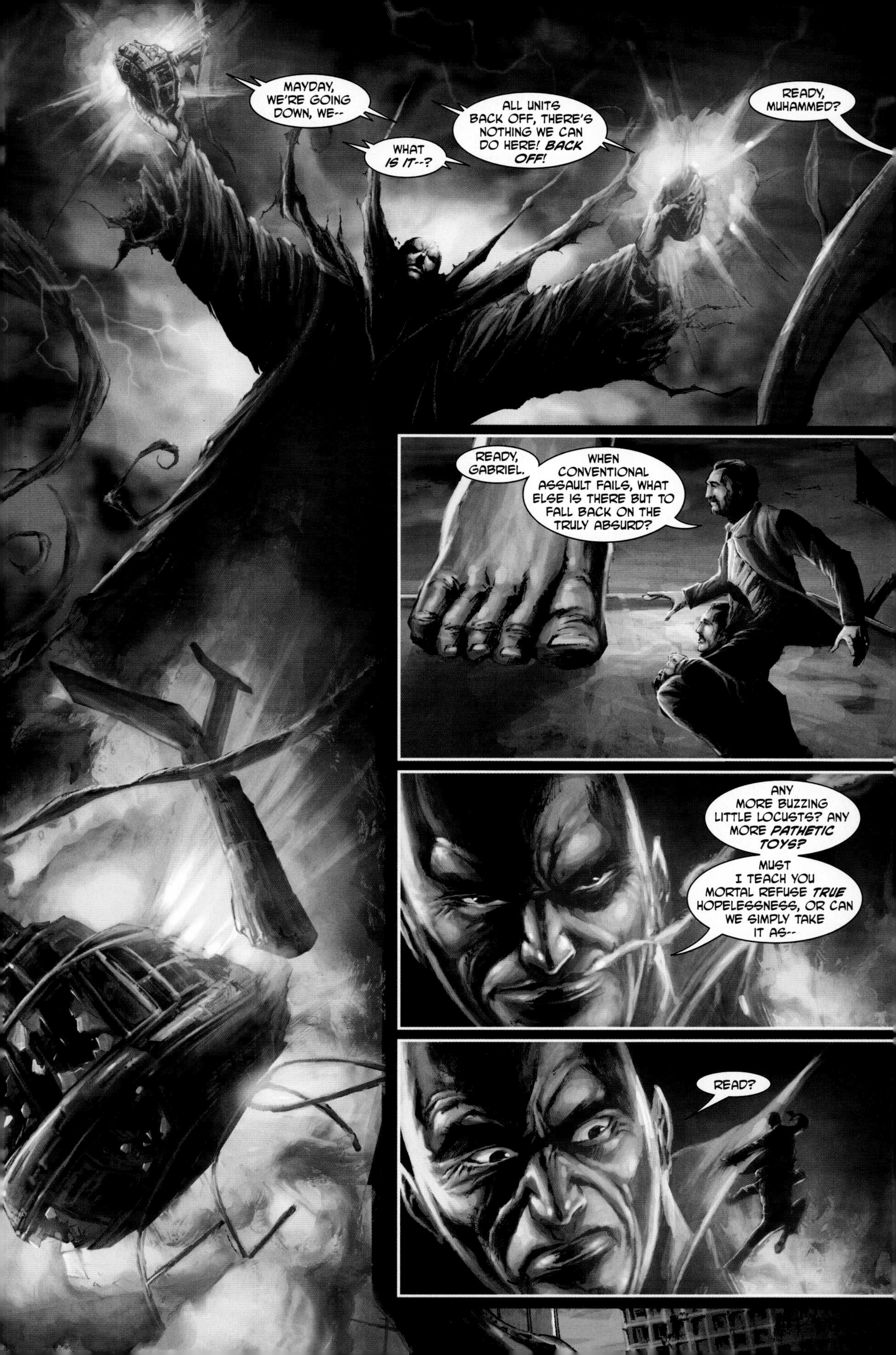
MAYDAY, WE'RE GOING DOWN, WE--
WHAT IS IT--?
ALL UNITS BACK OFF, THERE'S NOTHING WE CAN DO HERE! BACK OFF!
READY, MUHAMMED?
READY, GABRIEL.
WHEN CONVENTIONAL ASSAULT FAILS, WHAT ELSE IS THERE BUT TO FALL BACK ON THE TRULY ABSURD?
ANY MORE BUZZING LITTLE LOCUSTS? ANY MORE PATHETIC TOYS?
MUST I TEACH YOU MORTAL REFUSE TRUE HOPELESSNESS, OR CAN WE SIMPLY TAKE IT AS--
READ?

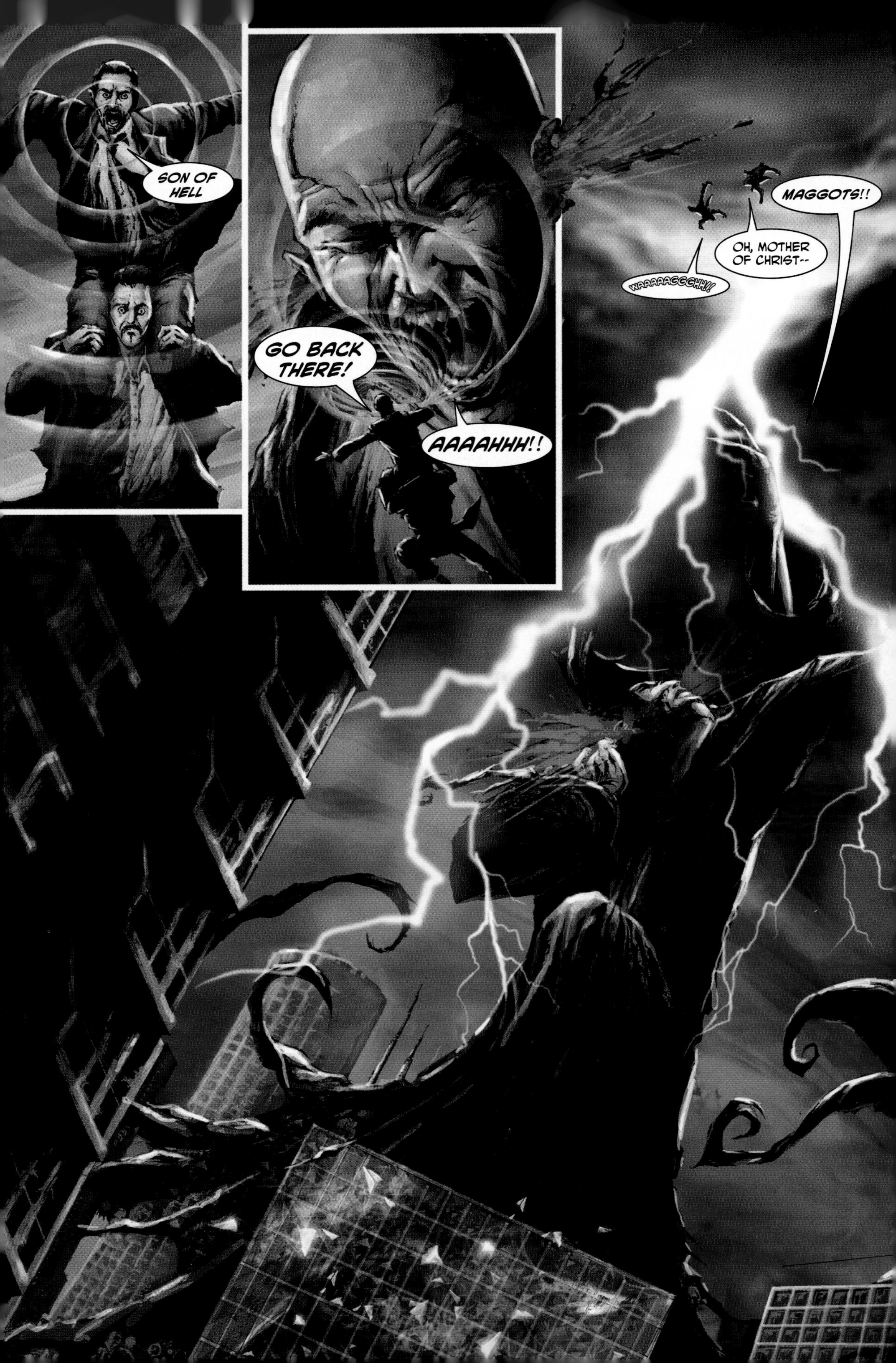
SON OF HELL
GO BACK THERE!
AAAAHHH!!
WAAAAAAGGGHH!!
OH, MOTHER OF CHRIST--
MAGGOTS!!

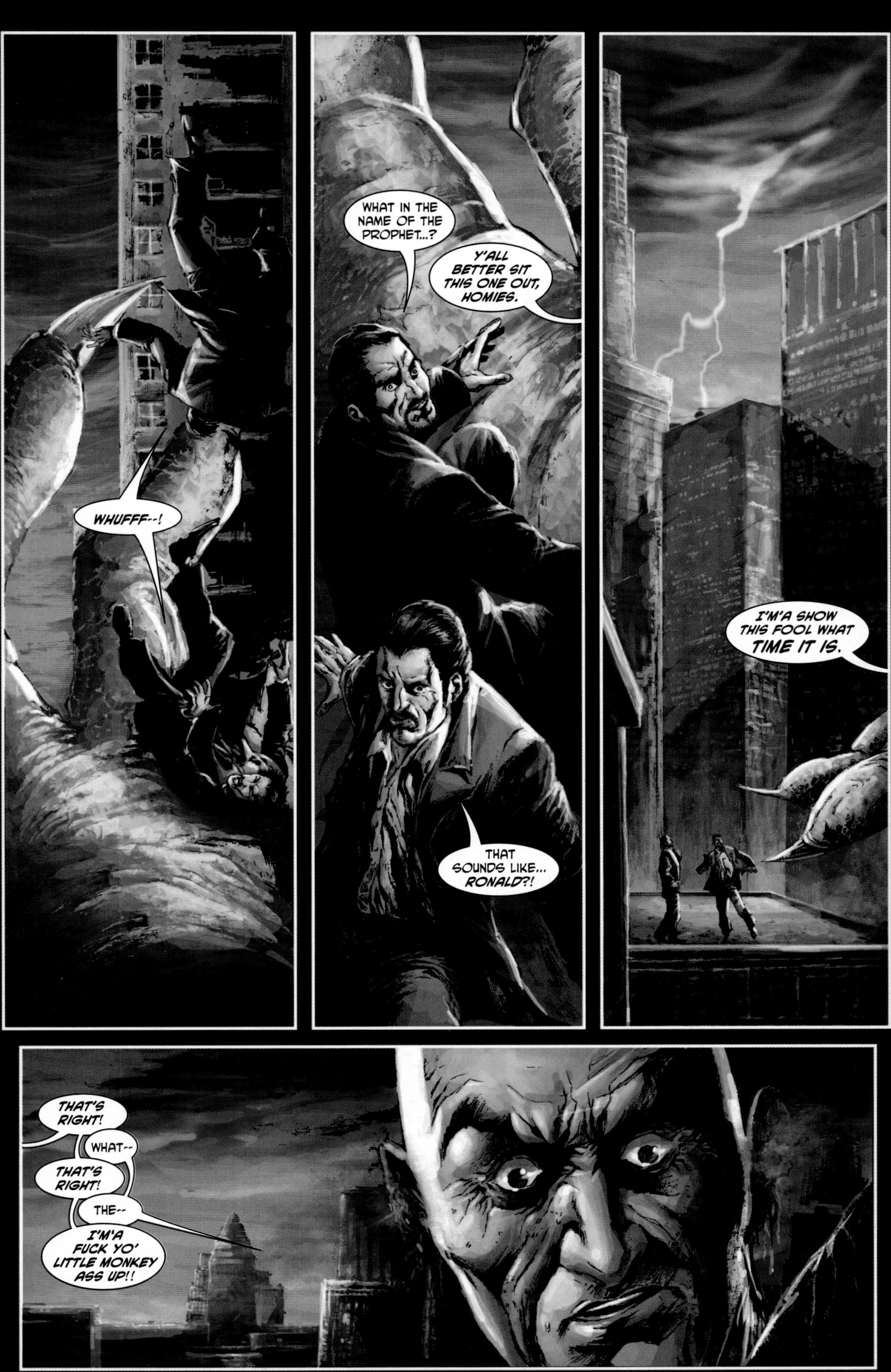
WHUFFF--!
WHAT IN THE NAME OF THE PROPHET...?
Y'ALL BETTER SIT THIS ONE OUT, HOMIES.
THAT SOUNDS LIKE... RONALD?!
I'M'A SHOW THIS FOOL WHAT TIME IT IS.
THAT'S RIGHT!
WHAT--
THAT'S RIGHT!
THE--
I'M'A FUCK YO' LITTLE MONKEY ASS UP!!

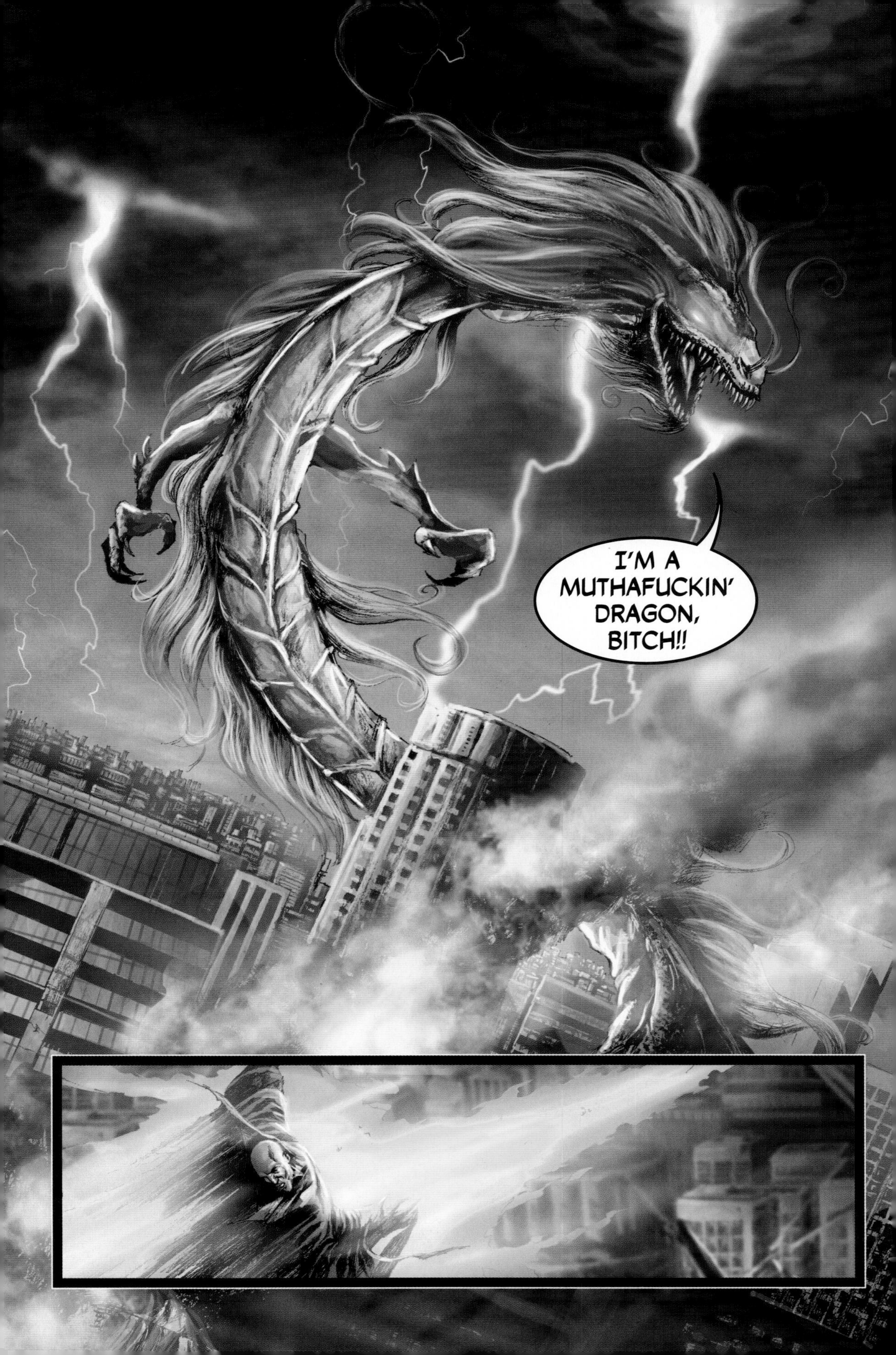
I'M A MUTHAFUCKIN' DRAGON, BITCH!!

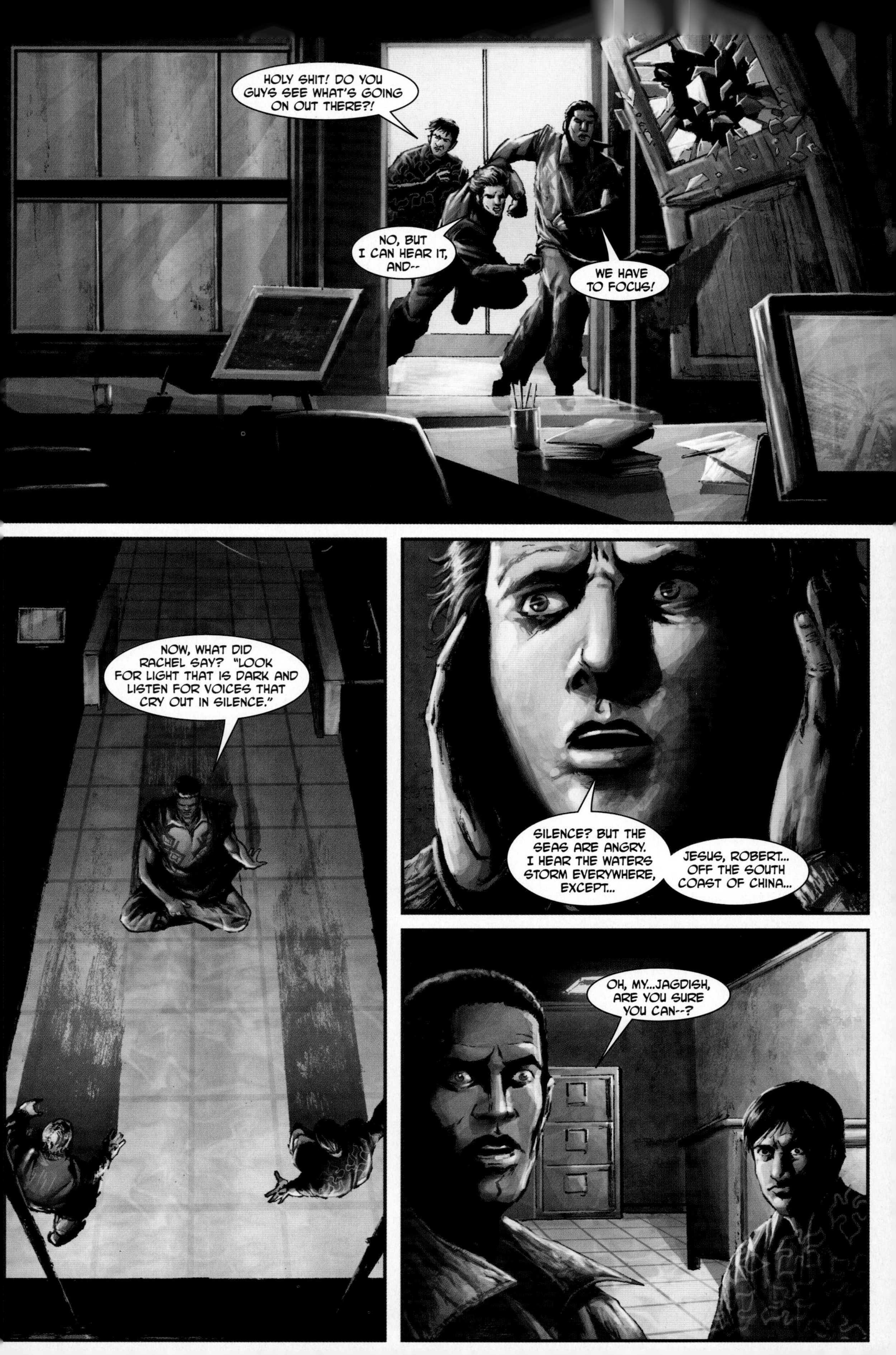
HOLY SHIT! DO YOU GUYS SEE WHAT'S GOING ON OUT THERE?!
NO, BUT I CAN HEAR IT, AND--
WE HAVE TO FOCUS!
NOW, WHAT DID RACHEL SAY? "LOOK FOR LIGHT THAT IS DARK AND LISTEN FOR VOICES THAT CRY OUT IN SILENCE."
SILENCE? BUT THE SEAS ARE ANGRY. I HEAR THE WATERS STORM EVERYWHERE, EXCEPT...
JESUS, ROBERT... OFF THE SOUTH COAST OF CHINA...
OH, MY...JAGDISH, ARE YOU SURE YOU CAN--?

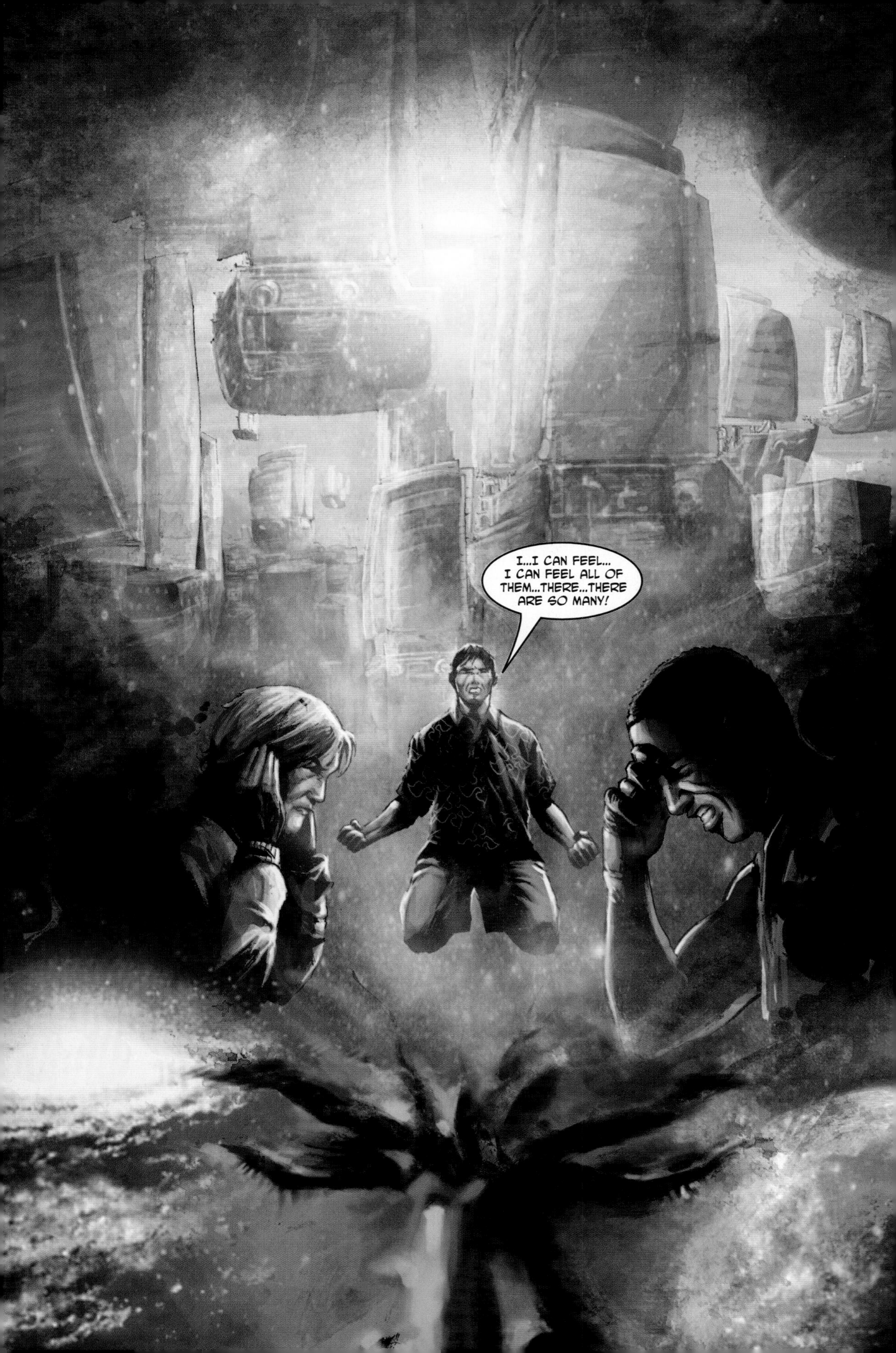
I...I CAN FEEL... I CAN FEEL ALL OF THEM...THERE...THERE ARE SO MANY!

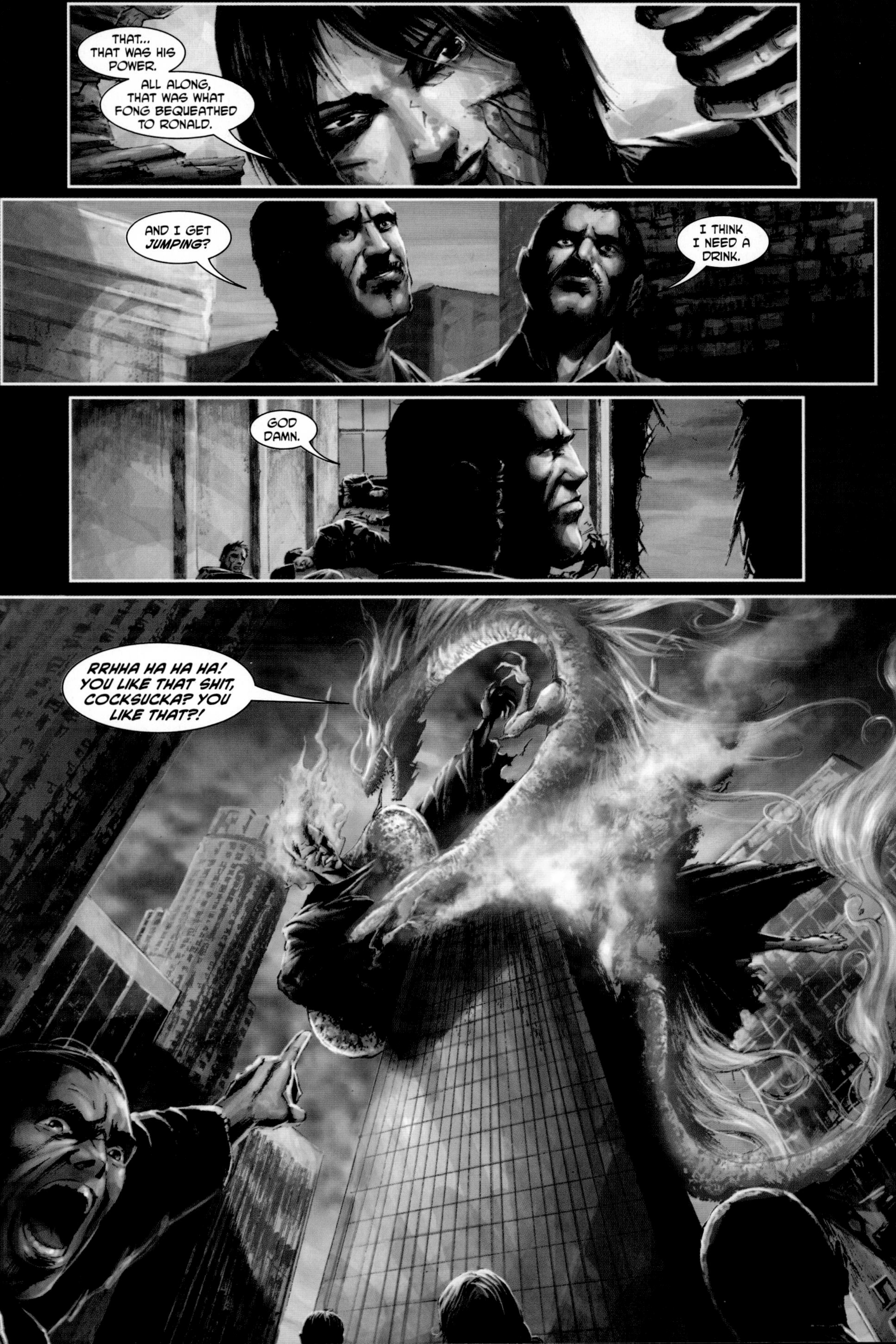
THAT... THAT WAS HIS POWER.
ALL ALONG, THAT WAS WHAT FONG BEQUEATHED TO RONALD.
AND I GET *JUMPING*?
I THINK I NEED A DRINK.
GOD DAMN.
RRHHA HA HA HA! YOU LIKE THAT SHIT, COCKSUCKA? YOU LIKE THAT?!

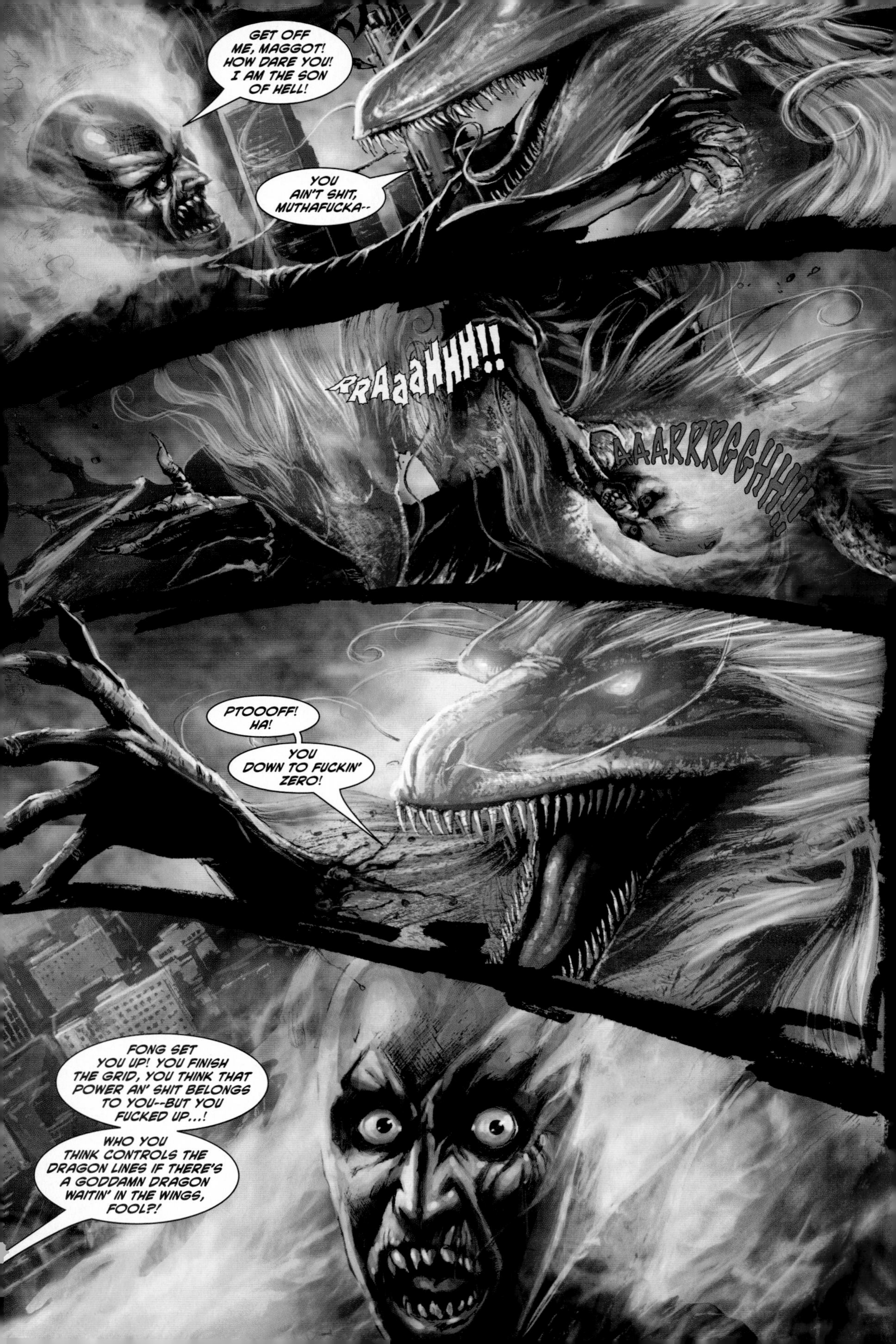
GET OFF ME, MAGGOT! HOW DARE YOU! I AM THE SON OF HELL!
YOU AIN'T SHIT, MUTHAFUCKA--
RRAAaAHHH!!
AAARRRGGHH!!
PTOOOFF! HA!
YOU DOWN TO FUCKIN' ZERO!
FONG SET YOU UP! YOU FINISH THE GRID, YOU THINK THAT POWER AN' SHIT BELONGS TO YOU--BUT YOU FUCKED UP...!
WHO YOU THINK CONTROLS THE DRAGON LINES IF THERE'S A GODDAMN DRAGON WAITIN' IN THE WINGS, FOOL?!

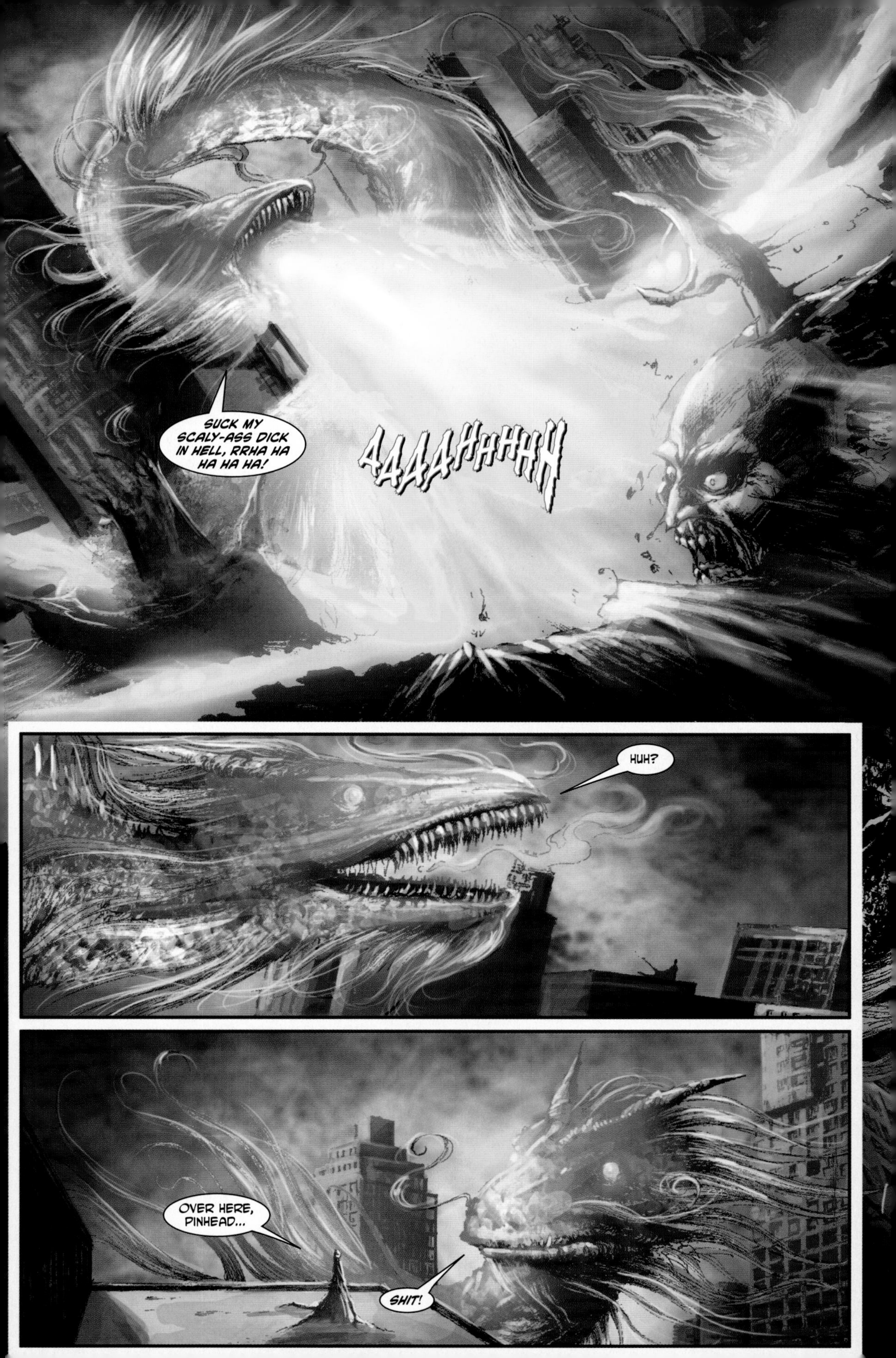
SUCK MY SCALY-ASS DICK IN HELL, RRHA HA HA HA HA!
AAAAHHHHH
HUH?
OVER HERE, PINHEAD...
SHIT!

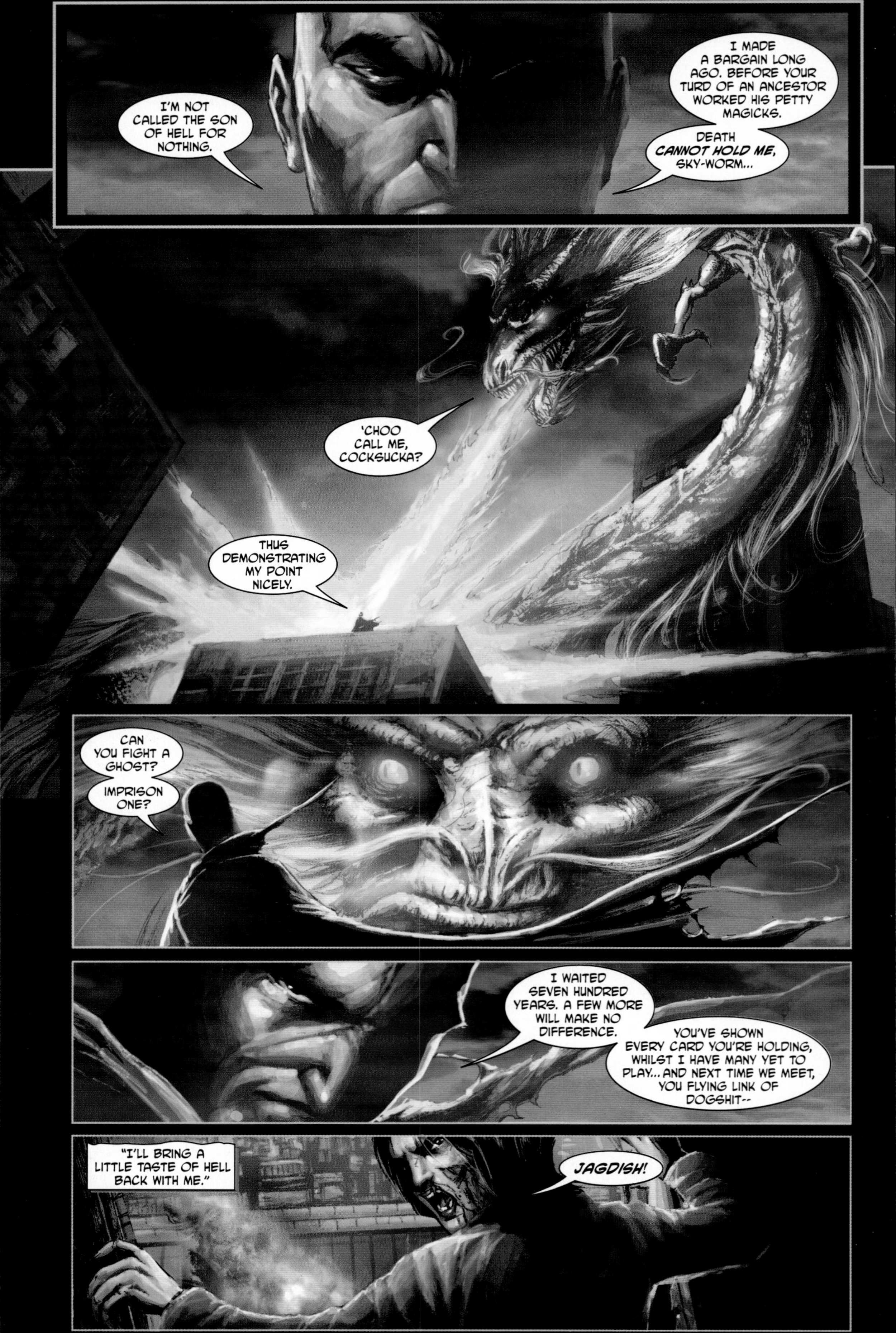
I'M NOT CALLED THE SON OF HELL FOR NOTHING.
I MADE A BARGAIN LONG AGO. BEFORE YOUR TURD OF AN ANCESTOR WORKED HIS PETTY MAGICKS.
DEATH *CANNOT HOLD ME,* SKY-WORM...
'CHOO CALL ME, COCKSUCKA?
THUS DEMONSTRATING MY POINT NICELY.
CAN YOU FIGHT A GHOST?
IMPRISON ONE?
I WAITED SEVEN HUNDRED YEARS. A FEW MORE WILL MAKE NO DIFFERENCE.
YOU'VE SHOWN EVERY CARD YOU'RE HOLDING, WHILST I HAVE MANY YET TO PLAY... AND NEXT TIME WE MEET, YOU FLYING LINK OF DOGSHIT--
"I'LL BRING A LITTLE TASTE OF HELL BACK WITH ME."
JAGDISH!

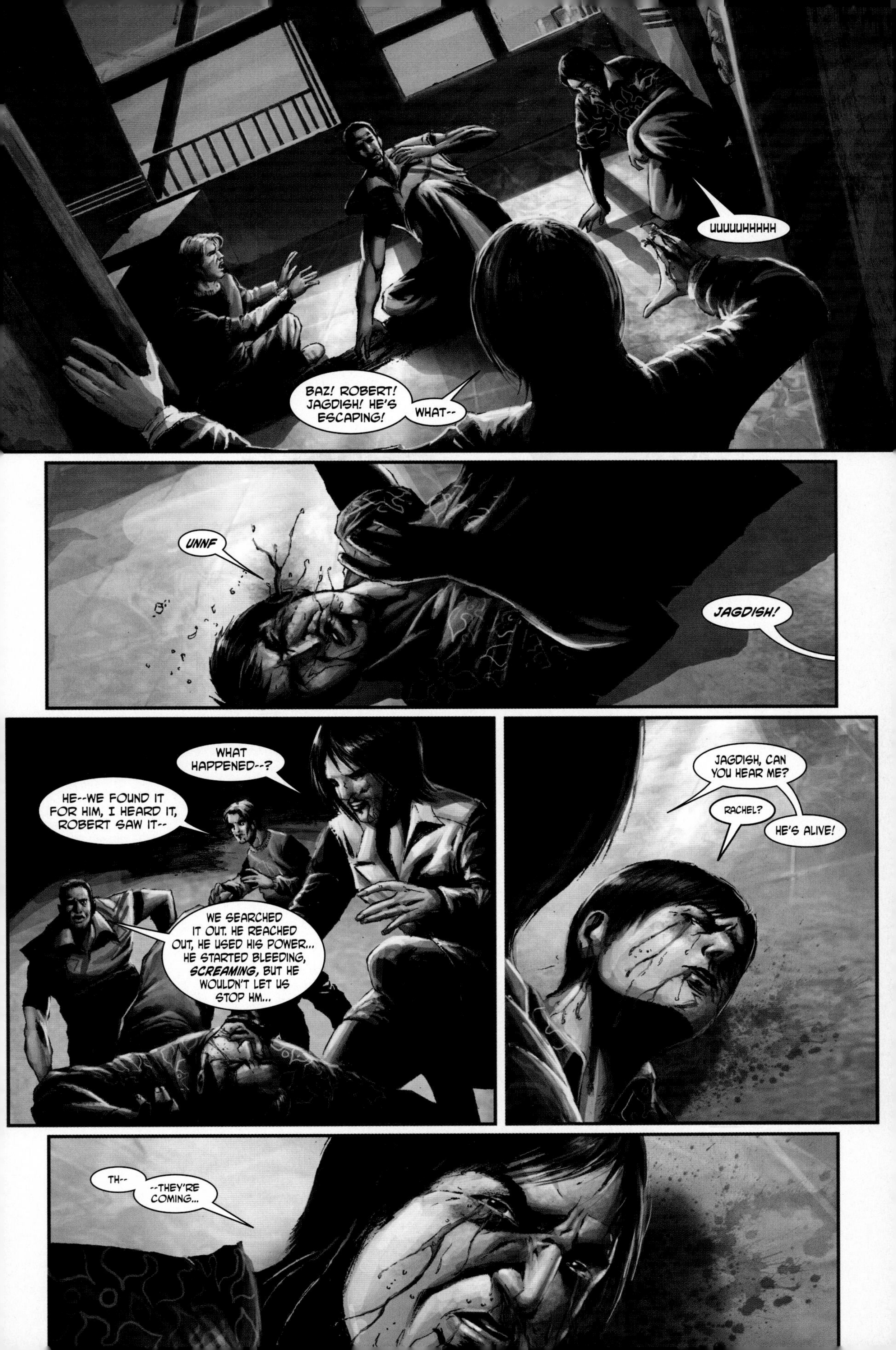
UUUUUHHHHH
BAZ! ROBERT! JAGDISH! HE'S ESCAPING!
WHAT--
UNNF
JAGDISH!
WHAT HAPPENED--?
HE--WE FOUND IT FOR HIM, I HEARD IT, ROBERT SAW IT--
WE SEARCHED IT OUT. HE REACHED OUT, HE USED HIS POWER... HE STARTED BLEEDING, *SCREAMING*, BUT HE WOULDN'T LET US STOP HM...
JAGDISH, CAN YOU HEAR ME?
RACHEL?
HE'S ALIVE!
TH--
--THEY'RE COMING...

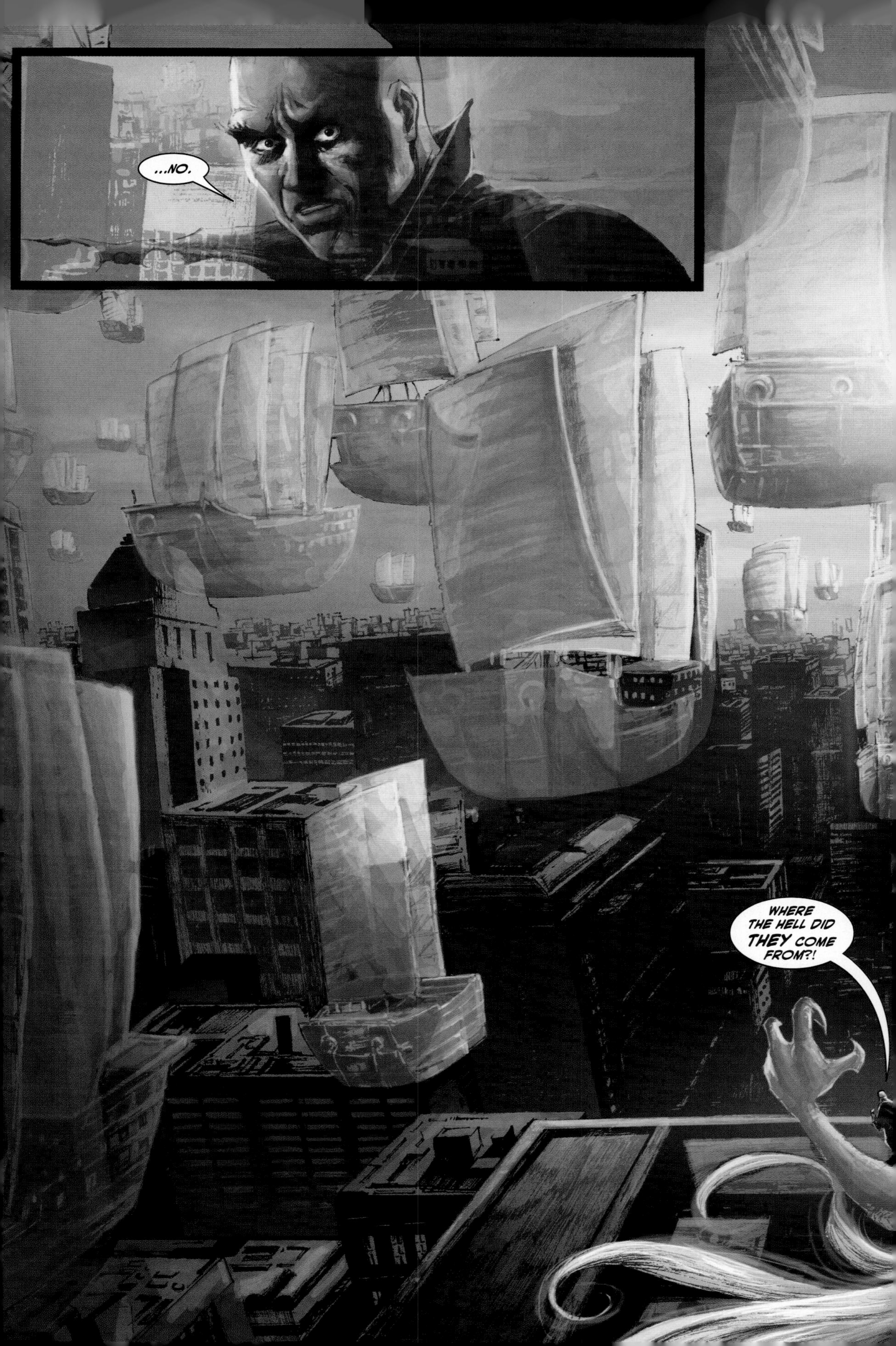
...NO.
WHERE THE HELL DID THEY COME FROM?!

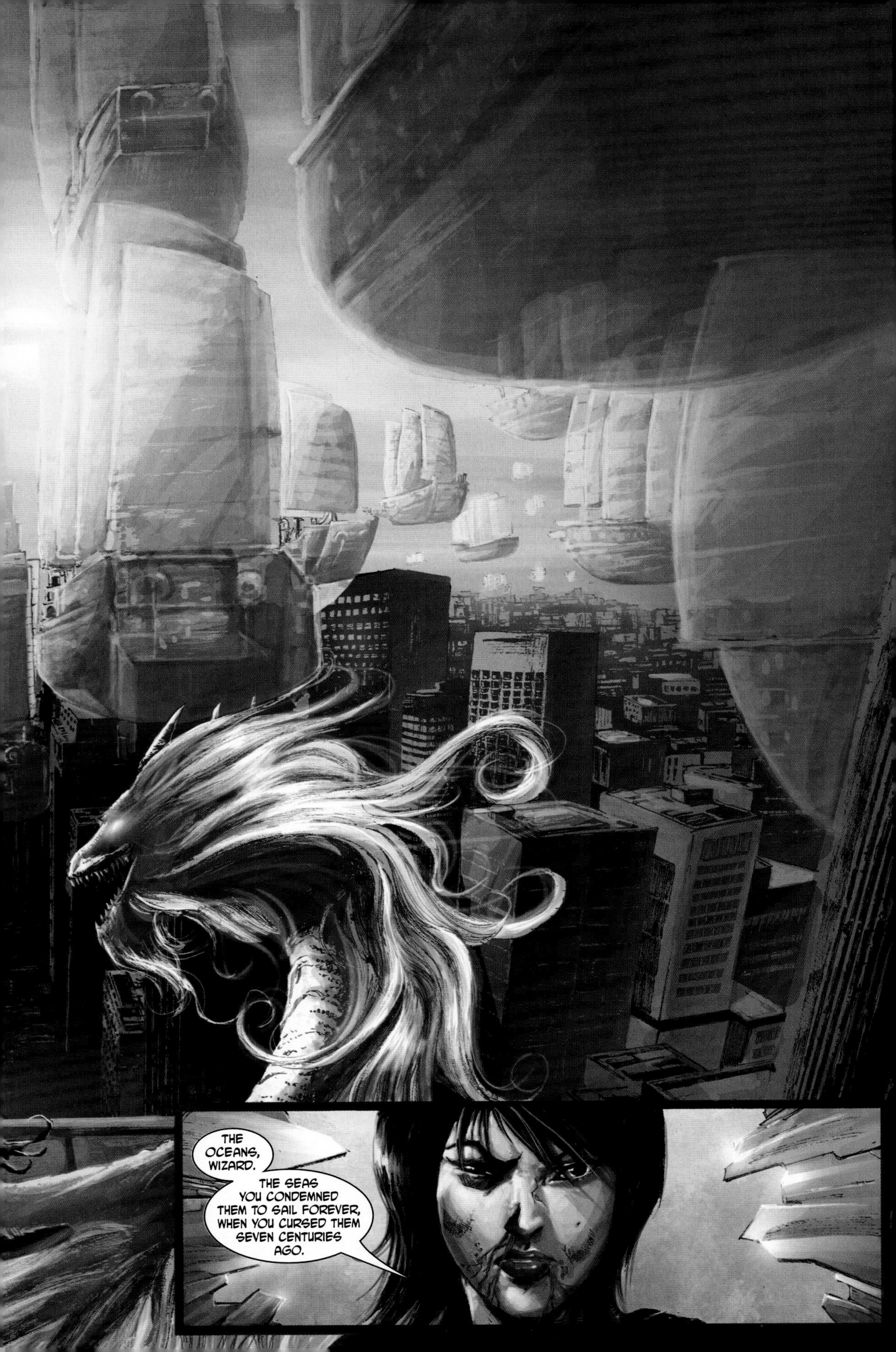
THE OCEANS, WIZARD.
THE SEAS YOU CONDEMNED THEM TO SAIL FOREVER, WHEN YOU CURSED THEM SEVEN CENTURIES AGO.

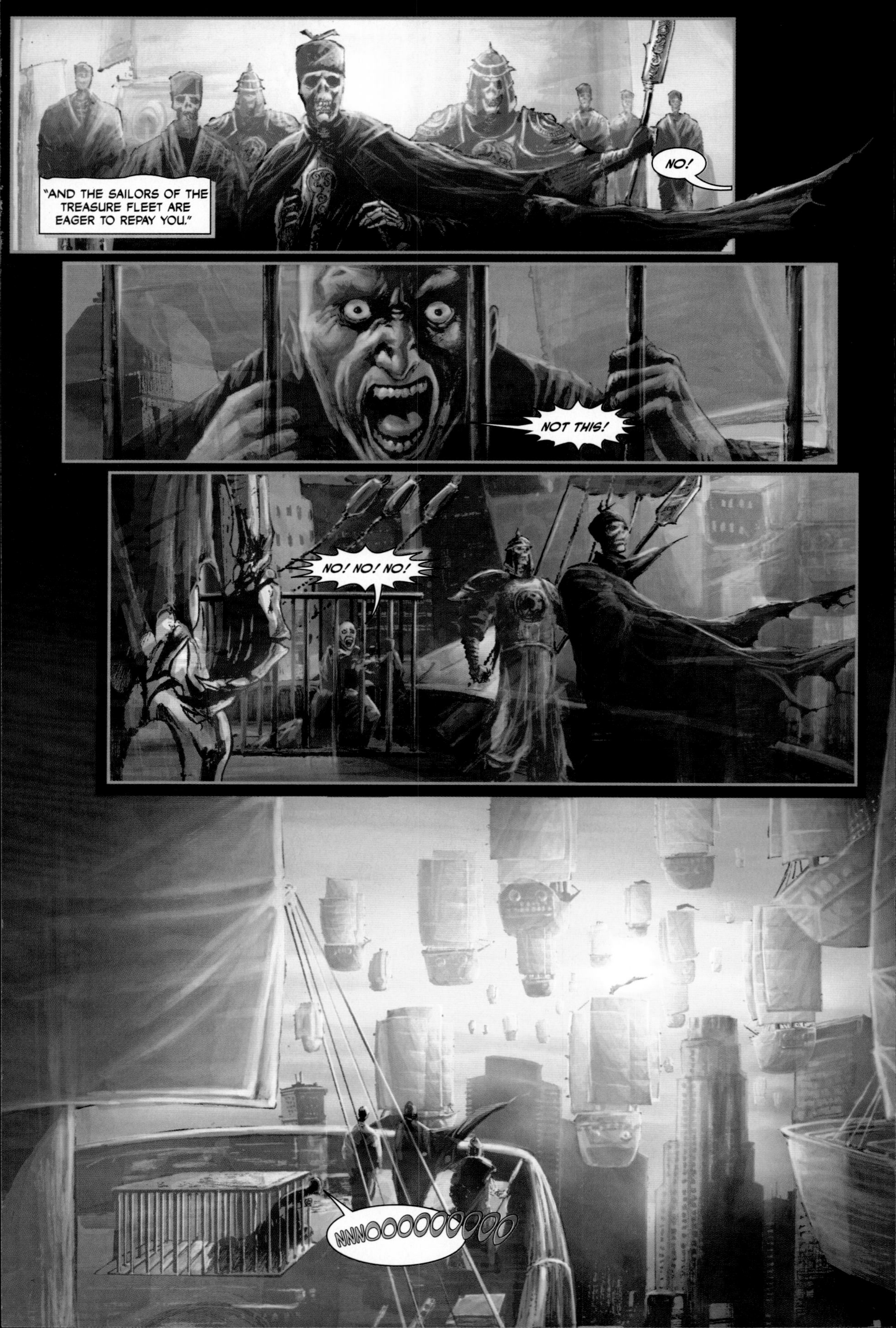
"AND THE SAILORS OF THE TREASURE FLEET ARE EAGER TO REPAY YOU."
NO!
NOT THIS!
NO! NO! NO!
NNNOOOOOOOOOOO

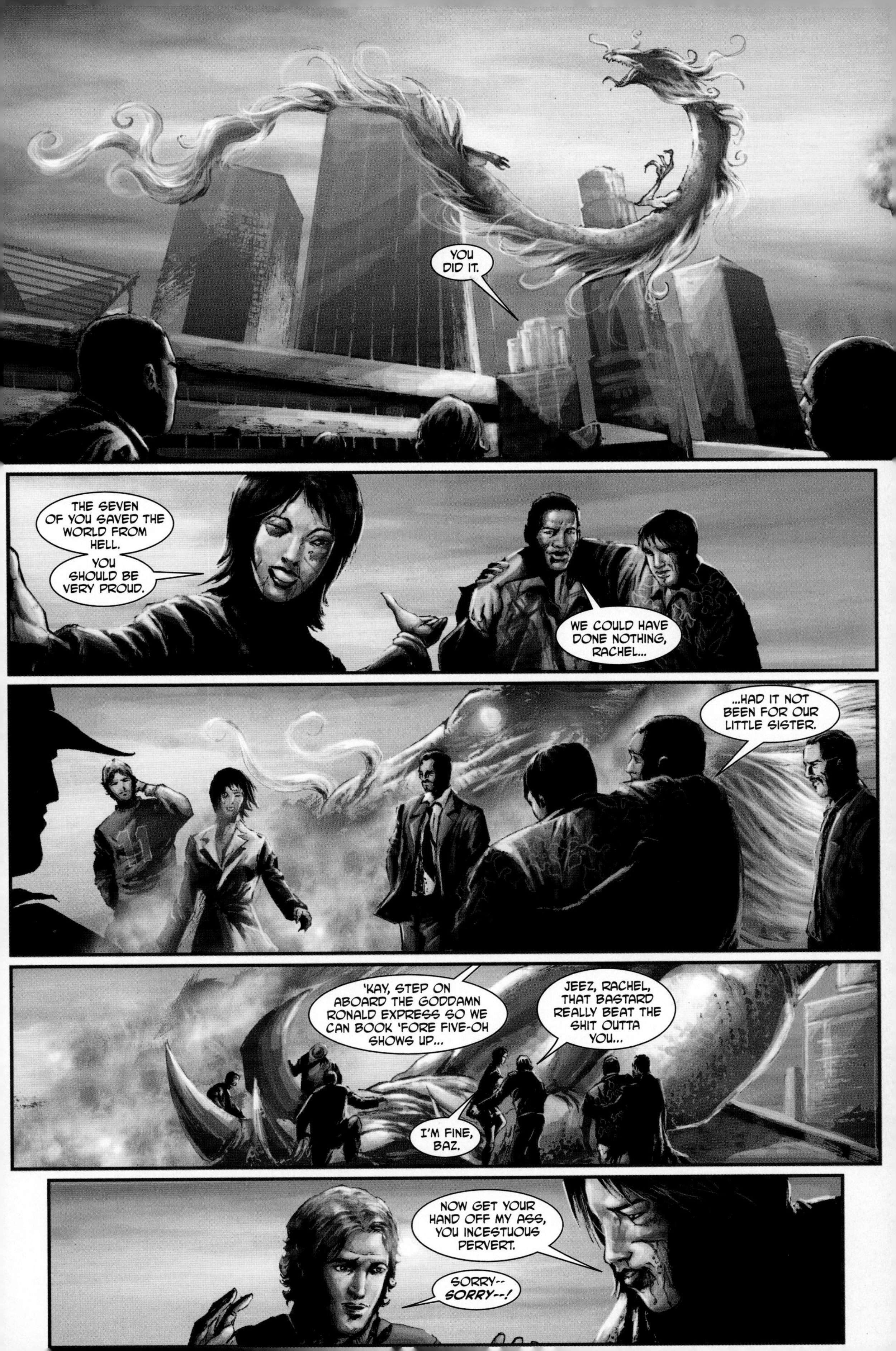
YOU DID IT.
THE SEVEN OF YOU SAVED THE WORLD FROM HELL.
YOU SHOULD BE VERY PROUD.
WE COULD HAVE DONE NOTHING, RACHEL...
...HAD IT NOT BEEN FOR OUR LITTLE SISTER.
'KAY, STEP ON ABOARD THE GODDAMN RONALD EXPRESS SO WE CAN BOOK 'FORE FIVE-OH SHOWS UP...
JEEZ, RACHEL, THAT BASTARD REALLY BEAT THE SHIT OUTTA YOU...
I'M FINE, BAZ.
NOW GET YOUR HAND OFF MY ASS, YOU INCESTUOUS PERVERT.
SORRY-- SORRY--!

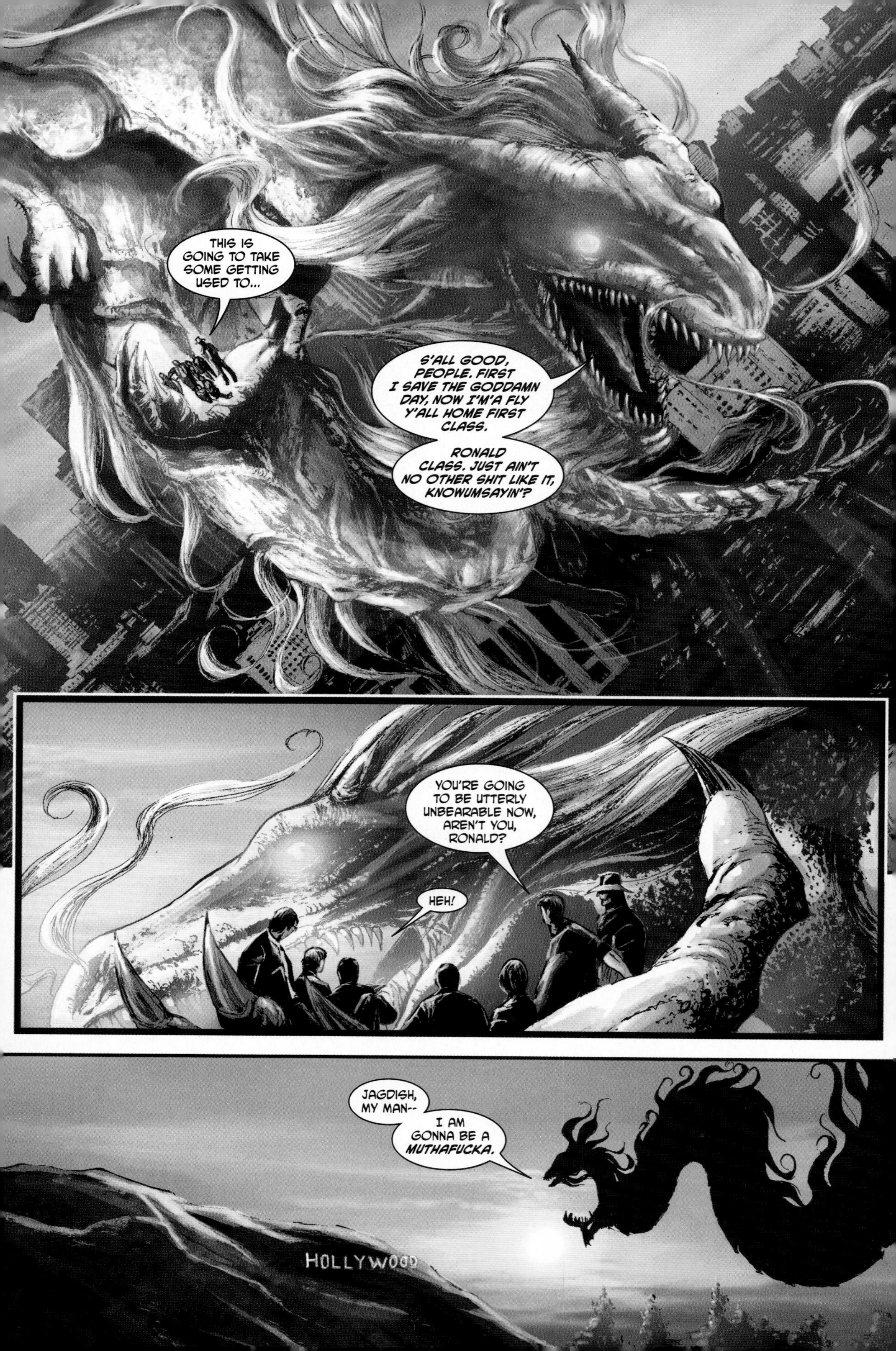
THIS IS GOING TO TAKE SOME GETTING USED TO...
S'ALL GOOD, PEOPLE. FIRST I SAVE THE GODDAMN DAY, NOW I'M'A FLY Y'ALL HOME FIRST CLASS.
RONALD CLASS. JUST AIN'T NO OTHER SHIT LIKE IT, KNOWUMSAYIN'?
YOU'RE GOING TO BE UTTERLY UNBEARABLE NOW, AREN'T YOU, RONALD?
HEH!
JAGDISH, MY MAN--
I AM GONNA BE A MUTHAFUCKA.
HOLLYWOOD

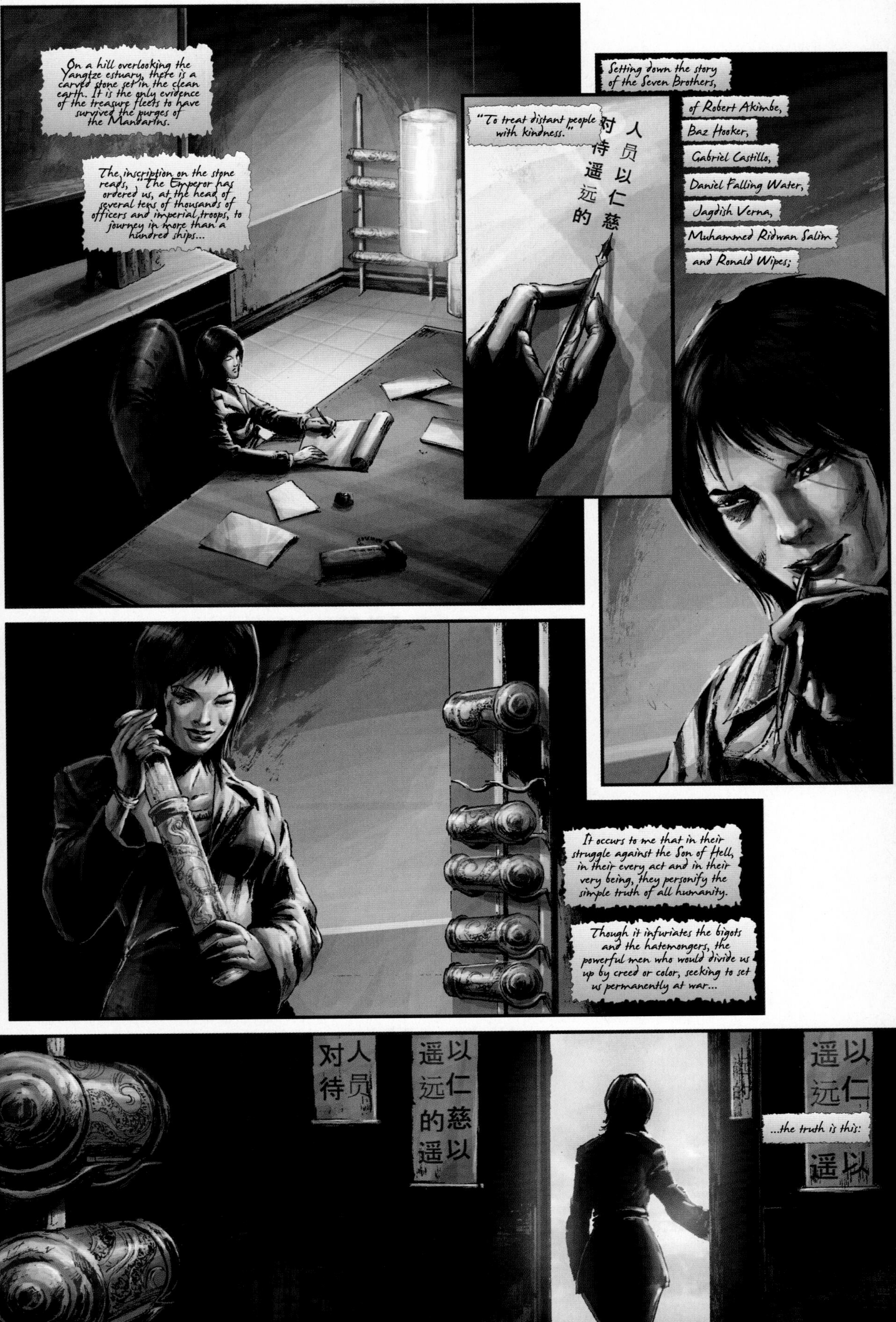
On a hill overlooking the Yangtze estuary, there is a carved stone set in the clean earth. It is the only evidence of the treasure fleets to have survived the purges of the Mandarins.
The inscription on the stone reads, "The Emperor has ordered us, at the head of several tens of thousands of officers and imperial troops, to journey in more than a hundred ships...
"To treat distant people with kindness."
人员以仁慈
对待遥远的
Setting down the story of the Seven Brothers,
of Robert Akimbe,
Baz Hooker,
Gabriel Castillo,
Daniel Falling Water,
Jagdish Verna,
Muhammed Ridwan Salim
and Ronald Wipes;
It occurs to me that in their struggle against the Son of Hell, in their every act and in their very being, they personify the simple truth of all humanity.
Though it infuriates the bigots and the hatemongers, the powerful men who would divide us up by creed or color, seeking to set us permanently at war...
人员
对待
以仁慈以
遥远的遥
以仁
遥远
...the truth is this:
以
遥

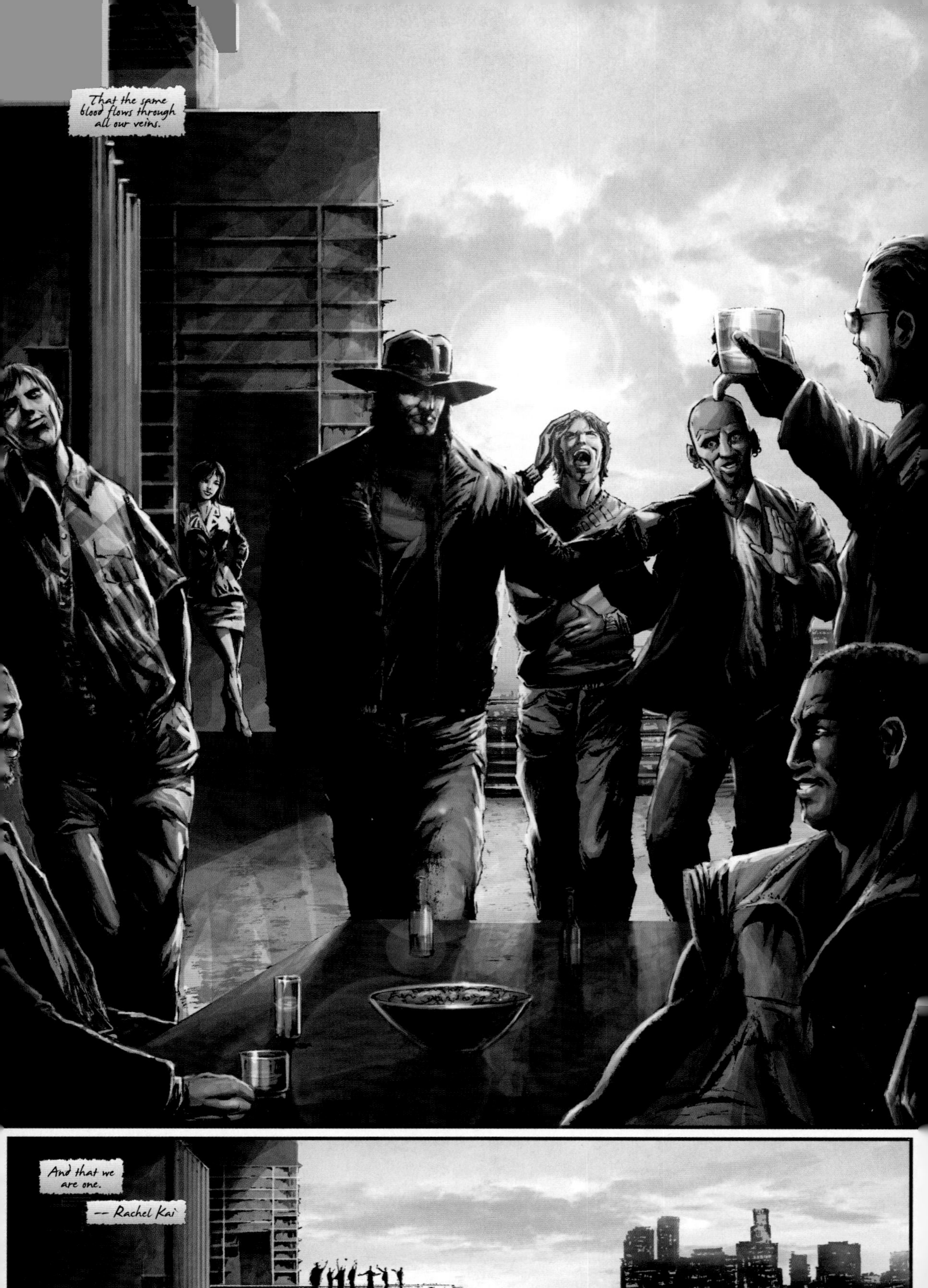
That the same blood flows through all our veins.

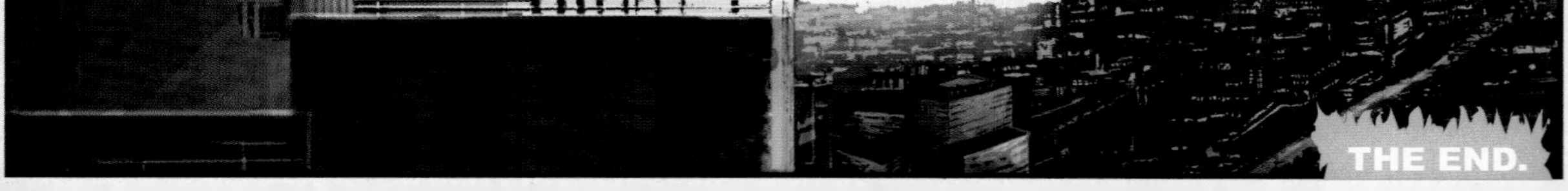
And that we are one.
-- Rachel Kai
THE END.

Hey Rachel! Here's that background info you asked for! Could you have picked seven guys who were farther apart? I've taken so many airplane flights in the last few weeks for this job, I could recite the entire in-flight movie to you in Spanish, Japanese and Hindi (I've included receipts for the plane tickets, by the way, to add to my normal fee). Talk to you later!
-L. R.

Subj: Castillo, Gabriel   Age: 29
Location: Buenos Aires, Argentina

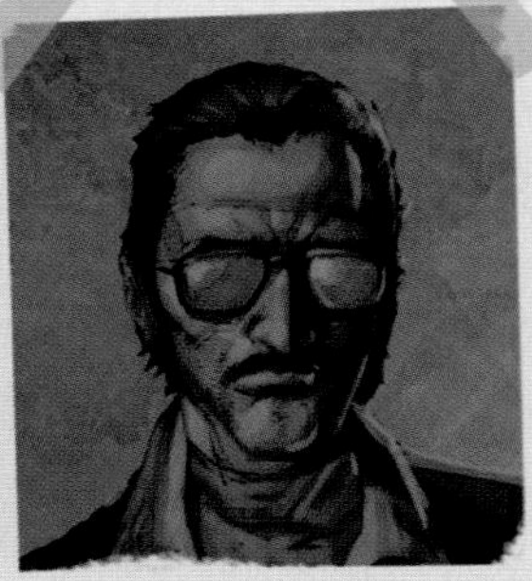

Gabriel's power is super-jumping, a skill that he doesn't flaunt, but certainly doesn't guard closely. Posing as a student on her study abroad year, I spent several hours talking to him at a local bar. He comes across with a very cool attitude (okay, so the ascot he usually wears is a little out there). He actually demonstrated his ability for me as he walked me home, plucking a flower from a window box five stories up, though I think his openness with his power was more due to the drinks we had. He told me of the first time he discovered he could do such things. He was ten years old, watching the sunset over the Andes, and, hoping to be able to see the sun for one instant more, He leapt with all his might. The next thing he knew, he was standing on the highest peak of the mountain range, watching the sun set over the Pacific. Above all, he is a rationalist, and has no problem giving an opinion, nor pointing out the problems with the opinions of others.

Subj: Verna, Jagdish   Age: 24
Location: Sitapur, India

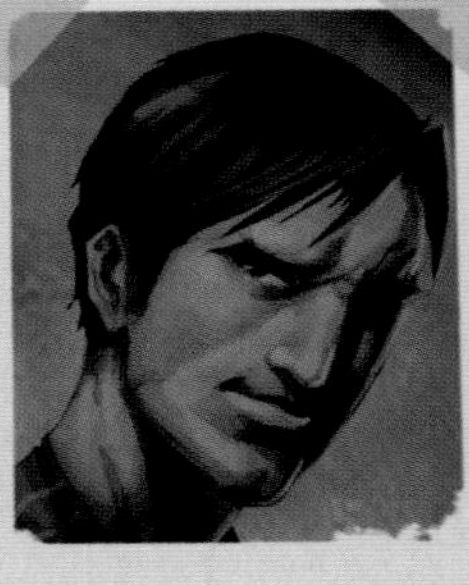

Jagdish (or "Jag" as his friends call him) has the ability to bring objects from great distances to where he is. The process seems to take a great effort on his part. While doing surveillance of the family home, where he lives with his brother and sister-in-law (and the rest of his immediate family), I witnessed his sister-in-law lament the loss of a necklace during a recent trip to New York City. Then, returning to his own room, I saw Jagdish grab the necklace out of the air. That is, it appeared out of nothingness. I'm not sure who these guys are supposed to be, Rachel, but they can do some weird shit.

Subj: Fallingwater, Daniel Age: 35
Location: New Mexico, United States

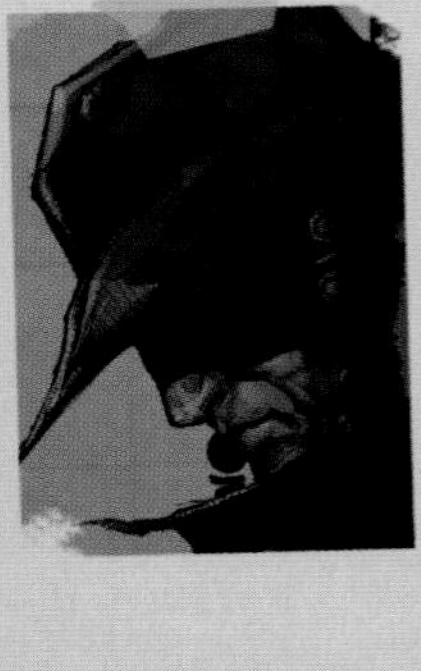

Daniel appears to have an ability of super speed and force. One incident recounted to me by a cousin of his on the Reservation happened when young Daniel was surprised by a mountain lion. He retreated, but ended up running so fast that he ran through several houses. Now, as an adult, he leads a stoic and solitary existence, and rarely speaks. He exhibits only the most selfish of tendencies, and is immediately suspicious of altruism in others. He looks out for number one, first and foremost.

Subj: Wipes, Ronald   Age: 33
Location: Los Angeles, California

Of all the people you had me track, Rachel, Ronald was
by far the most ridiculous. It would have been funny if
it weren't so pathetic. I've seen this guy get beat
down more times than I care to count (13 times over a
week), and yet, he still let's his mouth get him into
trouble. It's obvious that he'd like to be an
underworld bad-ass, but all he can seem to muster is
more swearwords than the entire navy. You mentioned
that he was different than the rest, Rachel, but all
I can see from here is a sad man with no promise, no
future... no redeeming qualities whatsoever. I hope you
didn't have high hopes.

Subj: Salim, Muhammed Ridwan Age: 36
Location: West Bank, Middle East

A family man, Muhammed is an active member in his
community. He is thoughtful and introspective, and is a
firm believer in an ethical and moral way of life.
His ability is to speak in an unbelievably loud voice;
I was unable to learn this by merely observing him—it
appears he takes great care never to use it.
I discovered it by recovering an Israeli military
intelligence file on Muhammed, recounting an episode
where an Israeli gunship was mysteriously downed near
Muhammed's home; apparently, the pilot could only
recount hearing Muhammed's booming voice (from inside
the cockpit, several thousand feet above the ground)
saying "Not my wife! Not my children!" The pilot's
visor shattered and blinded him, and he only just
escaped from his plane. But, as long as his family
isn't involved, Muhammed will certainly be easier to
manage than some of these other characters.

Subj: Akimbe, Robert   Age: 32
Location: Ikara, Nigeria

Robert was difficult to tail. Naturally suspicious and
very self-confident, he is also ultimately a good person
(though he wears that quality inside a very stand-offish
overcoat). His power is super-sight, though it took me a
good four days to find out (by far the longest of the
seven). The local bartender related Robert's dark past
to me. Apparently, as a young boy he had a pre-vision of
an invading troop of rebel soldiers, but could not
convince anyone else in his village to run or hide—he
was the only member of the village to survive. He has
carried the weight of that incident through to
adulthood, and takes nothing lightly.

Subj: Hooker, Baz Age: 26
Location Melbourne, Australia

Baz's ability is super-hearing—he recounts in a journal
from several years back that he was able to hear his
father's heart stop beating, even though he was diving
off the Great Barrier Reef and his father was in a
hospital in Melbourne. Elsewhere, he recounts being
able to hear whales sing, even when their migratory
pattern has them in the Arctic. However, Baz also seems
to be rather able with the ladies (I should note that
he hit on me on several different occasions—different
disguises each time—and had I not been on the clock...),
and seems to be clinically unable to pass up a beautiful woman. I'd watch out, Rach...

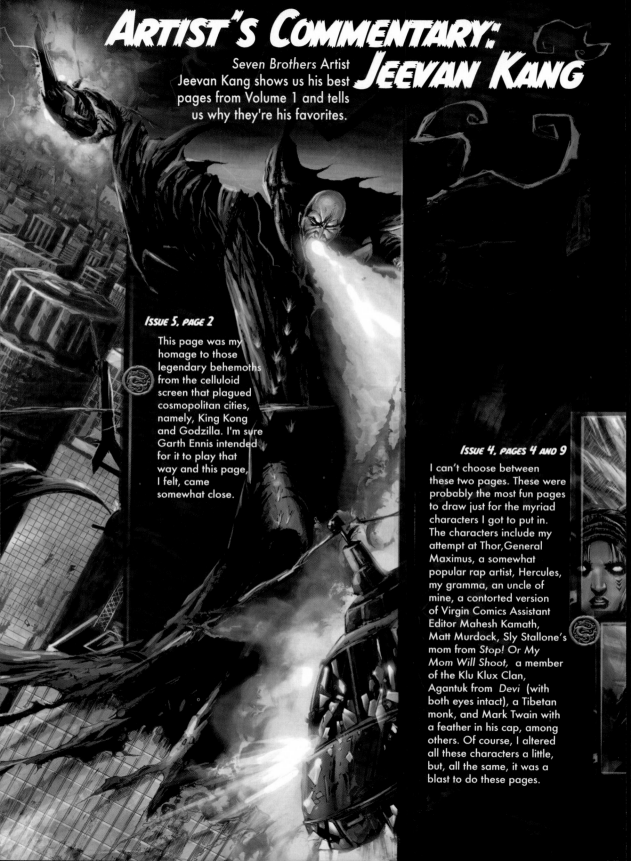

Artist's Commentary: Jeevan Kang

Seven Brothers Artist Jeevan Kang shows us his best pages from Volume 1 and tells us why they're his favorites.

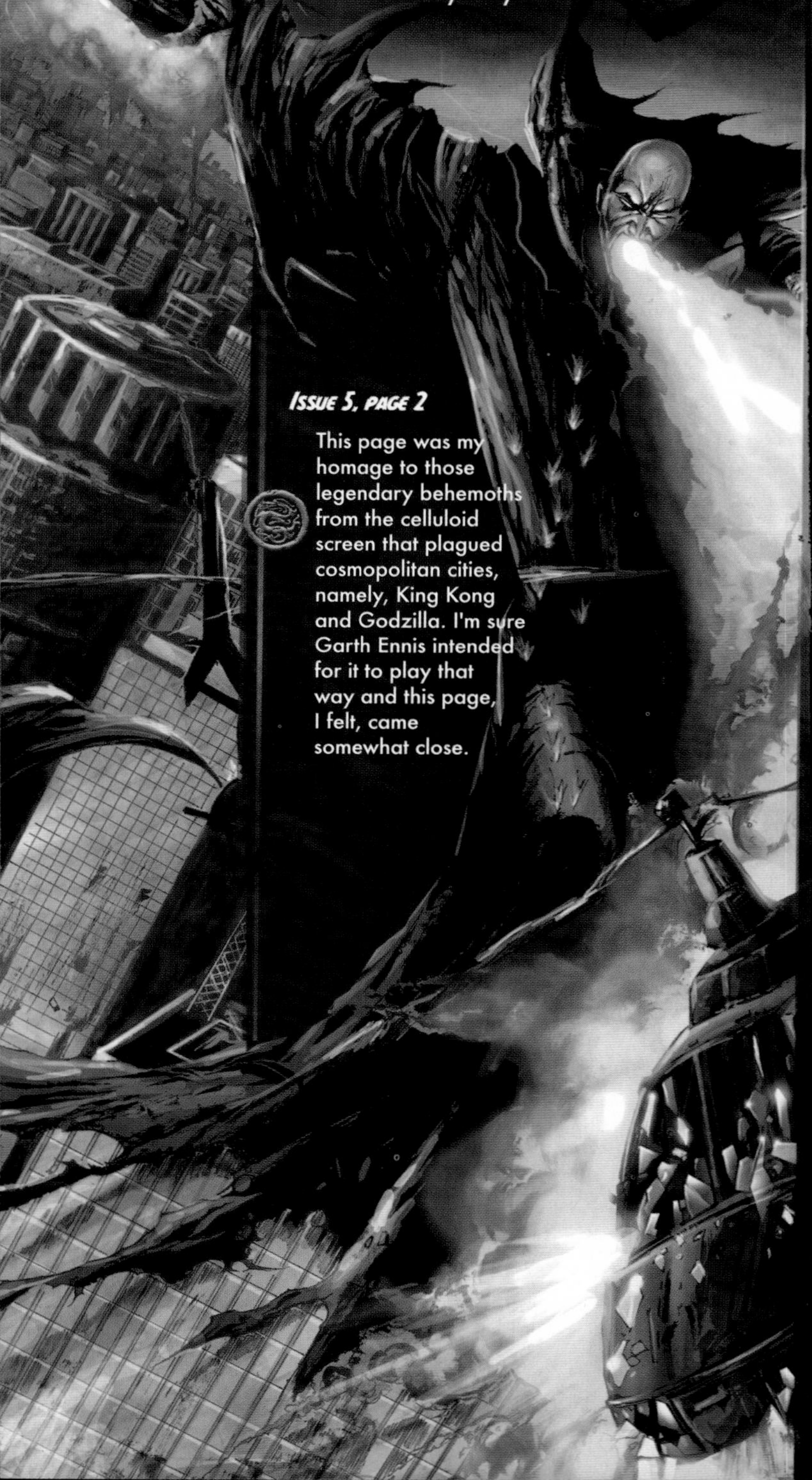

Issue 5, page 2

This page was my homage to those legendary behemoths from the celluloid screen that plagued cosmopolitan cities, namely, King Kong and Godzilla. I'm sure Garth Ennis intended for it to play that way and this page, I felt, came somewhat close.

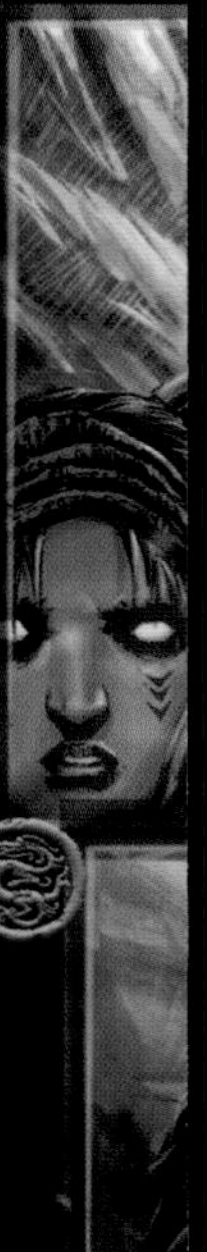

Issue 4, pages 4 and 9

I can't choose between these two pages. These were probably the most fun pages to draw just for the myriad characters I got to put in. The characters include my attempt at Thor,General Maximus, a somewhat popular rap artist, Hercules, my gramma, an uncle of mine, a contorted version of Virgin Comics Assistant Editor Mahesh Kamath, Matt Murdock, Sly Stallone's mom from *Stop! Or My Mom Will Shoot,* a member of the Klu Klux Clan, Agantuk from *Devi* (with both eyes intact), a Tibetan monk, and Mark Twain with a feather in his cap, among others. Of course, I altered all these characters a little, but, all the same, it was a blast to do these pages.

Issue 5, page 19

This double-page spread was inspired by the ominous shot of the alien ship hovering silently over the Empire State Building in New York in *Independence Day*. I was also inspired by scenes from *The Fifth Element*.

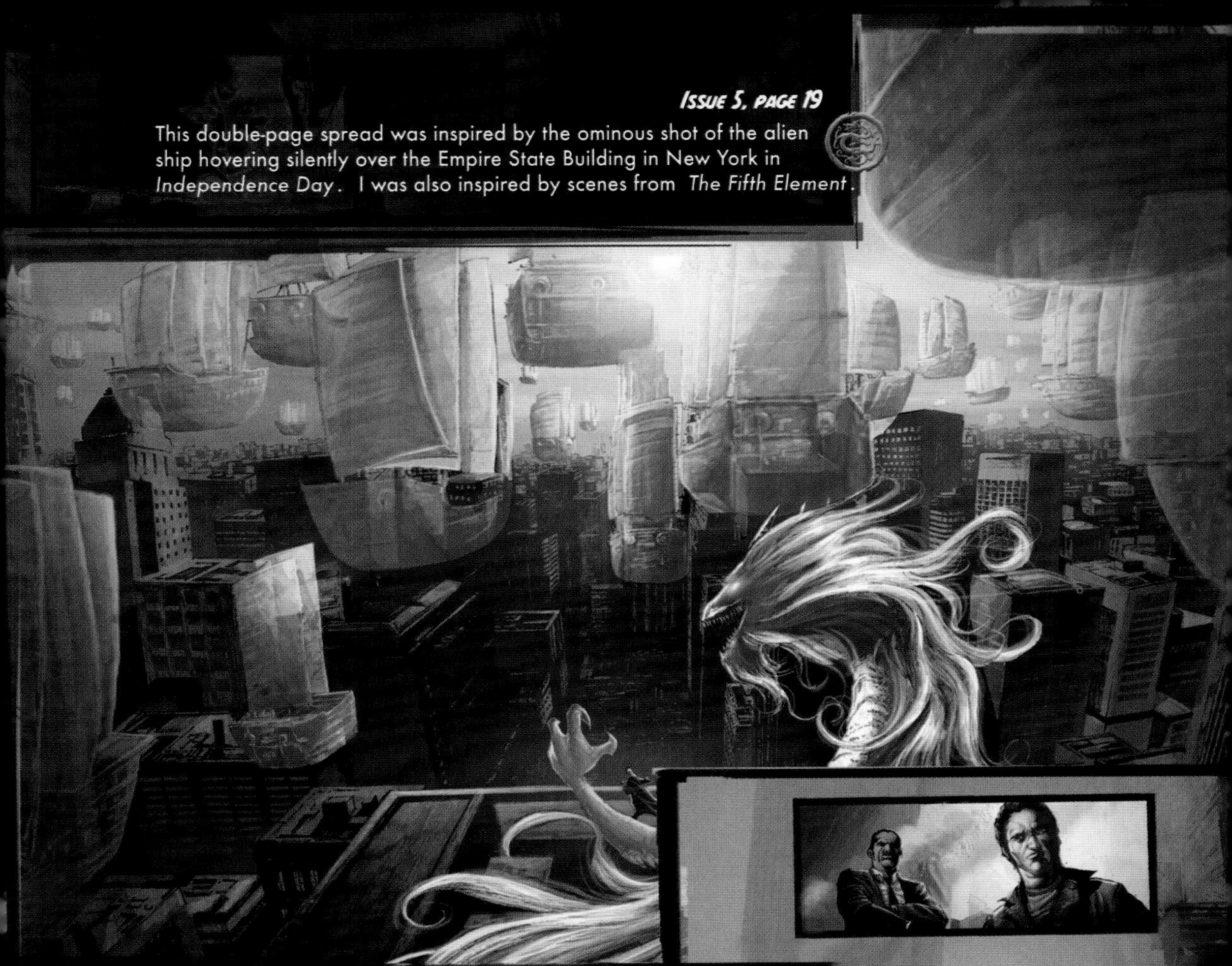

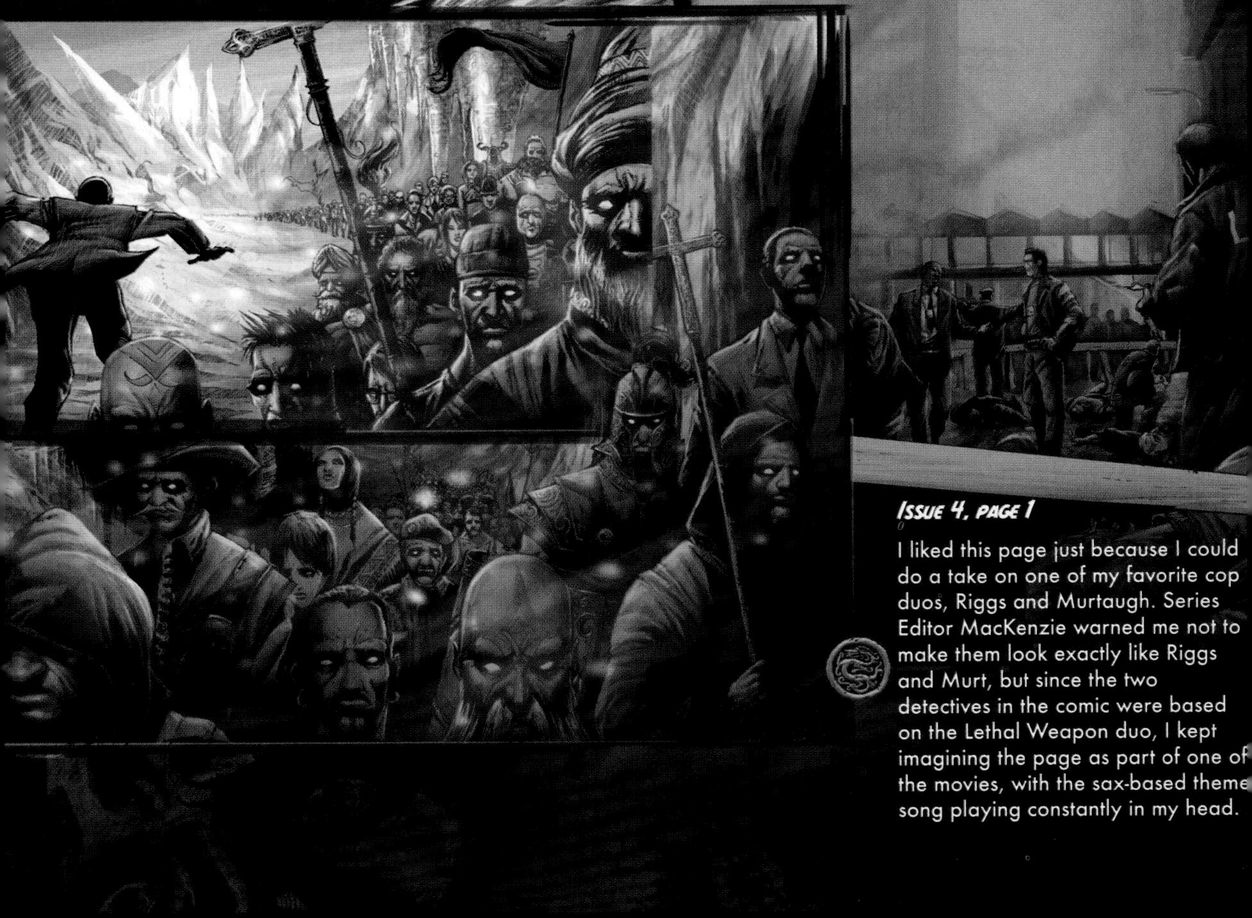

Issue 4, page 1

I liked this page just because I could do a take on one of my favorite cop duos, Riggs and Murtaugh. Series Editor MacKenzie warned me not to make them look exactly like Riggs and Murt, but since the two detectives in the comic were based on the Lethal Weapon duo, I kept imagining the page as part of one of the movies, with the sax-based theme song playing constantly in my head.

ART EVOLUTION

SEE HOW SELECT SCENES FROM SEVEN BROTHERS EVOLVED FROM PANEL DESCRIPTION TO LAYOUT TO PENCILS TO FINAL COLORS.

Issue 4, Page 15:
Rear view as they stagger on up the slope away from us. In as much as we can see who's who, Muhammed is last in line, nearest us, then it's Jagdish, Daniel, Gabrielle, Baz, Robert and Ronald, all holding hands. High above them, at the top of the slope, is a blazing, blinding ball of yellow light.

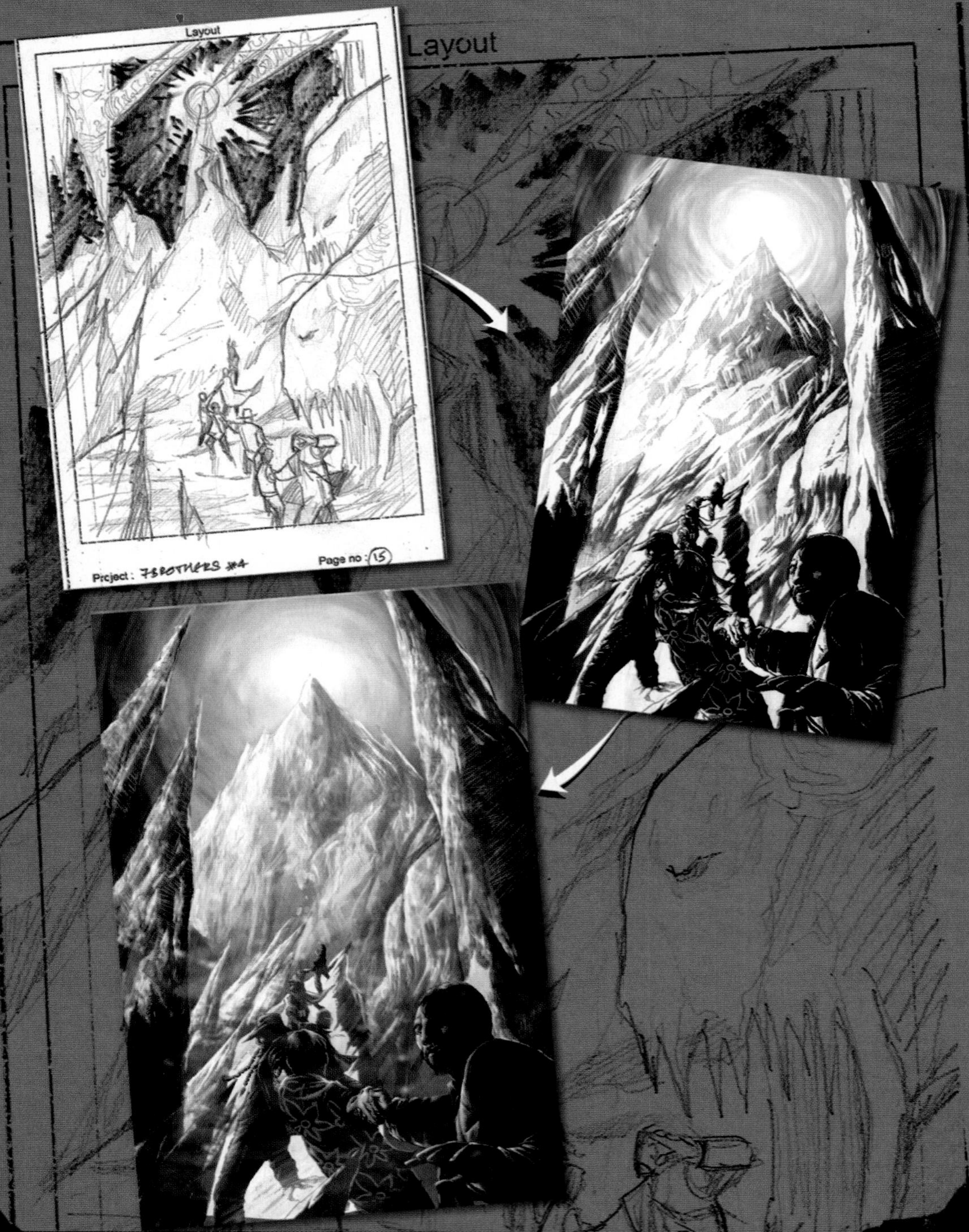

Layout
Layout
Project: 7BROTHERS #4
Page no: 15

Layout

Issue 3, Page 22
Panel 1: Big. The seven brothers lie dead in the street, blood all over the place. Zheng walks calmly over to Rachel.
Panel 2: Close up on Rachel as Zheng's foot comes down on her neck, gently but firmly pinning her to the ground. She gazes wretchedly up at us, utterly miserable, beaten.

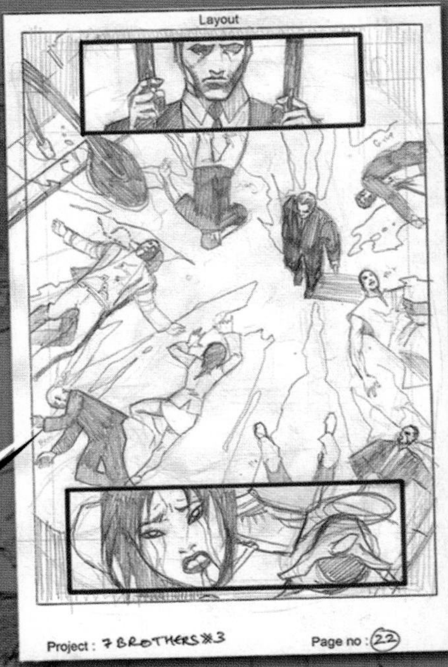
Layout
Project : 7 BROTHERS #3
Page no : 22

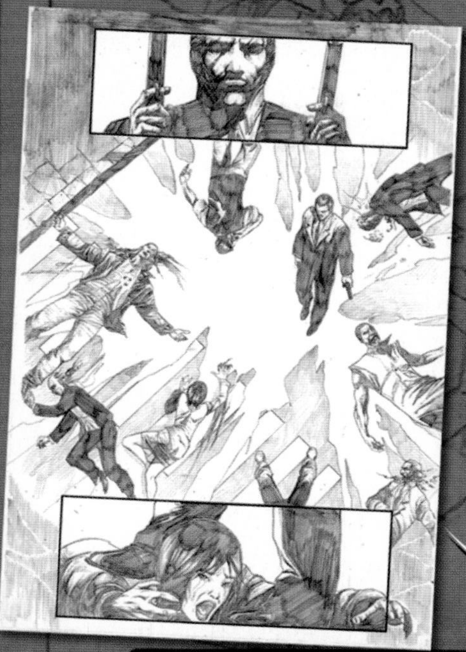

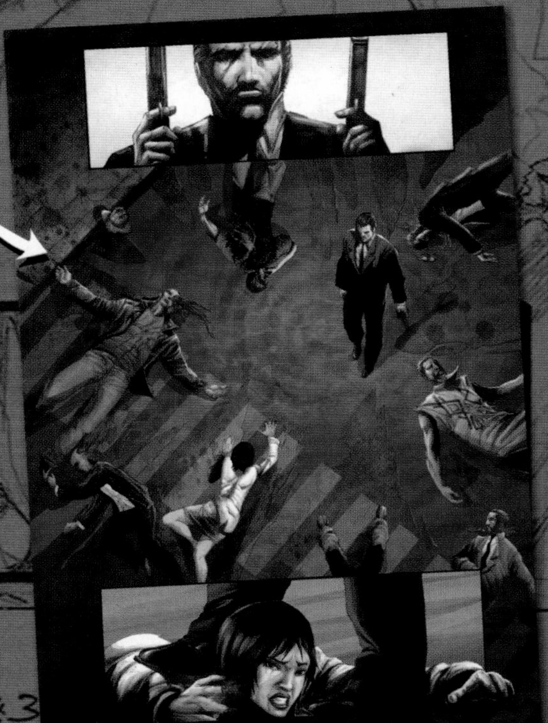

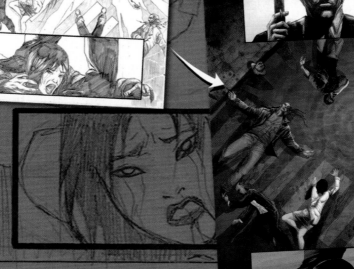

Project : 7 BROTHERS #3

SEVEN BROTHERS: VARIANT COVERS

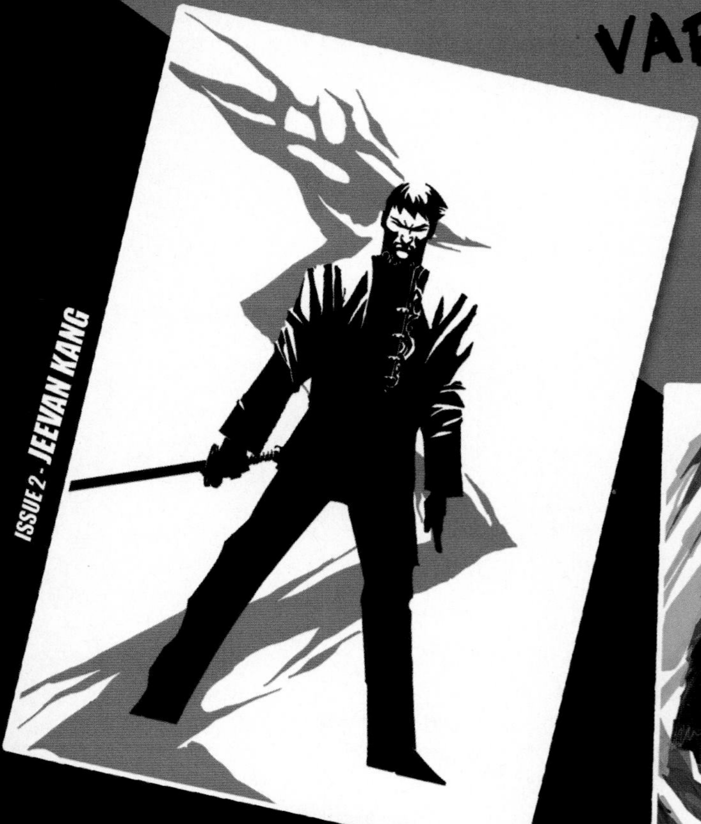

ISSUE 2 - JEEVAN KANG

ISSUE 4 - JEEVAN KANG

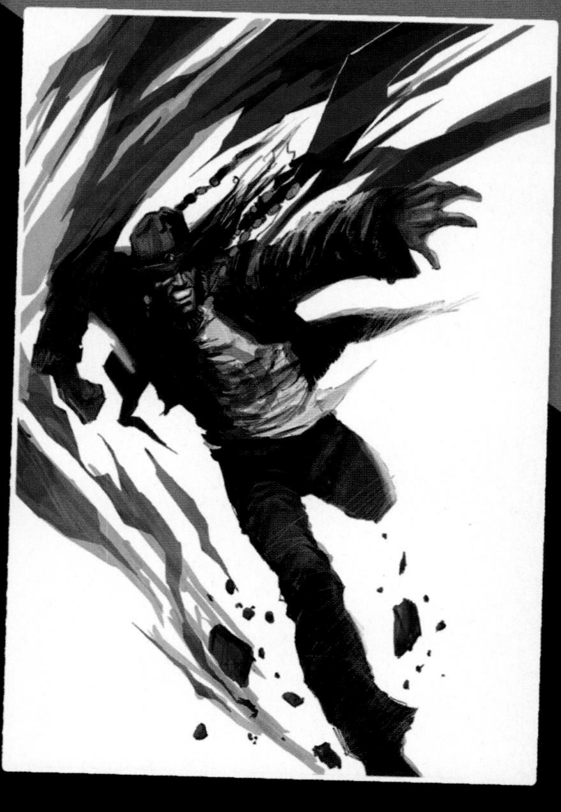

ISSUE 3 - JEEVAN KANG

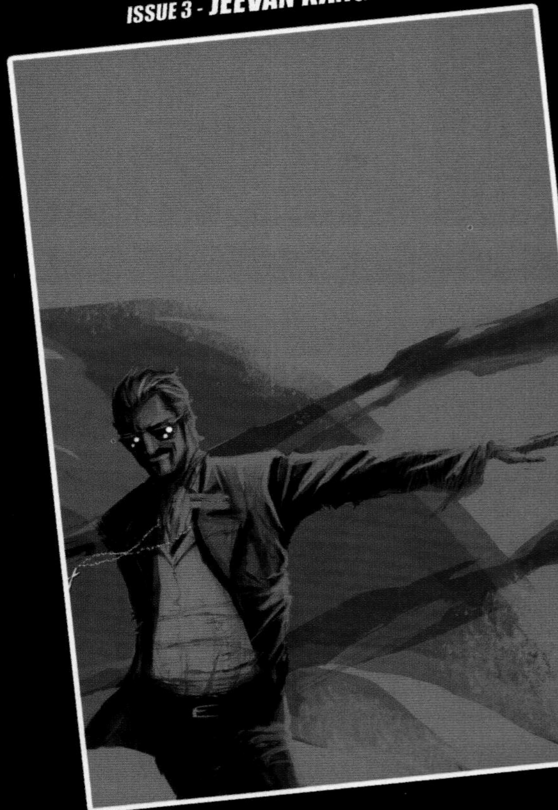

ISSUE 1 - GREG HORN

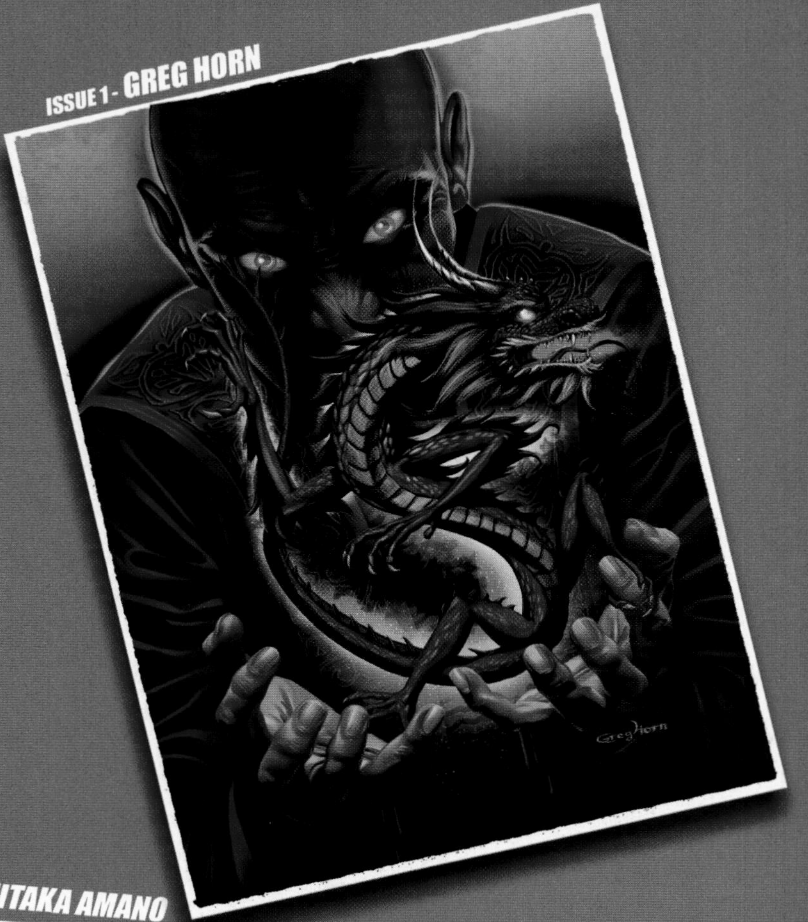
Greg Horn

TPB HARDCOVER - YOSHITAKA AMANO

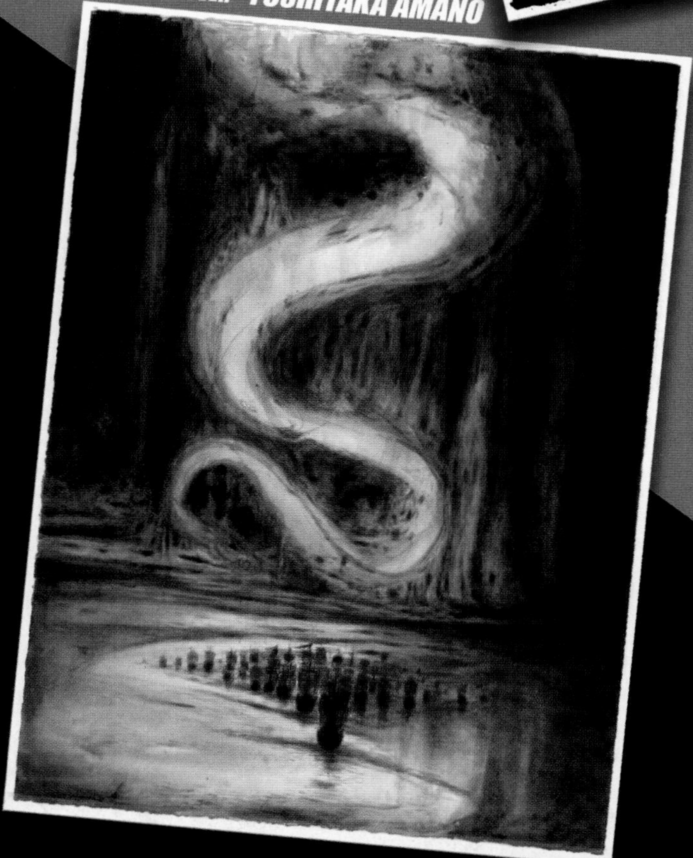

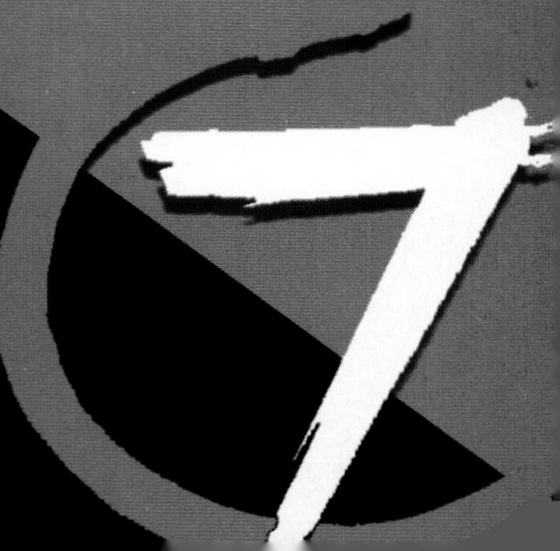

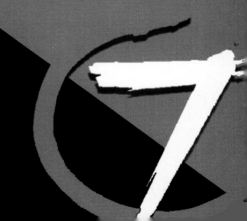

SEVEN BROTHERS:
THE RE-CREATION OF A MYTH

What is the "stuff of legends" exactly? An impressive tale of action and suspense, mystery and adventure, heroes and heroines? Well, that's one way to look at it. Or, the "stuff" could be a legend's capacity to inspire. A story can enter our minds, and leave bent, morphed, and distorted by that magnificent beast within that makes life a bit more interesting... our imagination. That's why we'll never have just one version of a legend. Because there are a million ways to tell a story and about 6 billion people willing to tell their version of it. And the more wild the imagination, the more wild the transformed legend is.

From those 6 billion, Virgin Comics brought together two very unconventional, maverick storytellers: filmmaker John Woo and comics scribe Garth Ennis. Their untamed imaginations push the limits of storytelling, shocking, mystifying, and sometimes, appalling audiences the world-over. Simply put: John loves the extreme, and Garth loves the profane. The pairing could only yield explosive results. As creators and purveyors of this sensationalized world of folklore and drama, we at Virgin Comics live for those results, seeking the stories that will seep into the recesses of cerebral fantasy and re-emerge more outlandish, more alluring, more kick-ass. Together, Woo and Ennis have turned that into a science as they experimented on the mythic tale of ten unique Chinese Brothers.

Thought to have been written around the construction of the Great Wall of China, the earliest version of the tale of the Seven Brothers is the oldest story in Chinese history to feature "superheroes". The original tale itself is simple: ten brothers with exaggerated, odd characteristics come together to defend one another and the exploited workers of the Great Wall. As with all superheroes, the brothers save the day, realizing that in these strange features lay great abilities and even greater possibilities when used in tandem with one another. Theirs is a message that resonates no mater how much the story is twisted and redefined, be it with the Woo style wickedness or Ennis style wildness: in the bonds of brotherhood lies a strength that can be super human. Here are ten brothers, whose features would seemingly make them outcasts, yet they transform them into something powerful, particularly when working together. They are a band of brothers that become a band of heroes.

What's relevant about the Woo/Ennis collaboration is that they take a poignant and powerful theme and distort it according to their fantasies of what modern outcasts-turned-superheroes should be. They're version is told through a grimy lens that magnifies and contorts the original myth, rendering it severely perverted, but startlingly more appealing to a contemporary audience. From their imaginations spawns a new vision of these modern-day heroes: there's a pimp, a promiscuous wizard, and a gun-wielding babe. Not traditional storybook characters, but modern spins on familiar archetypes. Our characters retain their awesome abilities, but they're real and they're flawed. They're pariahs in their own homes, brought together by the want of money, and lack of anything else left in their lives. They are unlikely heroes, but that makes us like them even more, because really, *we could be them*. Or so we think – because even as super heroes, we'd have our flaws that would make us human. This isn't a tale fit for a bedtime stories, but it's tale fit for legends. Seven special, but lonely souls become a part of something greater than themselves—a real family. And so, a band of heroes become a band of brothers.

But hey, that's just what we think. Take a read and decide for yourself.

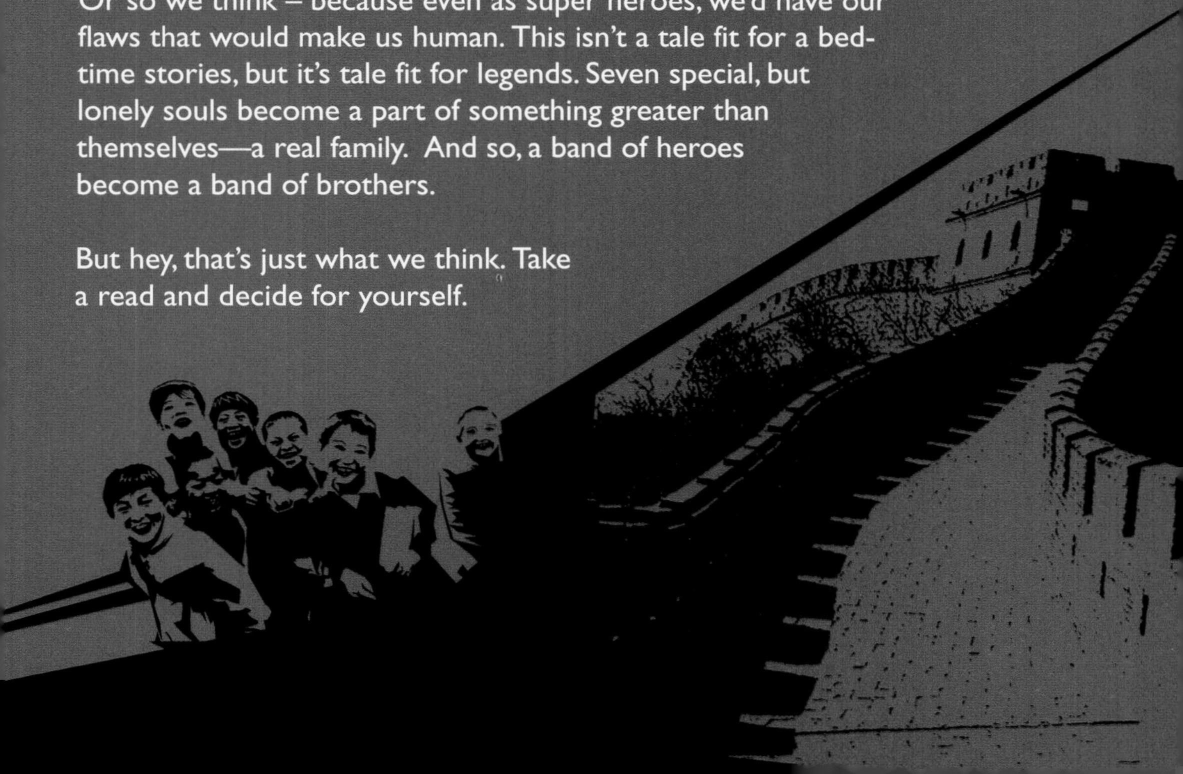

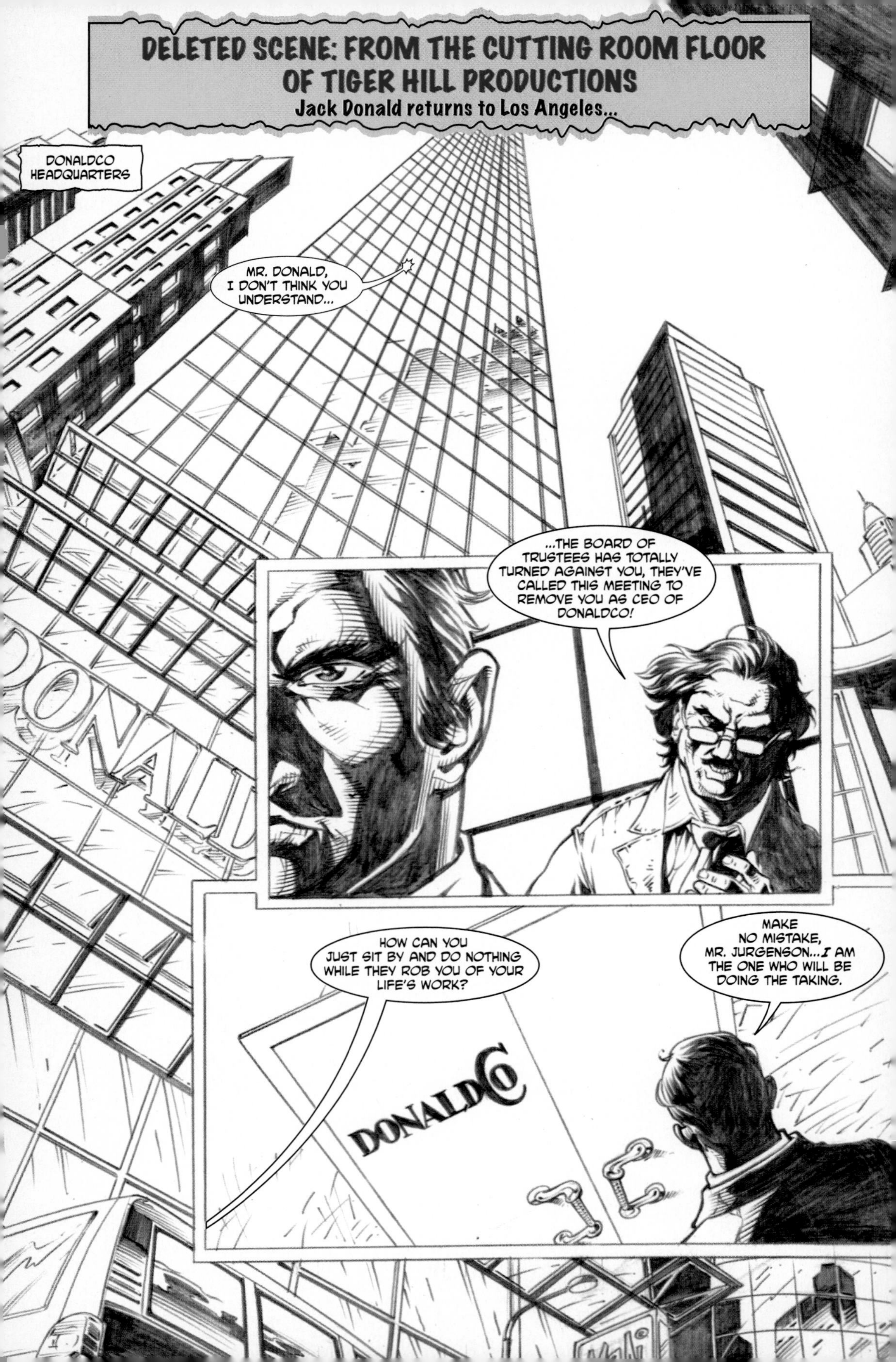
DELETED SCENE: FROM THE CUTTING ROOM FLOOR OF TIGER HILL PRODUCTIONS
Jack Donald returns to Los Angeles...
DONALDCO HEADQUARTERS
MR. DONALD, I DON'T THINK YOU UNDERSTAND...
...THE BOARD OF TRUSTEES HAS TOTALLY TURNED AGAINST YOU, THEY'VE CALLED THIS MEETING TO REMOVE YOU AS CEO OF DONALDCO!
HOW CAN YOU JUST SIT BY AND DO NOTHING WHILE THEY ROB YOU OF YOUR LIFE'S WORK?
MAKE NO MISTAKE, MR. JURGENSON...I AM THE ONE WHO WILL BE DOING THE TAKING.
DONALDCO

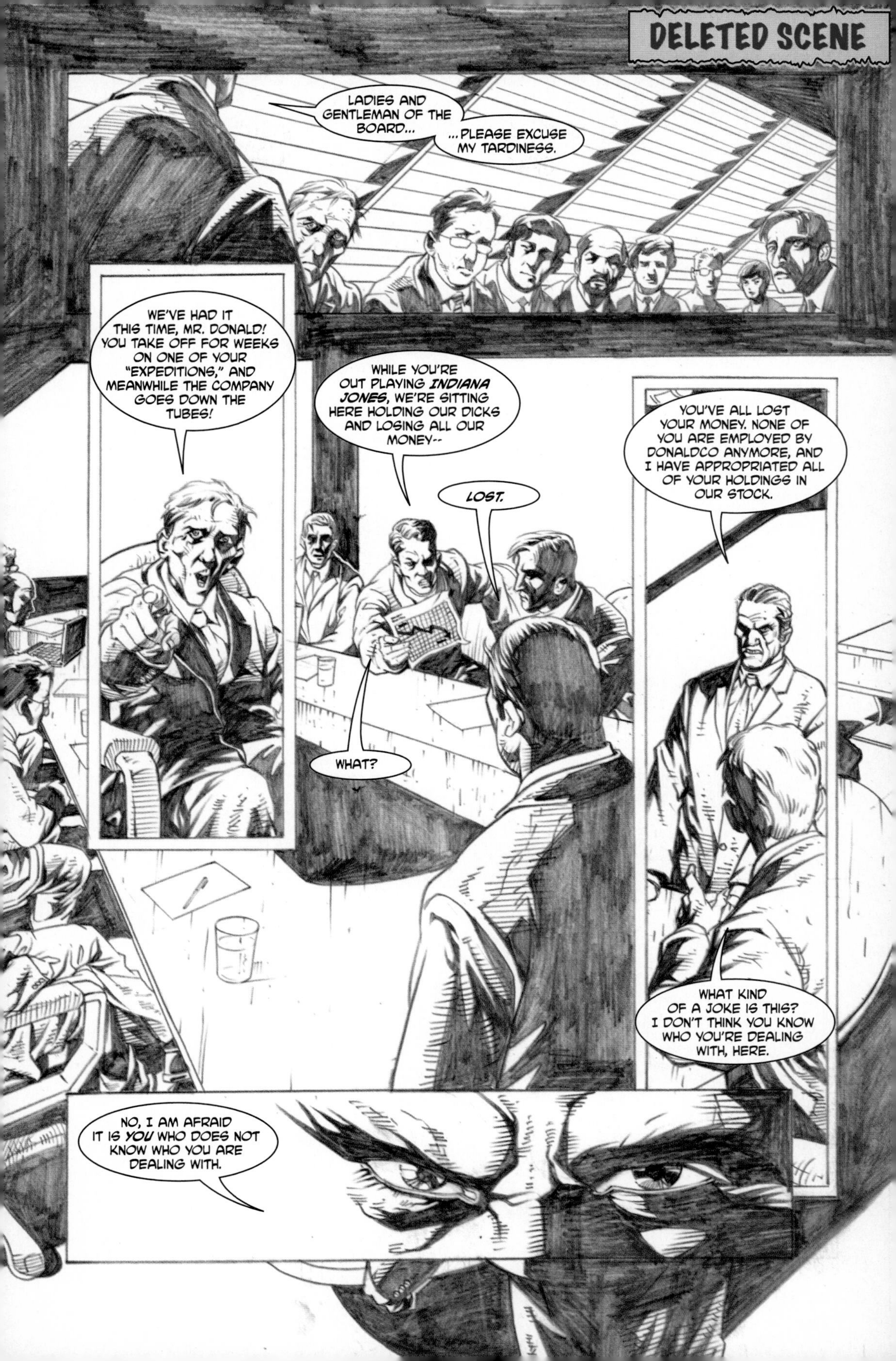
DELETED SCENE
LADIES AND GENTLEMAN OF THE BOARD...
...PLEASE EXCUSE MY TARDINESS.
WE'VE HAD IT THIS TIME, MR. DONALD! YOU TAKE OFF FOR WEEKS ON ONE OF YOUR "EXPEDITIONS," AND MEANWHILE THE COMPANY GOES DOWN THE TUBES!
WHILE YOU'RE OUT PLAYING *INDIANA JONES*, WE'RE SITTING HERE HOLDING OUR DICKS AND LOSING ALL OUR MONEY--
LOST.
WHAT?
YOU'VE ALL LOST YOUR MONEY. NONE OF YOU ARE EMPLOYED BY DONALDCO ANYMORE, AND I HAVE APPROPRIATED ALL OF YOUR HOLDINGS IN OUR STOCK.
WHAT KIND OF A JOKE IS THIS? I DON'T THINK YOU KNOW WHO YOU'RE DEALING WITH, HERE.
NO, I AM AFRAID IT IS *YOU* WHO DOES NOT KNOW WHO YOU ARE DEALING WITH.

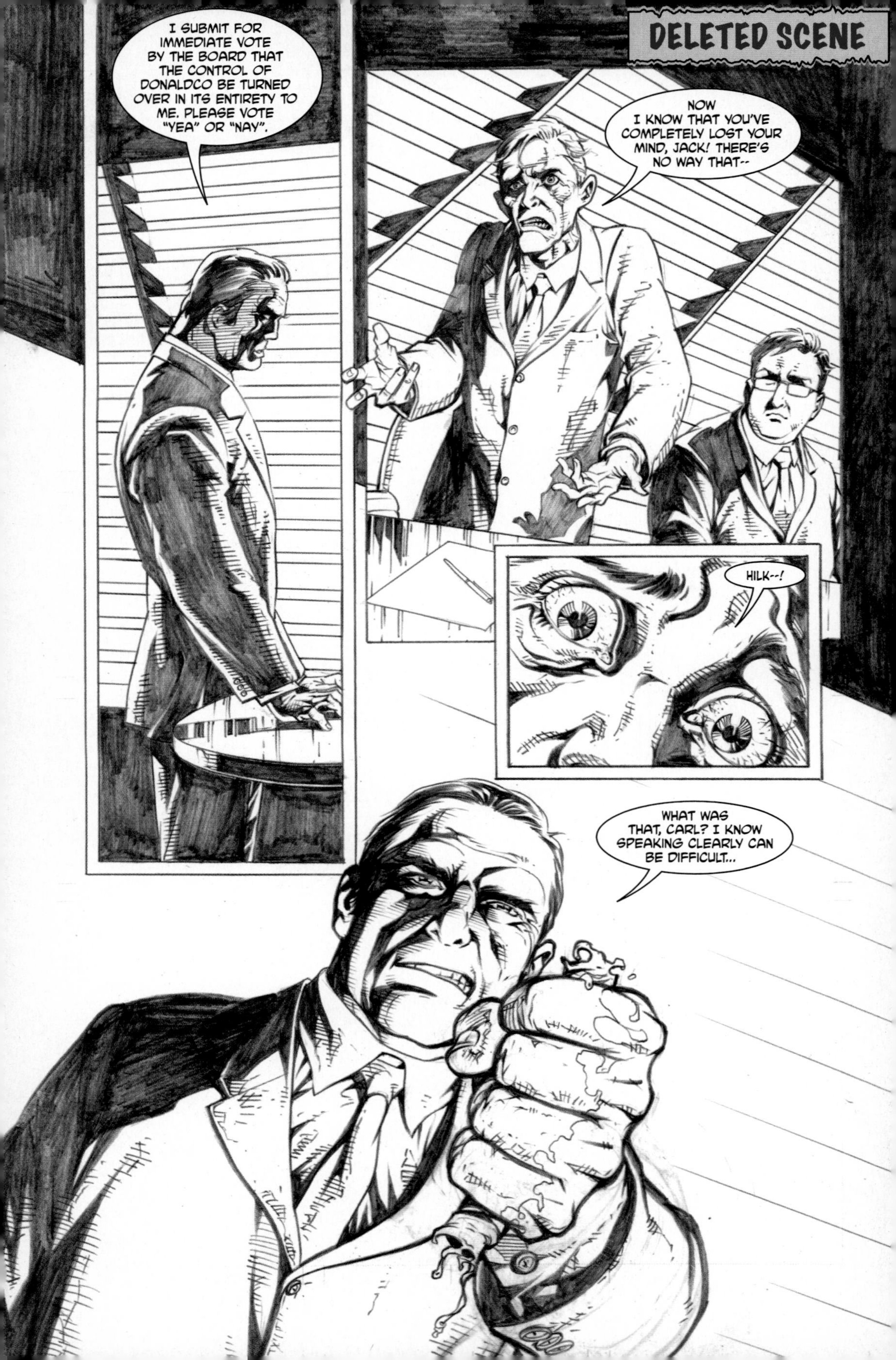
DELETED SCENE
I SUBMIT FOR IMMEDIATE VOTE BY THE BOARD THAT THE CONTROL OF DONALDCO BE TURNED OVER IN ITS ENTIRETY TO ME. PLEASE VOTE "YEA" OR "NAY".
NOW I KNOW THAT YOU'VE COMPLETELY LOST YOUR MIND, JACK! THERE'S NO WAY THAT--
HILK--!
WHAT WAS THAT, CARL? I KNOW SPEAKING CLEARLY CAN BE DIFFICULT...

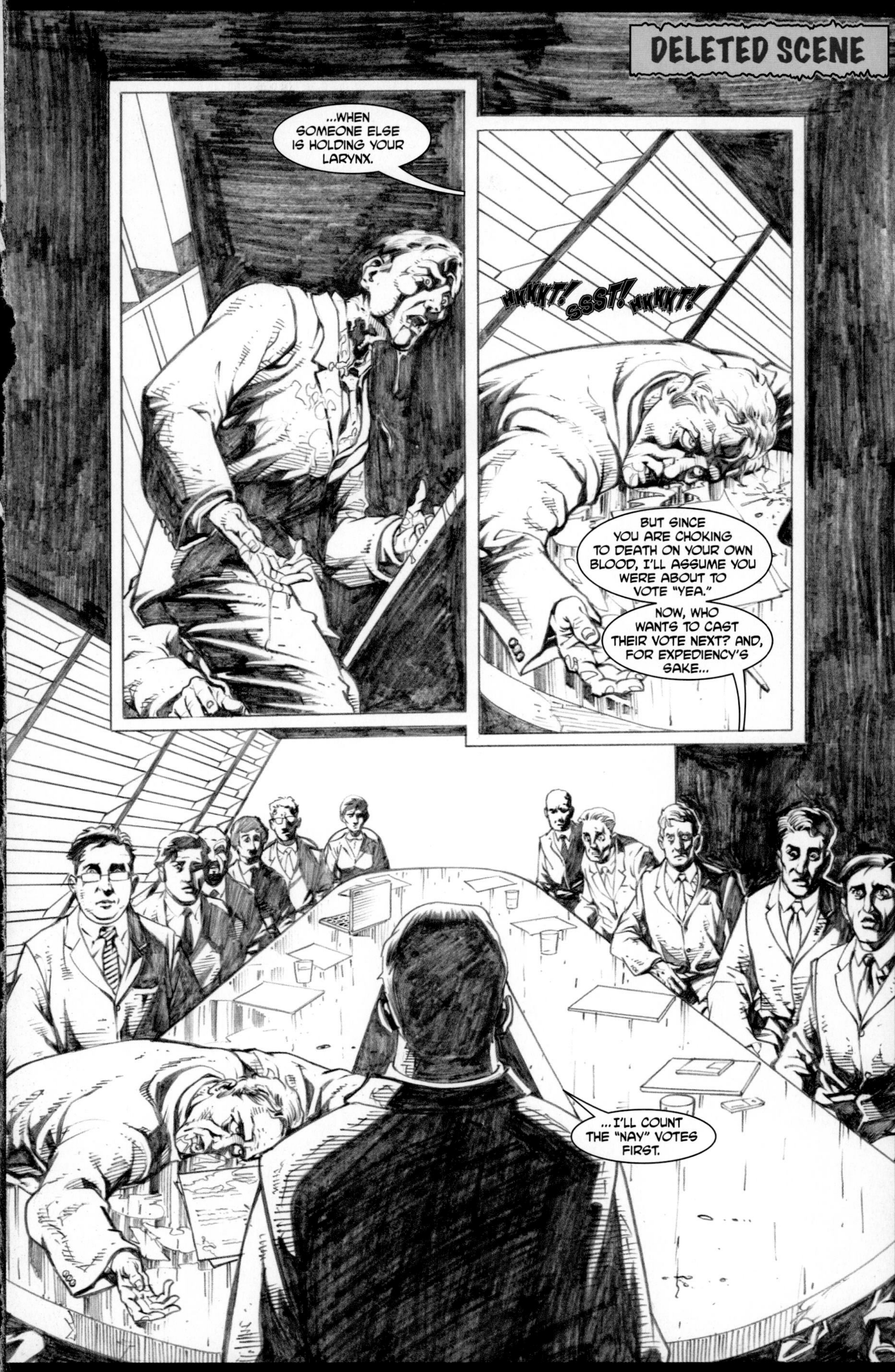
DELETED SCENE
...WHEN SOMEONE ELSE IS HOLDING YOUR LARYNX.
HKKKT! SSST! HKKKT!
BUT SINCE YOU ARE CHOKING TO DEATH ON YOUR OWN BLOOD, I'LL ASSUME YOU WERE ABOUT TO VOTE "YEA."
NOW, WHO WANTS TO CAST THEIR VOTE NEXT? AND, FOR EXPEDIENCY'S SAKE...
...I'LL COUNT THE "NAY" VOTES FIRST.

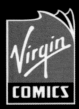

VIRGIN COMICS
COLLECTED EDITIONS

ON SALE JUNE 2007

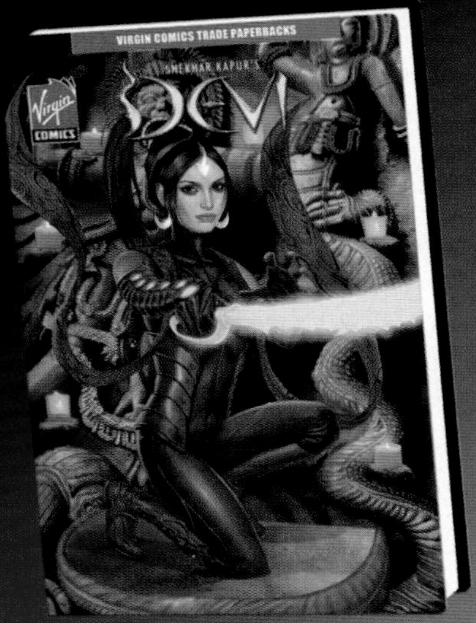
VIRGIN COMICS TRADE PAPERBACKS
Virgin COMICS

DEVI VOL.1

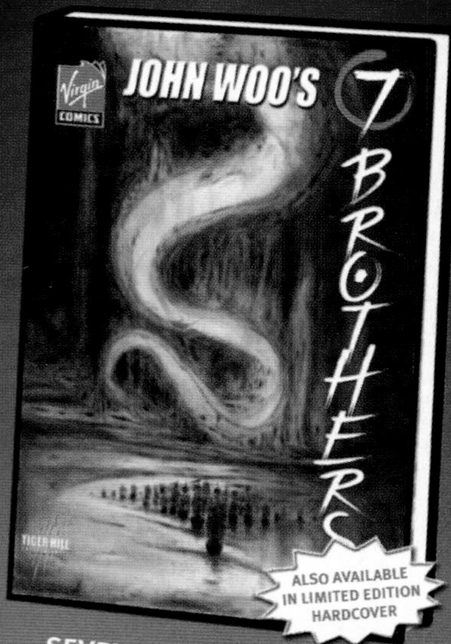
Virgin COMICS
JOHN WOO'S
7 BROTHERS
ALSO AVAILABLE IN LIMITED EDITION HARDCOVER

SEVEN BROTHERS VOL.1

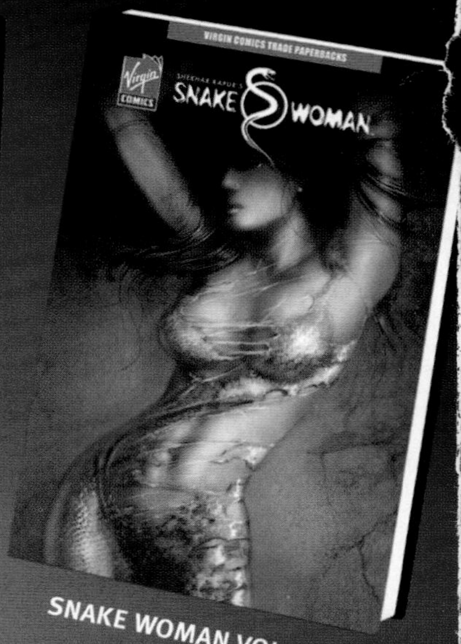
VIRGIN COMICS TRADE PAPERBACKS
Virgin COMICS
SNAKE WOMAN

SNAKE WOMAN VOL.1

ON SALE JULY 2007

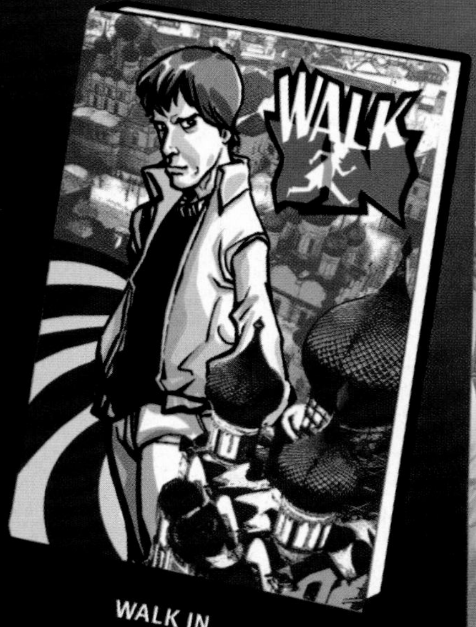
WALK

WALK IN

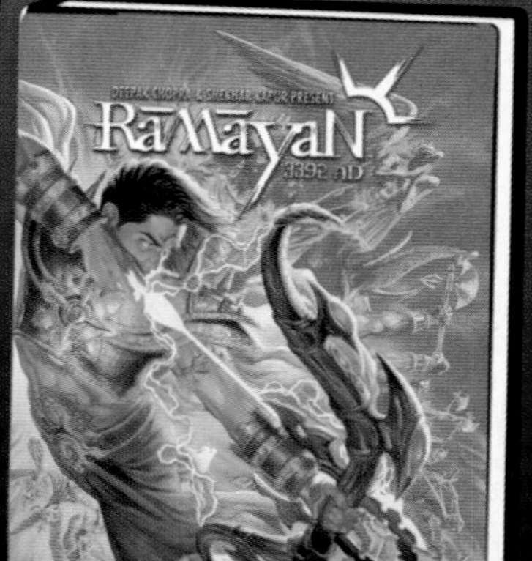
DEEPAK CHOPRA & SHEKHAR KAPUR PRESENT
RaMayaN
3392 AD

RAMAYAN 3392 A.D.
VOL.1

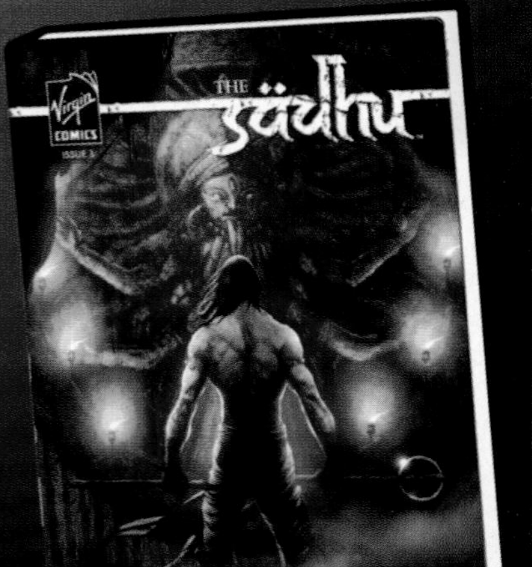
Virgin COMICS
THE
sadhu

THE SADHU
VOL.1

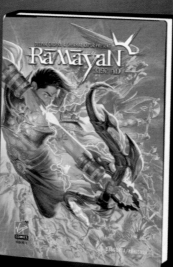

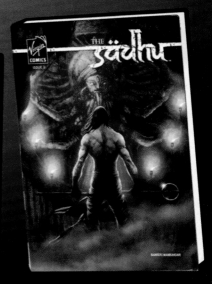